CLOUDS OF GLORY

A Hoxton Childhood

BRYAN MAGEE

PIMLICO

Published by Pimlico 2004

4 6 8 10 9 7 5

First published in Great Britain in 2003 by Jonathan Cape

Pimlico edition 2004

Pimlico
Random House, 20 Vauxhall Bridge Road,
London SW1 2SA

Addresses for companies within The Random House Group Limited can be found at:
www.randomhouse.co.uk/offices.htm

The Random House Group Limited Reg. No. 954009

A CIP catalogue record for this book
is available from the British Library

ISBN 978-0-7126-3560-8

The Random House Group Limited supports The Forest Stewardship
Council® (FSC®), the leading international forest-certification organisation.
Our books carrying the FSC label are printed on FSC®-certified paper.
FSC is the only forest-certification scheme supported by the leading
environmental organisations, including Greenpeace. Our
paper procurement policy can be found at
www.randomhouse.co.uk/environment

Typeset in New Baskerville
by Palimpsest Book Production Limited,
Polmont, Stirlingshire
Printed and bound in Great Britain by Clays Ltd, St Ives PLC

to
Norman Tillson

CONTENTS

CONTENTS

CHAPTER ONE

One of the most extraordinary things about being a human being is that we just wake up in the world and find ourselves here, though what 'here' is is something we never discover. Existence is something that happens to us, and then remains a mystery. There is no question of our having any say in it: a light comes on in a new centre of consciousness, and it is another one of us.

We find ourselves not awarenesses only, but bodies also, and perhaps other things besides – whatever we are, it is certainly complex. And we inherit a going concern. We know nothing about any of it until after it is well under way, by which time we are already a particular person, born a while back to two other persons embedded in particular circumstances; and everything that has happened to us since then constitutes what is already a life; and already we are partially-formed personalities. Everything about the situation is specific in the highest degree, a fate, a destiny, already in full swing when it is imposed on us, so that we ourselves are a *fait accompli* with which we are presented.

Later this will confront many of us with the question: 'What is this "I" that I am?' But to begin with, at any rate, our conscious-ness is not a consciousness of self. The reality of the situation is not that our awareness starts by being an awareness of our own existence as unique persons, and then extends outwards from this as a starting point to become an awareness of the world around us. The process moves in the opposite direction: we start by being aware of things outside ourselves – light, space, movement, objects, colours, people – and at first these fill our consciousness; and it is only by degrees that we become aware of our selves as centres of these experiences, as entities distinct, and to that extent separate, from what is going on outside us. Quite a lot of people, either underdeveloped people or people in underdeveloped societies, never securely establish a sense of self. But whether we as individuals become self-aware or not – and whatever we do, and whatever happens to us – it is inescapably us that we are, and this is the life we have; and whether we die in infancy or live to be a hundred, it is for all time true that each of us has existed in the world as a distinct human being who lived that life.

What I want to do in this book is tell the story of one such life, the only one I know better than anyone else knows it. I shall do everything in my power to tell the truth, and nothing but the truth; but I shall not attempt to write the whole truth, for that would be boring; in fact the most important task of all will be the task of selection. Everything here will be as I carefully remember it, but not everything I remember will be here. Memory can err, of course, so I shall make use of all the checks on mine that are available, chiefly older relatives and surviving documents. If, in spite of this, mistakes occur, I apologise in advance. If the reader thinks of the book as being called *As I Remember*, that will give him the right perspective. It is a report of experience, not a record of events.

The earliest recollection I have is of being surrounded by a fuzzy yellow light, known somehow to be in an enclosed space like a room, I think our kitchen, in which there were two giant figures standing, blank as silhouettes but blurry as the light, and slate grey, as if they were solid shadows. I was perceiving them from somewhere around their feet. High above me, from the tops of these giant figures, were coming noises that were directed not at me but at one another, top to top, like signals passing between radio masts. I understood that some kind of communication was going on between the two of them, and it absorbed them, so that they were not aware of me. It was all taking place above my head in both senses of that phrase. But I knew, somehow, that these high objects that were making these sounds were different from other objects, and were what mattered to me; and I have an idea that speech became, or already was, of commanding interest to me, even when not directed at me.

I remember a much loved companion of the same size as me who was a black dog called Robert; and I remember what he looked like, though he was no longer with us by the time I was three. I have an incisive memory of crouching in the darkness inside his kennel under the kitchen table, no one knowing where I was, and feeling breathlessly excited that I was genuinely hiding – not playing at hiding but really hiding, successfully. I could hear people running about and raising the alarm at my disappearance.

The first extended scene I recall involves a girl called Pam Ainsworth, who was probably between nine and eleven, and used to wheel me about in a push-chair. Once, at the door, as we were on our way out, my mother said to her: 'Don't give him any sweets. He's got a tummy ache.'

I piped up: 'I haven't got a tummy ache.'

'Yes you have,' snapped my mother. 'Shut up.' And my whole body boiled over with resentment that she was lying to prevent me getting any sweets. As soon as we were out in the street and passing the sweet shop two doors away I twisted myself round in the chair and called to Pam: 'Buy me some sweets.'

'Your mum says you can't have any. You've got a tummy ache.'

'I haven't got a tummy ache.'

'Your mum says you've got one.' And on we pushed, past the sweet shop. I remember every aspect of both of these scenes: the three of us at the door and the two of us in the street – the visual settings, Pammie Ainsworth and what she looked like, our words, and my consuming frustration and rage at what was happening.

When I was as small as that my face was so near the ground that I saw in vivid close-up everything that was under my nose. I knew each paving-stone in the street immediately outside where we lived, each with its own actual shape and colour. The existence of each seemed to be important, as if I had a relationship with it. Then there were the kerbstones, longer and thinner but harder and chunkier, and of a different stone – one had a plum colour, and I liked that one particularly: I often used to give it a special kick, or something of that sort. Once, standing there, I looked over the road and saw my father on the pavement opposite, talking to the man who lived in the flower shop facing us. My inside irradiated with joy at the sight of him, and I darted out across the road to be with him. An almighty screaming of brakes overwhelmed me, and a car was almost on top of me. It hit me, and knocked me sideways, but not off my feet; so, uninterruptedly, I ran curving round to my father's side and stood there, shaken but smiling up at him, putting my hand into his. He gripped my hand hard and jerked me to his side, and to my total incomprehension exploded down at me with a violent roar even louder than the brakes.

'What are you doing?'

I was thunderstruck. He was red-faced with rage, and I had taken it for granted that he would be pleased to see me, and would enjoy my being with him. Why didn't he want me there? I stood bewildered.

'You could have been killed. You nearly were.' Still shouting, beside himself. 'Don't you EVER do that again. Never, never, never cross this road by yourself again. Never. Do you hear me? Listen to what I'm saying to you.'

And then I understood that his anger had something to do with the car hitting me, which I could see might have been dangerous; and I realised that he would be even angrier if I were to get myself run over; so obviously I mustn't.

I continued as a normal thing to be out of doors by myself – my mother sent me out every day to get me from under her feet. 'Go out and play,' were the words I heard from her more often than any others, usually as part of a question uttered in a harsh, annoyed tone, like an order: 'Why don't you go out and play?' I needed no further encouragement. From soon after I could run I did a lot of my growing up on the street, even before I was allowed to cross the road.

Between where we lived and the end of the road on our side there were three shops and a bit of blank wall. The shops were small, though not perceived as such by me at the time. When you reached the corner the pavement ran downhill to the right. That new bit was called Whitmore Road, and had another three shops in it before you came to the next street, which was Phillipp Street. Among the shops in Whitmore Road was the baker's, Vooght's (pronounced Voots), where we bought freshly baked bread every day, still warm if you were lucky; and also rolls and cakes. In their shop window they had a display that reached down below my eye level, and was differently laid out every day – cream horns, jam tarts, almond meringues, always something made with lemon curd, various things with sugar icing, God knows how many kinds of cakes, and goodness knew what else too: doughnuts, ginger nuts, flapjacks, biscuits, scones . . . Cream horns were so much my favourite that there were things I never got as far as looking at. The fact that Vooghts was just round the corner meant that it was out of sight of home yet still only thirty yards away, and I could get there without crossing a road. I was frequently sent there to fetch things.

I remember going into the shop one day by myself – unlike our shop, you went down a step to get into it – and there in the centre of the space stood the round, heavy Mrs Vooght, with her

5

black hair and her loud voice, chattering with a woman customer. She said something about me to the other woman as I came in, and then addressed me.

'How old are you?'

'Free.'

'No you're not.'

'Yes I am.'

'You're not free. You're three. Say three.'

'Free.'

She was a mountainous woman, or seemed so to me, and she bent down over me until her huge face was immediately over my upturned one, almost touching it. To my astonishment her tongue, yards long, came out right in front of my eyes until the tip of it was resting on her great big bosom – an illusion that must have been caused by the angle I was seeing it at.

'Thhhhhree,' she said, with that incredible tongue right in my face, pink and vast, shaped like a pointed spade. 'Say thhhhhree.'

'Free.'

I could hear perfectly well what she was saying and thought I was saying it too, so what on earth was all this about? Why did she keep saying I wasn't three, and then saying I was? However, the dominant element in the memory, the chief reason I remember it, is nothing to do with the word, it is the tongue, which I found alarming. To this day, in the silence of my mind, this memory remains for me the most concrete connotation of the word 'tongue'.

If I was heading for the baker's I started off down our street. The other way was up. It was up, but only a few yards up, that I had, some time before this, got involved in a fight with the boy from the sweet shop, whose name I eventually knew to be Norman Tillson. I find, incidentally, that most of my earliest memories involve physical, emotional or sensory violence of some sort – no doubt this is why they impinged on me as they did and are now memories. As a street kid I was fairly violent myself, involved in fights every day as a matter of course, and I soon made the discovery that by unbridled fury of attack I could rout boys bigger or older than myself – within a certain size-gap, of course, which I learnt to estimate fairly accurately, though not infallibly. It did not work with Norman, though. He was three at a time when I had not yet reached that age; and although he was no taller than me he was more stockily built. I laid into him with my customary fury – and I have little doubt that it was I who was the aggressor – but was disconcerted not just by the effectiveness with which he fought me off but, even more so, by the untroubled air with which he did it. He was not in the least alarmed by my onslaught. He treated the demands it made on him as if they were a nuisance but all in a day's work, which I expect they were. I rushed back at him again and again, on repeated assaults, each time to be punched off in what seemed to me an insultingly offhand manner. It was as if he were being relaxedly good-natured about it all – no hard feelings, chum, but if you're really sure this is what you want, *biff*! Our fight took us off the pavement and into the roadway. Somebody from one of our families either saw or heard us, and shouted that being in the road was dangerous, and stopped us, and made us go back indoors to our respective homes. The contest was never resolved. But from that moment Norman was the best companion of my early years, and has remained a friend ever since.

These earliest memories carry within themselves the sense of an already embodied past. Things had been going on for some time before they happened, and I was already somebody. I felt as one feels on waking from a long, nourishing sleep – fresh and alert, and ready to begin, yet aware that a great deal has been going on that cannot be remembered. This, I take it, was some sort of subliminal awareness of the first couple of years of my life, years that I already carried within me as part of the person I was.

They must have been years of primal emotion, violent reaction, and intense learning: and now, deep within me, was an obscure, remote, inaccessible turmoil like the apprehension of an unremembered dream, not unhappy-making that I was conscious of, but unrestful. I was all the time avid for something, and I did not know what, so I wanted to absorb everything.

CHAPTER TWO

I was born into a shopkeeping family in a little community of shops. The year was 1930, a round number that made my age always easy to remember, and was later to make me feel a decade younger than people born any time in the 1920s. Our shop sold men's and boys' clothes, and belonged to my grandfather, whose name stood over the door: E. J. MAGEE. The initials stood for Edgar John. Everyone knew him as Edgar, though he had one or two amazingly old and privileged friends who, to my wonderment at their temerity, addressed him as Eggs. His son, my father – who within the planetary system of the family was the sun round which I moved – was Fred Magee. He worked for my grandfather for a weekly wage of three pounds fifteen shillings, which was about average in the '30s; though he also lived rent-free in the rooms over and behind the shop, which were home for him, my mother, my sister and me.

As a family of four we did most of our domestic living in the single back room on the ground floor behind the shop, which we called the kitchen. The dominant fact about this room was its littleness: when I was fully grown I could come within a couple of inches of touching the side walls simultaneously. When my memories begin there was, in the middle of one of these side walls, a black, open-grate fireplace with little ovens on each side of the fire and a hob on it for boiling a kettle, and a fender all round it with tiny padded seats at the corners on which we children loved to sit. One of my earliest memories is of two loud men in overalls coming into the kitchen and tearing all this out and replacing it with a light-coloured tiled modern fireplace, me watching with misgiving but also fascination. They, or somebody, installed a gas cooker in the dark corner behind the door that led into the shop. What space was left for the other corner on that side of the room was occupied by a deep, cubic, ochre-coloured earthenware sink with a cold-water tap. Pushed hard up against the other side wall was the kitchen table, round which there was just room for the four of us to squeeze past one another, or sit and eat. A tiny armchair was pinched between it and the doorway into the shop. Against the wall farthest from this door a sideboard stood under the kitchen's only window, which had metal bars outside and faced north-east, so the room was darkish most of the time. There was always a bowl of fresh fruit on the sideboard, but I was supposed to ask before taking any of it. There was also a big 1930s radio set, the chief daily source of music. In the remaining corner was the door into the back yard: you opened it and went down a couple of stone steps into an open-air, concrete-covered square not much bigger than the kitchen, surrounded by a high wall; and there in the far corner was the lavatory, where you had to stand holding the chain down till it finished flushing, otherwise it stopped in mid-flush.

Just inside the back door a forbiddingly steep and enclosed wooden staircase led to the rooms above, so narrow that adults had to swing their shoulders to one side to get up or down it. One of my earliest recollections is of lying on my back on the tiny landing at the top and thinking it would be interesting to find out how far it was possible to push myself out over the stairs without falling down them. It did not occur to me that only if I exceeded the limit could I find out where it was. First I pushed my head out, looking up at the ceiling; then my shoulders; and at that point I started to be careful: I pushed my torso out a bit more, and then another bit, and then, concentrating, edged myself out a little further, inch by inch; and then, I thought, just a tiny squeeze more, holding my breath now, thinking that either this was it or I could manage *just* one more teeny weeny little – *bangety-bang-bang-wallop-crash*, down I went, head first, over and over. By chance, not only was the door open at the foot of the stairs but so was the back door, so after hurtling down all the wooden stairs I carried straight on down the stone steps and out into the back yard. In addition to the racket this made I yelled, and people came running. A quick discussion took place about whether I should be whipped off to a doctor, but this was decided against; and I was bundled in somebody's arms to the chemists up the road to have my cuts and bruises tended, and no doubt to get his expert opinion about whether I ought to see a doctor. When I woke up next morning the bumps on my forehead were fascinatingly immense, and the pain from them was a new experience that might have been interesting too, had it not been so painful.

Off the landing from which this venture had begun, three rooms opened. On the left, in the smallest one, which looked out over the back yard, I slept in a large single bed with my sister Joan, who was three and a half years older than me. The room straight ahead, facing over the street, was our parents' bedroom, and they had a double bed, in which I had been born. But we were never allowed to go in there. This was far and away the most forbiddingly expressed and reiterated domestic taboo of our childhood: never, ever, no matter what the circumstances, were we to open the door of our parents' bedroom. But I was occasionally summoned in by them, so I knew what was there. The chief thing was a large, free-standing sewing machine referred to as the Singer. It was worked by a treadle, and on it all the family's clothing repairs (and perhaps a few simple alterations for the shop) were made. I longed to play with it, but was forbidden to touch it. The other main item was a dressing-table with three high mirrors that moved on hinges. One of my earliest memories is of standing in front of this dressing-table screaming with agony: I had drunk a bottle of eau-de-Cologne that I found there, and my insides were on fire.

The room to the right of my parents' bedroom, up a step from the landing (my bedroom was down a step) was the living-room, also facing out over the street, and bigger than the others. Against the far wall as you entered was a black open fireplace, and to the right of this a bookcase. By the right-hand wall was an upright piano, and opposite that, running along the wall under the window over the street, a sofa. Into the two far corners snuggled comfortable armchairs. Against the wall immediately to your left as you went in was a sideboard. In the middle of the room stood a dining-table, with leaves at each end that opened out; normally it stood shut, with upright chairs pushed in under it and standing there unused, stiff, like sentinels that you had to edge past. The fact that you could pull the leaves of the table out and make a bigger table was something that fascinated me, and my interest was intensified by the fact that there were three choices: you could pull one leaf out, or the other, or both; and this plus the table in its original state gave you four options. Sometimes I would pull a leaf out and just stand there looking at the table as remade. The contemplation of it gave me a pleasure that I often felt with any-thing in my environment that was unobvious or could be changed. But if I then just went off and left it I would get a serious ticking-off from my mother, so it could be a dangerous thing to do.

Actually there were a lot of things in that room that fascinated me. Across the shelf over the fireplace walked elephants, and at each end of it horses reared up with reins made of wire held by naked men. Somewhere in a different position each time you went into the room would be the wind-up gramophone, in its royal blue box, so heavy I could lift it but not carry it. Actually I was forbidden to touch it at all, but that only made it an object of greater interest. Hanging from the walls were two pictures. One was of a man whom I identified with my father: he wore a stove-pipe Puritan hat and was standing looking alarmed, with a woman on either side of him. When I learnt to read I discovered that it was called 'Between Two Fires', and this surprised me, because I had never noticed any fires in the picture, and even now I was unable to see any. The other picture was called 'The Boyhood of Raleigh' and showed an old man, whom I identified with my grandfather, pointing out across the sea, his muscley arm extended to its full length, while he was talking to two boys squatting at his feet. I identified myself with the farther one of these, the one in black, and assumed that the old man was pointing something interesting out to them: it never occurred to me that he was holding them spellbound with stories of distant lands beyond the horizon. I cannot put into words the piercingness or depth of the nostalgia I felt when I stumbled unexpectedly across the originals of some of these things, which I began to do in my teens. The first were the equestrian statuettes on the mantelpiece: at seventeen I found myself looking at them as the large statues on either side of the entrance to the Champs Elysées in Paris.

The table and the upright chairs matched the sideboard, and the armchairs matched the sofa. The upholstered furniture started out as a rather depressing gingery-brown leather with rounded backs, but one day it had all changed into something covered with a light-coloured new-looking fabric and square corners. A lot of my early memories have this character of something that I knew as having been always there changing suddenly into something different. Presumably it was the change that impinged on me and was the experience that is now the memory. I nearly always had a preference for the new over the old, so although I was startled by these changes I usually liked them. I now understand that those were years in which Britain was coming out of the Depression, and the living standards of families such as mine were going up steadily throughout the '30s (and were then to leap sharply upwards during the Second World War, never to return to the pre-war poverty that was the normal standard for most British families), so that I was experiencing, at the coal-face of childhood experience, the beginnings of a long-term social shift of historic proportions. Needless to say, I knew nothing of this at the time.

My parents would often spend evenings in our living-room after my sister and I had gone to bed, and we could hear their voices in our darkness, which I liked. We children played in the living-room on rainy days, and when other children were visiting us. And the whole family used it whenever all four of us were together for more than just a meal, which meant that we spent all day Sunday there, and ate our midday Sunday dinner at the dining-table. We used it also whenever we had guests or visitors, so it was automatically the room for special occasions, like Christmas and birthdays. Although it was in constant use it came to be associated in my mind with treats. Workaday life was carried on downstairs in the kitchen, but fun was more usually upstairs in the living-room. The reason we all made so little use of it during the daytime on weekdays was that people needed to be popping in and out all the time, either in and out of the shop, or the street (for which you needed to go through the shop), or the lavatory in the back yard; and the stairs were a disincentive, especially to someone carrying dishes of hot food, or for that matter carrying anything at all. There were no utilities upstairs except for the electric light: we had no indoor lavatory or bathroom, and our only water supply was the cold tap in the kitchen sink. But all this meant that during the day on most days we were perpetually squeezing past and round one another in that tiny kitchen.

Because of this, the kitchen was the only room that was always heated – by the cooking, whether we liked it or not, and by a coal-fire whenever we wanted one. The bedrooms were never heated, and the living-room only in winter when the room was being used. So for half the year there was a practical question attached to going upstairs, namely: 'Is it worth lighting the fire?' Inertia on that point saw to it that we made much more use of the room in the warmer half of the year.

In the cold half we would get out of bed and put our clothes on straight away in the mornings, and then go downstairs and wash. Our getting-up times were staggered so that we could take it in turn at the kitchen sink; and while each of us was washing, the kettle would be boiling for the next one. Saturday night was bath-night, at least as far as the children were concerned. A zinc bath would be carried into the kitchen from the yard and set on the hearthrug in front of the fire. Water was boiled up in every available cooking utensil simultaneously. My sister, being a girl, was given the clean water, and I would clamber into it the moment she got out so as to catch it while it was still warm. ('*Come on, hurry up, it's getting cold!*') We had two zinc baths, a small one for us children and a full-length one for our parents. Both hung from iron nails in the brickwork of the house's back wall, where their position helped them to dry out, though they got rained on a lot. Our parents always bathed when we were not around, and I simply do not know when they did it: I think they must have bathed more often than we did, for they always seemed to me unnaturally clean. But I never saw either of them naked.

Because we had no indoor lavatory, the use of chamber pots was part of our everyday life, and I took them for granted. There were always two under each bed upstairs – my sister and I each had our own, as did our parents. They were referred to as 'the po', as in 'I want to use the po', and were the first focus of repression I can remember. I was supposed to try hard not to use the po, and to use it only when I had to, and to crap in it only when I *absolutely* had to, and given clearly to understand that the whole thing was really a bloody nuisance, which obviously it was.

CHAPTER THREE

The reason we had three rooms upstairs and only one down is that the shop had once been two shops that were then knocked into one, and in the conversion one of the two ground-floor back rooms had been incorporated into the new shop, making it L-shaped, quite large by local standards. So we had the upstairs rooms from two shops but the ground-floor room from only one.

Outside, narrow alleyways ran along both sides of the enlarged shop. One of them, no more than a slit, cut through to what had been stables at the back and were now two minuscule cottages in a space next to our back yard. In the corresponding space on the other side lived a cow which belonged to the Jenkinses. They kept what everyone called a dairy. From the street, a tunnel you could walk through ran alongside our shop and opened out into the yard where the cow lived. In the rooms above this tunnel lived the Jenkinses. At the tunnel's mouth was a nook of a shop with not even a door on to the street but only a window, through which old Mrs Jenkins sold milk and her other dairy products to people on the pavement. Her own front door was in the tunnel. She was a fat, much-chinned old woman with gold-rimmed glasses and piled grey hair, and she always wore a loose black dress down to her ankles, as did most elderly women in the Hoxton of that time. For almost the whole of every day she would sit unbudging in her window at the point of sale. When I caught a sight of her walking I saw she limped heavily, dragging one foot in a built-up surgical boot. I was often sent with a jug to buy milk from her, but although I had frequent exchanges with her I did not like her – she was too snappish. She spoke differently from everyone else, with what I now realise was a Welsh accent.

She had a grown-up daughter called Bessie, whom I liked immensely but who was only seldom on duty in the window nook. Bessie did all the work behind the scenes, including not only housework and shopping but looking after the cow. Sturdily built and handsome, she was a country woman rather than a townee, with a strong physical presence and an outflowing warmth that children especially responded to: talking to Bessie gave me a glow. From what my parents said about her I picked up the fact that they regarded her as stupid, but to me this appeared either untrue or unimportant. She had a daughter, Mary, a year or two older than me, who skipped everywhere instead of walking, and was always referred to in our family as 'Mary in the dairy'. The Jenkins household contained no men. When I asked Mary where her father was, she told me he was in prison for stealing old Mrs Jenkins's money. Looking back, and remembering remarks over-heard from my parents, I realise now that Mary was illegitimate, and that the prison story had been given to her as a cover.

When I was sent for milk I would hand the jug up to old Mrs Jenkins and she, with a cylindrical ladle that was also a half-pint measure, would dole the milk out from a churn at her side, a churn bigger than me. I enjoyed watching the milk overflowing the measure and pouring back into the churn. Usually I was sent to buy half a pint, so I would see this happen only once, but if I was lucky enough to be buying a pint I saw it twice. Half a pint was three farthings, a pint a penny farthing. Farthings were beginning to lose their grip even then, and I remember only three things for which I used them regularly: milk, the cheapest sweets, and the cheapest cigarettes.

However, in the shop on the other side of ours from the

Jenkinses they were standard currency. This sold women's and girls' clothes, and everything in their display was priced at so many shillings and elevenpence three farthings. The idea was that if you bought something priced, as half their items seemed to be, at nineteen shillings and elevenpence three farthings, you got change from a pound. This shop had once been my grandmother's. She and my grandfather had run the two shops side by side, complementary in their merchandising for the two sexes, ready between them to clothe persons of all ages from the nape of the neck to the ankles. (Neither of them sold hats or shoes.) When my grandmother started to have children – two girls and two boys, one of whom died in infancy – she found it impossible to bring up a family while at the same time running a business separate from my grandfather's. So she sold it to an immigrant Jewish family whose name had been Zuckermann and was now Sugar. I vaguely remember an elderly couple who, by the time my memories begin, were semi-retired and took so little notice of me that I hardly knew them. The driving force of both family and shop was their grown-up daughter Doris. Nothing against the Sugars was ever said in my hearing, but I grew up realising that my family regarded them as selling shoddy stuff, and having shoddy attitudes, no longer providing for women a complement to our shop, where plenty of things cost less than a pound but a garment was more likely to be made of green cheese than to sell at nineteen shillings and elevenpence three farthings.

On the other side of Sugar's was a newspaper shop run by Jim Cohen and his wife Mabel. Everyone referred to this as Pemberton's, which was the name over the door, but the Pembertons had gone away for ever, and I never set eyes on them, though I often heard them talked about. Mabel Cohen was Mrs Pemberton's sister. Not only did the shop have to cope with a crack-of-dawn delivery of morning papers, but London at that time had three evening papers which came out at about eleven in the morning and then kept issuing new editions throughout the afternoon, with ever fresh and up-to-the-minute racing results; and for each of these there was a delivery round. The Cohens had no children, and were coming up to middle age, so to manage these newspaper rounds they took in a homeless young couple called Ling, who had a boy smaller than me called Brian (the only other person of that name I ever came across in Hoxton). Somehow it was known to one and all, even us children, that the Lings had no money; and we were all supposed to feel sorry for them.

Beyond Pemberton's was a shop that was empty when I knew it: it had been a second-hand furniture shop that people still referred to as Dirty Harry's. Then came the corner shop, with its little front door, like the front door of a tiggywinkle house, slanted diagonally across the street corner; and you had to open the door by the brass knob and walk up a step to get in. It was run by a little old lady called Mrs Benson, who seemed all ribbon and lace, which was what she sold, together with needles and thread, buttons and buckles, and all the rest. New then, I believe just coming in, were zip fasteners. One of my earliest memories is of standing in that shop with my mother, surrounded by all those sparkling and colourful yet pleasingly small things, examining them while the two women were chattering.

Once you turned the corner past both windows of the corner shop and started downhill you were in Whitmore Street, and there immediately was Vooght's. All this was what happened if you went down Hoxton Street, turning right as you came out of our shop. If you went left there was first the dairy and then Tillson's sweet shop. Albert Tillson, who ran this, had shock-red hair and a face like the film actor Claude Rains. His wife Beattie ran a bigger sweet shop further up the street. They were great friends of my parents. They had two children who were similar in age to my sister and me, the older a girl called Eileen, the younger Norman. The Tillsons had not had the larger of their two shops for long, and shortly after I became aware of them they moved their living-quarters to it from the small one. This meant that no sooner had Norman and I become friends than he moved away. It was only two or three hundred yards away, but the distance seemed an obstacle at the time. I had other friends at my end of the street; but as I grew bigger and more mobile, and also more independent, I used to wander more and more up to Norman's, to see him – and also because that was where the market was.

The shop beyond Tillson's was a barber's shop run by a blue-chinned man with a big head and black hair called George Pope. In one corner of his shop a parrot cage hung by a chain from the ceiling, and every time anyone went in or out the parrot shouted: '*Shut the door!*' A shave was fourpence and a haircut six-pence. In those days, men who could afford it would more freq-uently be shaved by a barber than by themselves, so at different times of each day, when things were quiet in our shop, my father or grandfather would slip three doors up for a shave, my grand-father usually announcing this by saying: 'I'm just going to have a dig in the grave.' About Mr Pope there was something heavy and dark, forbiddingly saturnine, and I was always wary of him, uncomfortable in his presence. I was also unsettled by the ugly screeching of his parrot. To my relief I did not have my hair cut by him, and nor did my father, in spite of his having an almost daily shave there. For our haircuts we walked together up to Kingsland Road, to a likeable barber called Morrie. Looking back, I realise that George Pope was a depressive. He committed suicide a few years later, during the blitz, because he could not stand the nightly bombing. It was my father who found him. Before man-oeuvring his head into the gas oven he rolled himself in the carpet so that he would not flop out when he fell unconscious.

Even as a child I often heard about people committing suicide in Hoxton. There seemed to be two ways they did it, one by putting their head in the gas oven and the other by cutting their throat.

All men had cut-throat razors (and leather straps to hone them on, these providing the normal weapon for chastising children) so this was a means universally to hand. It also equipped violent criminals with a terrifying weapon – but that is something we shall come to later. I recall my father making the changeover from a cut-throat to a newfangled safety razor, and trying to persuade my grandfather to do the same, and my grandfather refusing, and the two of them having a heated discussion about it.

Beyond Pope's was Burch's, the shoe-menders. Two men worked here all day, perched at lasts, side by side, repairing boots and shoes. Of the two of them one was unobtrusively pleasant but the other, Mr Barrett, was a natural bully with a square head and thick neck who got pleasure out of frightening children. I did not like going into his shop, but I frequently had to. The compensation was the smell of fresh leather, so wonderful it made your head swim. Huge strips of it, toffee-coloured, the size and shape of a door split in half down the middle, stood propped up on their long sides against the wall; and out of these the two men would cut the various shapes they needed for their work. Mr Barrett had a handsome white dog which was always running out into the street when not supposed to, at which he would drop whatever he was doing, grab a long thin strip of leather kept for the purpose, and rush out after it, swearing violently. Every time a customer opened the door he would shout: 'Don't let the dog out!' But the dog escaped daily; and as I grew bigger I met Mr Barrett ever further and further afield, usually pounding down the middle of a roadway, looking up all the side streets, cursing loudly, waving his leather strap and shouting threats at the invisible animal. 'Seen the dog?' he would call to me. I always said No, whether I had or not – quite frequently I had, but I was on the dog's side, as was everyone else. My parents almost never said derogatory things about any of our neighbours in my presence, but for Mr Barrett they made an exception: he was a brute, and they said so. I fear it may have been this licensed disapproval that led me and Norman Tillson occasionally – and shamefully – to terrorise his two unfortunate sons, who were smaller than us, and were probably already having a violent time of it at home.

Their shop had two windows with the front door between them, and in the inlet to their front door there was dirty white tiling on the ground with the name Tubb picked out in black tiles. It was explained to me that this had once been a shop like ours, belonging to a Mr and Mrs Tubb, and that my grandfather had worked in it before acquiring his own shop. A number of local people still referred to the shoe-menders as Tubb's. Shops' names in Hoxton had, perhaps still have, a tendency to outlive their owners. There is still a paper shop called Pemberton's, now owned by Asian immigrants.

The liveliest premises on our side of the road that were at all near us were those of a pub, perhaps a hundred yards up, called the Admiral Keppel – which until quite a few years later I took to be the Admiral Kettle. We referred to it usually as 'the pub', since it was the nearest one on our side, and was such a hive of activity; all other pubs were given their name, but just 'the pub' meant this one. As a child I was forbidden by law to enter any of them. During the middle hours of each weekday, when the men were working, the Keppel would be full of women, and the cluster of prams on the pavement outside its closed doors would be so dense that you had to step out into the road to pass. Usually one or other of the babies in the street would be yelling, and a steady succession of women emerged through the pub door, drink in hand – each mother seemed to know when it was her child crying – and give the baby a drink from her glass to tranquillise it, and go back into the pub. The men who filled it in the evenings were involved with racing, and they organised regular day-outings to race meetings. On those days they would gather together at the bar from opening time onwards, to prepare for the day's racing with some serious drinking; and then, when it came time, climb aboard the charabanc outside and set off. This vehicle (pronounced by us sharrabang, or more usually just sharra) was the most wonderful land vehicle I ever set eyes on. It was the length and width of a London bus, but only one-storey, and completely open. It carried something like forty people. I found it amazing just to look at. It was crucially important to be standing beside it when it drove away, because when the men took their seats in it they would sort out the coppers from their loose change while waiting for it to start, and then, the moment the wheels began to move, hurl the coins out into the road. So forty men simultaneously showered the street with money as their vehicle drove off to the races. Crowds of children on the pavement waited for this moment, getting more and more impatient; and a great cheer went up from them when the money was hurled into the air. They scrambled out into the space left by the departing sharra as pennies and ha'pennies ran around criss-cross all over the road, bouncing off the walls and running along both gutters. Appallingly, some of them always rolled into the drains. The worst thing was to see sixpences and shillings going down the drain, because there were always some of the men who were drunk by this time and got their coins mixed up, or simply hurled all the change from their pockets overboard. The best thing was to position yourself well away from a drain and alert yourself to pick out silver from copper with your eye while the coins were still flying around, and then reach a bit of silver before it stopped rolling – and before anyone else got to it. Fights broke out everywhere in the scrum of children clambering to get past one another, pouncing on the same coins simultaneously; but these were sorted out by the women who had come to share a departing drink with their men, and were now left behind. Their separation of the fighting children was a standard part of the ritual. The children, adrenaline running, would rush into the market with whatever money they had managed to grab, and the women would turn back into the pub and take over there until the men returned.

When I was a bit older I learnt that this pub was among the favourites of the criminal fraternity, and that it was from this that its special connection with racing derived. Crimes were hatched and discussed here, and the recruitment for them carried out among its regulars. On the whole my father and grandfather steered clear of it, going instead to a quiet pub on the other side of the road, nearer to us, called the King's Arms. This was run by a couple, Jimmy and Betty Ainsworth, who were special friends. It was their daughter Pam who wheeled me about in my push-chair; and they had two boys, dissimilar twins, who were nearer my age but older enough to be uninterested in playing with me.

One of the boys I played with a lot lived diagonally opposite the Ainsworths, on our side of the road, in a shop a few yards up from Barrett's. His name was Davy Franks, though I could not pronounce this properly and used to say 'Damy Franks', which is what he became known as in my family. His parents' shop was dark, dim, and empty of furniture or fittings. It was full, from floor to ceiling, of piles of American comics, which they either sold or bartered: if you already had two you could take them there and they would give you one in exchange. This meant that the ideal number to have was four, because then, when you had finished them, you could get another two, and *then*, in a moment of special bliss, exchange those for a culminating one, so that your four became seven.

I was playing with Davy Franks in the street one day when three or four boys bigger than either of us appeared out of nowhere and started chanting '*Jewboy! Jewboy!*' and then ran towards Davy shouting '*You're a Jew! You're a Jew!*' I was impressed by the way he unflinchingly hurled a cry of 'What of it?' into the oncoming charge, but they bore down on him just the same, barged into him, pushed him around, and then ran off chanting, '*Jewboy!*

Jewboy! He shouted 'What of it?' again after their retreating backs.

When they had gone I said: 'What did they do that for?'

'Coz I'm a Jew.'

'What's a Jew?'

'I don't know.'

'How d'you know you're one, then?'

'Coz my Mum and Dad said so.'

'What d'you mean?'

'My Mum and Dad say we're Jews.'

'What does "What of it?" mean?'

'I don't know.'

'What did you say it for then?'

'My Mum and Dad told me to.'

'What d'you mean?'

'My Mum and Dad said if anybody says "Jewboy" to me I've got to say "What of it?" to them.'

'Why?'

'I don't know.'

When I got home I asked my parents: 'What's a Jew?'

I wish I could remember their reply. Probably I understood less than half of it. But I know that from then on I had some notion what a Jew was, and that there were people who were horrible to Jews.

Beyond the Franks's shop was a cheap outfitters that sold the same sort of clothes for men as Sugar's did for women. They called themselves 'Wingo: The Dollar Tailor', and on the outside brick wall over their front door was painted the sign for five shillings, (5/−), big and bold. It was from asking what this meant that I discovered that five shillings was a dollar, and that half a crown was called half a dollar; and today the word 'dollar' often brings to my mind a visual image of that sign.

Next up from The Dollar Tailor was a shop of real importance

25

in my life, the fish and chip shop. Chips I adored, and used to buy them sometimes instead of sweets: they would sell you a penn'orth. The cheapest fish cost tuppence. This was so-called rock salmon, a scavenger. To get cod you had to pay threepence, which is what my parents usually did. There were more expensive fish than that, such as plaice, haddock and skate, but these were special-occasion stuff, like for when we had unexpected visitors. It was for fast food in emergencies that my parents used the shop mostly, and this resulted in our having fish and chips about once a week. For me a grown-up, big-wide-world thing was when we used the shop as a restaurant and took our guests there, and sat at one of the marble-topped tables, and were waited on by the man behind the counter. In the middle of each of these tables stood salt, pepper and vinegar in jumbo containers, the first two in metal canisters so big I could scarcely get my hands round them, and the vinegar in quart bottles. The rougher grown-ups used to dowse the fish and chips in vinegar, but children found it too sour.

Up from the fish and chip shop was a wireless shop. I grew up taking wireless for granted, but in fact, unrealised by me, it was a newish thing, and we were still in the period when the poor were getting it for the first time. The shop's window was full of second-hand wireless sets and spare parts. After that came Wilmer Gardens, the first turning on the left from our shop, less than a hundred yards up. It was a notoriously rough, tough street, and I was forbidden to go down it. I did, of course, but each time something would happen that I was afraid to tell my parents. Eventually my visits there were outed. I got involved in a gang fight with some boys, and we all took our belts off and started whirling them round our heads like flails, trying to hit one another with the buckles. Suddenly I had what seemed to me a good idea. I nipped back home, took the belt off my other pair of trousers, fastened the two belts together to make a double-length flail, and hurried with it back to the fight. But I was so small that I did not have the strength required to twirl a flail of that length at the speed needed to make it effective. It flagged, and the far end flip-flopped. The boy I was fighting grabbed it, yanked it out of my grasp, ran off with it at top speed, and disappeared through one of the street doors.

Dreading what I knew must come, I returned home. Scarcely had I got there than there came the inevitable question: 'Where's your belt?' To lose one belt might be regarded as a misfortune, but to lose two was unpardonable carelessness, and what with that and going into Wilmer Gardens *and* getting into a gang fight I got an angry slapping from my mother.

It was just past Wilmer Gardens that Hoxton Street became wider and the street market started: so the mêlée of the market began about a hundred yards from our shop. As a tot I was not supposed to go into the crowds by myself, though I went in amongst them almost daily with my mother or my sister, and I loved them. Wilmer Gardens was so narrow, and so few vehicles ever went down it, that I was allowed from the beginning to cross it by myself, though at first only to go to the Co-op, three doors further on – and then it was always with two strict injunctions: 'Keep on the pavement!' and 'Come straight back!'

On the far corner of Wilmer Gardens was Costers' Hall, a mission hall where my grandparents had met. They were totally irreligious, both of them, but the mission had organised some sort of social club for young people who went there to meet one another. This had happened when my grandparents were eighteen and nineteen, the normal age then for most people to marry. I myself went there one evening a week for a while, when I was about seven or eight: it must have been a different clientele, obvi-ously – they probably took in different age-groups on different evenings. I used to take along a penny, and was given a mug of cocoa and a couple of hours' organised games with other children.

It was the only place I ever got cocoa, which we did not have at home. I liked the place, and quite liked cocoa, though I didn't think it was as good as tea.

Next to the mission, which was quite a big building, was the small front door of Dr McCurry's surgery. He was a diminutive Scotsman, swarthy and hunched, our family doctor. He had delivered both me and my sister, and came to see us in bed every time any of us got ill, always carrying his battered old leather bag. When he talked to our parents he jerked up and down on his toes all the time, but he did not do this when he talked to us. We liked him, but were a little in awe of him, for our parents told us that he knew everything and was always right, and that we must do whatever he said. Each time he came he would examine us thoroughly and then sink his chin into his chest and say 'Hmmmm!' forbiddingly to himself, and start jerking up and down on his toes while deciding on his diagnosis. Whenever he spoke it was in a peculiar way that I never heard from anyone else: sometimes he had to repeat himself before I understood. My parents said this was called a Scottish accent, and said they liked hearing it. I was puzzled by the notion that there could be anything about it to enjoy.

After Dr McCurry's front door came the Co-op, a long low shop with more than one door on to the street and the most floor space of any shop near us. When I started being sent there my mother used to write down her Co-op number and give it to me to show in the shop, so that she would get her dividend; but I soon knew it by heart, and have never forgotten it: 179263. Many years later, when I was a Labour MP during the premiership of Harold Wilson, he and I found in conversation that we shared certain childhood experiences, and he told me that on his worldwide travels throughout his adult life he had always, whenever confronted by an official form that asked him to fill in his passport number (which he could never remember) put down his mother's Co-op number; and that no one had ever queried it. I was so intrigued by this that for a couple of years I did the same, and no one queried me either.

I realised as I grew older that my grandparents disapproved of my mother's shopping at the Co-op, on the ground that the Co-op put small shopkeepers like themselves out of business. She was undeterred by their disapproval, and said she wanted the dividend, and was damned if she was going to cut off her nose to spite her face. (This was one of her characteristic expressions.) Next to the Co-op was the Admiral Keppel, and the pram-jam on the pavement outside it that forced you to step out into the road – straight into the maelstrom of the market – so for a long time that was the farthest I went by myself.

Because I lived under such a draconian ban against crossing Hoxton Street by myself I was less well acquainted with the other side. The roadway at our end was not wide, but once I had ingested the taboo it might as well have been the Grand Canyon. However, there were many days when I went over there with someone; and once I started going to school, which I did when I was three, my mother took me across it and back twice a day. Even so, any attempts at exploration or hanging around were strictly forbidden when I was with her.

Directly opposite our front door was a flower shop belonging to the Taylors. Mrs Taylor ran it and did all the work, a fat, strong woman, tough and competent while being likeable and good with children. Her husband, a weaselly little man, was weak and shifty, and the two of them together looked like the married couple in the classic seaside postcards by Donald McGill. Mr Taylor never had a job, and no one ever saw him lift a finger in the shop. I once heard my father describe him as a hanger-on, and I came eventually to realise that he lived as a scrounger in the shadows of the world around us, a racecourse tout, a bookmaker's nark, but was not even trustworthy enough to take bets on street corners.

The Taylors had a son, Tom, who was a cripple and sat all day in a wheelchair on the pavement outside the shop. Tom was a teenager with a normal-sized body but legs that had not grown properly, and he could not walk. Also, he had a huge, misshapen, encephalitic head. His mental age was about the same as mine, so I enjoyed talking to him, and we had many interesting conversations. The flower shop's routine work was for such things as weddings and funerals, chiefly funerals, and this meant that there were always wreaths to be made up, which involved the intertwining of stalks with wire to provide a basis. Tom was able to help with this, so he would sit doing it in his wheelchair in the street, where he was always glad of someone to chat to. Some of the street kids occasionally tried to hassle him, but when they did, Mrs Taylor, who kept an eye on him through the shop window, would be out of her front door like an arrow and send them flying with great swipes from her meaty hand, followed by colourful abuse hurled after their disappearing backs, until she finally stomped back into her shop with a look of marvellous disgust on her face.

To the left of the Taylors as you looked over the road was a corset shop, run by two sisters called Blitz. In those days all females wore corsets from puberty onwards. I believe there was a workshop at the back in which corsets were repaired, if not made: the two women were constantly busy at sewing machines. One of them also gave piano lessons: everyone around us who learnt the piano was being taught by Miss Blitz. My sister and I understood from the earliest age that if ever we were to have piano lessons, that's who we would have them from.

Actually, in our house the piano was a bone of contention. My father and his two sisters had had lessons when they were small, and my father had turned out to be a good player. He was especially gifted as a sight-reader: he could put a difficult and unknown score on the music rest and simply play it. In fact he was an accomplished score-reader altogether: away from the instrument he could sing a strange score at sight and up to speed, which is something I have never been able to do. He wanted my sister and me to start piano lessons while we were still small, in the way he had, but my mother was opposed to this on the ground that it was a waste of money. It was a running dispute between them; and my mother started looking for a chance to settle it for good by getting rid of the piano. What made this a possibility was the effect the radio had on my father. The regular broadcasting of classical music was a recent innovation, and he had become a regular listener to it. The pianists he heard on the radio were so much better than himself that he preferred to listen to them rather than play, and he reached a point when he almost stopped playing. This gave my mother her chance. She complained of having to keep clean and dusted a piano that was 'never used', and accused it of aggravating our space problem, and pointed out that we could get good money for it. When my sister began to clamour for piano lessons, at the age of about seven, mother took decisive action. It resulted in one of the most astounding sights of my life. I was returning home one day along the street, past Pope's the barbers, when I looked up, and there, at what seemed to be rooftop level, was our piano hanging out of the sky. I stood transfixed, unable to believe what I was looking at. To this day that memory has something surreal about it, a piano floating high in mid-air over a street, surrounded by sky and clouds, as I might now expect to see it in a painting by Salvador Dali or Magritte. What had happened was that my mother had won her campaign to get rid of it – I suspect we were broke at the time, and desperately in need of cash – and had found it impossible to have the thing carried down our narrow staircase, so a pulley had been mounted on the roof and a rope used to swing it out through the upstairs window; and I had caught it at just the moment when it was hanging out there, about to be lowered into the street. This momentous departure of the piano put paid, as it was meant to do, to any prospect of my learning to play it in the foreseeable future. But I do not remember being especially upset about that. My sister was, though: she felt she had been sold out by my mother, and of course she had. No piano lessons from Miss Blitz, then, for either of us.

The next shop-front up from the Blitzes had a display window of frosted glass, and was not a shop but the surgery (which I read, when I first learnt to read, as 'sugary') of Dr Perkoff. He was a tall man with foreign-looking glasses, and he wore a sports jacket and flannels at a time when other doctors wore suits – I think he was being casually British. He spoke with a foreign accent, and in an unpleasantly peremptory manner, as if he were giving orders; and nobody liked him. None of his near neighbours had him as their doctor. He was known particularly for his meanness. He was the first, and for many years the only, man I ever saw carry his money in a purse. Everyone thought that, being a doctor, he ought to wear a suit but was too mean to buy one. When he took British nationality and changed his name to Perkins he asked all the neighbours beforehand what they thought of the proposed new name, and I recall everyone turning this question over in conversation – I think he wanted them to be reassured that he would still be the same person. When two men came and changed the name on his frosted-glass window people said he had chosen Perkins because it would cost him less money to have only three letters changed instead of the whole name. The workmen chiselled off the last three letters, and my sister and I stood across the street and watched while they did it. It seemed to me baffling that anyone should want to change his name at all, and I did not understand why, until it was explained to me that he wanted people to think he was English. I understood that all right, but how could anyone think Dr Perkoff was English? After that he got annoyed when people called him Perkoff, and corrected them in strident tones – 'I'm Dr Perkins now' – but people went on doing it just the same, because that was how they had got used to thinking of him.

What lay next to Dr Perkoff in that direction I no longer remember, except that you very quickly came to the Ainsworths' pub, which was only a skip and a jump from our front door. A few yards further on was a very tiny street called Clinger Street – pronounced to rhyme with ginger – so small that in my mind it scarcely counted as a street at all, though my opinion of it changed when I was told that my grandfather had been born in it. The idea of my grandfather being born was not an easy one to grasp, but I was quite pleased that it had happened so close to where I had been born myself.

If, from the flower shop opposite us, you went down the street instead of up, there was first of all a shop owned by a family called Goorwich (pronounced Gorridge). They dealt in much the same merchandise as the Sugars, but were bigger and more up-market, more solid, with not quite the same aura of trashiness. I recall watching a big square clock being hoisted up over their shop door as a street sign, pointing sideways out into the road so that people would be able to tell the time from both directions. The Goorwiches had a daughter Sadie, who was the same age as my sister, and the two girls played together. If, on a Sunday, Sadie wanted Joan to come out and play with her – our shop being closed, its shutters down, and we all upstairs in the living-room – she would stand in the middle of the road outside and toss something up at our closed window; and when she had gained Joan's attention she would mouth silently up at her, and Joan would mouth silently back, through the glass, while I looked on fascinated by this mode of communication. To me the two of them seemed like incredibly clever, sophisticated girls behaving in a marvellously grown-up fashion, when in fact they were seven or eight years old.

Joan mentioned to me one day that the Goorwiches were Jews.

Looking back, I realise that half our neighbours were – Cohen, Sugar, Franks, Perkoff, Blitz, Goorwich – but at the time it was not a conscious thought. I had a rough idea what Jews were, but did not identify somebody as one unless I was told. In a few years' time Oswald Mosley and his Fascists would make our area one of the focal points of their activity because of this racial mix; but until this happened, the question of who was and who was not a Jew was not one that preoccupied anyone I heard talking, though people were alive to the difference, and would mention it some-times. My parents had many Jewish friends. Our shop, being in the rag trade, bought most of its goods from Jewish suppliers. One way and another I grew up knowing a lot of Jews – so when in the late '30s the Blackshirts started beating up Jews in our local streets it had a colossal impact on me. But when I was very small this was still in the future, albeit the near future.

When I wrote the string of names in the last paragraph it trig-gered a wholly unrelated, and by comparison trifling, realisation in my mind, and that is that even the people we saw most often, saw perhaps many times a day, were invariably referred to by their full names: Jim Cohen, Doris Sugar, Tom Taylor, George Pope. Even when there were no two with the same first name it was never just Tom or Doris or George, not even when they were on terms of close friendship, as we were with Albert Tillson and Jimmie Ainsworth. These would be directly addressed as Albert and Jimmie, but always referred to by their full names. This applied even to children, and even among children: both I and my parents would always talk about Norman Tillson, Davy Franks, Sadie Goorwich. When I went to school, the same thing applied among the children there: even the tots talked about one another in this way. I have no ready explanation for it, nor of why or when it changed to today's practice.

On the far side of Goorwich's was a boot shop. It sold shoes too, but it was always referred to as 'the boot shop'. This was the last decade in which most people wore boots – shoes were coming in already in a big way. The difference was mostly a generational one, among adults at least: in Hoxton most middle-aged and elderly women wore boots, but the young ones all wore shoes. My grandfather wore only boots, but in my time my father did not possess any. I wore boots in winter and shoes in summer. I do not think my sister ever had boots, though a lot of small girls wore them, and nearly all boys. Children were a special case, because in most families clothes were passed down from one child to the next, almost regardless of sex – not frocks or trousers, but nearly everything else. One often saw a little girl wearing a boy's jacket and cap because they had belonged to her older brother.

It was when you got past the boot shop that you came to my favourite shop of all. This was Hunter's, often referred to as 'the chandler's'. It dealt in everything to do with the keeping of horses, though it also, as a sideline, provided for other animals, notably dogs, cats and birds. Motor vehicles were thin on the ground in the Hoxton of those days, as they were everywhere else in Britain, and nearly all supplies for Hoxton Street market came in horse-drawn vehicles, with which the streets around us were packed during the day. The local horse population was enormous. The perpetual background-noise of my childhood, never-ending in the street outside our shop, was the sound of horse-drawn vehicles passing by. It was a whole lot of different sounds integrated: the gratingly sharp-edged clip-clop of horseshoes on cobblestones, accompanied by a jangling of harness like tambourines, with a bass line of raw, flinty, linear grinding from the iron rims of the wheels along the cobbles, and above it all the crazy racket of the upper wooden chassis of the carts as they bounced and bumped wildly over the stones.

The chandler's was run by a Mr Saunders, a well-dressed man with a smart moustache. In winter his wife wore her fur coat every time she went out, whereas the womenfolk in my family wore theirs only on special occasions. Everything about their shop conveyed to me a sense of luxuriant pleasure. There were first the smells, different smells on all sides, at least a dozen, each as pungent and sumptuous as the leather in Burch's. It was like a shop of smells. A lot of them did in fact come from leather, dark brown and black, the harnesses and saddles hanging from the walls. Between the saddles dipped great loops of reins. To be used on all this leather were waxes and other sorts of jicker, in jars and boxes and free-standing blocks, all with their own different smells. Best of all, and filling the body of the shop, were huge standing sacks of barley and oats, and other kinds of grain, sacks bigger than me, with wide open mouths. An everyday sight in our streets was that of a horse having a nosebag fitted over its head, and here was where what was in those nosebags came from. When I thrust my face over one – or better still into it, like a nosebag – it made me swoon with the aroma, not shallow like other smells but a deep, solid smell, a smell you could almost sink your teeth into. I used to come out from that shop feeling high – unquestionably there was something in those smells that affected my brain. The sacks themselves, the sacking, had a different but also powerful smell if you pushed your nose into them. Their texture was so harsh that if you brushed past one hard enough it could scratch and hurt – and it was easy to do this, because there was scarcely any room to move between them. The floor was unlike any other I knew, in that there was no layer of anything else over the wooden floorboards – everywhere else had linoleum, if not carpets or rugs, but here there was only sawdust. Occasionally, to this day, if I find myself standing on a sawdust-covered wooden floor, I am transported, as if by some inner time-machine, to Hunter's.

With this exotic chandler's, Hoxton Street began its curve round to meet Pitfield Street, Hoxton's other main artery. The two streets run parallel for about three-quarters of a mile, and then curve in and meet. The core of Hoxton consisted of them and all the lesser streets that ran across and between them – and all the slits and walks that ran off *them,* a rabbit-warren of cut-throughs and alleyways, wood-yards and cobbled courts, teeming with humanity. I put the word 'consisted' in the past tense because this rabbit-warren has now disappeared. During the decades since the Second World War, council estates of multi-storey apartment blocks have been built over areas where whole streets were, so that the lines of the streets themselves have been obliterated. Hoxton and Pitfield Streets now provide services for a high-rise redbrick jungle through which they forlornly trickle. In this wan replacement the new shops, where there are any, have nothing like the distinctive character of the old. For instance, somewhere along that curve where Pitfield Street runs into Hoxton Street – where now there is nothing at all – there was a tobacconist's shop that specialised in cigars. Here was another intoxicating smell. What interested me more than the smell, even, was that on the customers' side of the counter, at the height of a man's head, burnt a tall flame from a gas-jet fitted to the wall, so that the instant you bought a cigar or a cigarette, even while you were being handed your change, you could light it. I was fascinated by the fact that the long flame stood upright, completely straight, so thin and yet so powerful, and was timeless, never not there. Another specialty of the shop was snuff. This was still in wide use then, and all tobacconists sold it, but this one made a point of giving his customers the choice of a dozen or more; and they all had delicious smells, so you were lucky to be there when some-body bought one.

Between two of the buildings that were just in Pitfield Street was a narrow slit that had been turned into a workplace for a cobbler. It was like the slit between our shop and Sugar's, except that someone had fitted a street door on to the end of it, and covered it over against the weather; and there, far back in the cave thus created, sat a cobbler at his last, facing the open doorway and shouting conversations with passers-by who stopped to toss greetings into the murk. The space he sat in was scarcely wider than his shoulders.

It was more or less opposite him, on the other side of the road, that Gopsall Street ran off Pitfield Street. And it was to the school in Gopsall Street, the school that my father and his sisters had been to as infants, that I was sent when I was three.

CHAPTER FOUR

I remember people saying to my mother, wasn't I much too young to be sent to school, and her saying I couldn't be if they were willing to take me, and anyway she was fed up with having me around all day and was sending me to get me out of the way. I think the situation was that according to law you had to be at school when you were five, so most kids went when they were four, and the schools were willing, if asked, to take you at three. The moment I was three my mother asked.

On the Day she led me across Hoxton Street, then across Pitfield Street, then the full length of Gopsall Street towards a gigantic building approaching us from the far end on the left. It is still there, jutting up into the sky and looking from a distance like a castle, the more so as the maze of streets that surrounded it has been demolished to make way for a park and some playgrounds. Schools based on the same design are still in use all over London, run up *en masse* a hundred years ago to cope with the then recent introduction of compulsory education for all, but so securely built that they look as if they will go on being used for ever. Huge buildings in three unusually high storeys, built with unmovable municipal stolidity, they all have the same internally windowed classrooms, the same parquet-floored corridors and assembly halls, the same asphalt playgrounds with pitches for games marked out in white, the same external colour schemes on their façades. In one of them you could be anywhere in Edwardian London.

Gopsall Street School had looked exactly the same when my father went to it in the first decade of the century, or so he said. The junior school behind our house, to which I moved a few years later, looked the same too, but it was its destiny to be demolished by a direct hit in an air raid – to the delight of its pupils, many of whom had daydreamt of doing the same if only they could.

When my mother and I arrived at Gopsall Street School we were directed to a classroom where other mums were waiting or arriving with their children. The teacher there to receive us was a Miss Wynter. It was not until my adult life, when I tracked her down after many years, that I came to realise that her name was spelt like that: throughout the years when she taught me I thought she was Miss Winter. And it seemed to me an appropriate name, for she was grey, severe and cold. She was then only in her mid-twenties, but I thought of her as a great deal older. Already her hair had gone an iron grey, and she wore it clipped off along the sides of her head. What with that and her tortoise-shell glasses she looked the image of a schoolmarm. The day I arrived, the school was starting an experiment: instead of moving each class up to a new teacher each year, as they had done in the past, they were trying out the idea of having one teacher stay with the same class all through the school. So from the age of three until I moved on to junior school I was taught by Miss Wynter.

On that first day I saw for the first time a classroom, with its rows of Lilliputian desks, thirty-five of them, confronting the teacher's giant desk out in front on a dais. As the children arrived, Miss Wynter ticked their names off in a register and allotted them their desks, at which they sat while their mums gathered in an ever-growing crowd near the open door, looking on, each continuing to communicate silently by hand and eye with her offspring. When all the desks were occupied, and no more mums with children were expected, something incredible happened. The mums all left. After words from Miss Wynter, and waving cheerily, and smiling, each calling out across the classroom in words of bright farewell to her own particular little one, and also to Miss Wynter, the mums trooped out in a gaggle. The children looked after them in perplexed silence, unable at first to believe the evidence of their widening eyes. Then as the last mum disappeared and the door closed behind her a fortissimo of wailing crashed out from half the throats in the room, as if brought in on cue by a director – a primal sound, a lamentation that was half grief and half incredulity. I was thrown by this. It never worried me to see the back of my mother, but these children were bereft, devastated. Then others, who had not at first cried, started to cry. And then I found I was crying with them. And there we were, thirty-five of us, sitting in rows at our tiny desks, crying our eyes out, the tears streaming down our faces, sobbing and yelling at the tops of our voices. It was the first consciously traumatic experience I ever had, but it was a powerful group experience too, and it has remained with me as one of the most vivid memories from any period of my life. Of how Miss Wynter coped with it I remember little, except that two or three of the children tried to hurl themselves out of the room, presumably to run home, and she manhandled them back from the door to their desks. She shouted at us a good deal, as if it were unreasonable of us to be upset, and smacked a few of us; and I suppose eventually we must have exhausted ourselves. I do know that next day the atmosphere was completely different, to my uncomprehending surprise. The children were subdued; and I suppose some kind of normality must then have begun. Going to school soon became an accepted routine for all of us.

There were no such things as school dinners: children went home in the middle of the day to eat. Fathers who worked locally – as most did, including mine – would do the same, so the whole family would sit down together to what was in fact the main meal of the day. Mothers, if they had left their children at school in the morning, did the shopping on the way home, there to prepare the midday dinner for their husbands and children. This sort of pattern was normal daily life for most of the British population before the Second World War. It was only when the war came, and most women got jobs, that most husbands and children started eating out in the middle of the day; and then the family's chief meal together shifted to the evening.

Another difference between now and then is that small children were nothing like as closely supervised out of doors: it was quite normal for little kids to be wandering around in the streets alone. Thus it did not seem at all odd that it was for only a brief period that my mother accompanied me all the way to school and back twice a day, making four journeys for her in all. Soon she was just taking me over Hoxton and Pitfield Streets and leaving me on the corner of Gopsall Street, with injunctions to look carefully both ways before crossing the side roads between there and school; and she would be on the same spot waiting for me when I returned, as if she had never moved. Then it was not long again before she pronounced that I was big enough to cross Hoxton Street and Pitfield Street by myself. This for me was the great liberation. Once it was accepted by my parents that I was able to cross main roads alone I could go anywhere I liked. The real exploration of my surroundings began, and then the whole world around me opened up at great speed. I started to become an independent person. But before talking about that I would like to say just a few more words about my infant school, which after all was my first peer group.

There were not only infants in that enormous building: there was also a junior school for girls, aged seven to eleven, and a senior school for boys, aged eleven to fourteen. Those were the three categories of elementary school in those days: Infants, Juniors and Seniors. The seniors left school and started work at fourteen, so the oldest boys seemed to me to be grown up already, with their long trousers and deep voices – huge great louts to be avoided, most of them, with no time for us infants except to cuff us out of the way, or crash through a group of us at the school gates, scattering us in all directions.

My class was in effect a permanent group of thirty people that I played with every day. We stayed together for three years, until we moved on to our various junior schools. At that point the girls stayed together in Gopsall Street but the boys were dispersed among surrounding schools, depending on where they lived. My memories of those three years form not a narrative but a picture, a single remembered way of life. I recall some of the individuals clearly. There was Bobby Meredith, round-headed and black-haired, who lived next door to the school and was the only child who was late every morning. If I saw him coming down his front steps I knew I was late too. There was Willy Humberstone, warm-natured, heavy-jawed and slow-speaking: he used to accompany me on part of my way home before peeling off on his. There was Georgie White, a scrawny kid, with arms and legs like sticks, and rabbity teeth; he had a laugh that was a chortle. There was Frank Lee, better dressed than the others, a mother's boy, who came from the paper shop just round the corner in Bridport Place. There were the two Harrys, Harry Green and Harry Messer: Harry Green the quiet one, a formidable fighter, Harry Messer more of a character. They always arrived and left together. They were dirty, and always in rags. Even the other children knew they were poor. But I looked on them with envy for their freedom of spirit. They would take anything they could get their hands on. If you were idling about daydreaming with a stick of something to eat in your hand, or a bit of fruit, one of them would slug you in the eye and be off with it before you knew what had happened. And then he would be nowhere to be seen.

Actually we were all a bit like that: it was the way of life. If you saw somebody with anything you wanted, and you reckoned you could beat him in a fight, you took it and dared him to do anything about it – unless he was with somebody else, in which case you kept your hands to yourself – unless again you were with somebody else, in which case you calculated whether the two of you could beat the two of them. You were always on the watch to catch prey alone – and that was why gangs formed, for safety in numbers. To keep anything, you had to be alert. If you had something that anyone bigger than you might want you were careful who you showed it to. Everyone lied a great deal, usually making it up as they went along, often with wild improbability. Normally you could tell who was lying, though not always. The touchstone of everything, and all that really mattered, was what you could get away with. There were two main ways you could come unstuck: one was by picking on a boy who, it turned out, could get the better of you, or, as we would say, could fight you; the other was being caught by a teacher and punished. 'Fight' was our expression for 'beat in a fight'. A common sort of exchange would be: 'Can you fight Charlie?' – 'No, but I can fight Johnnie, and Johnnie can fight Charlie, so if Charlie's around I keep with Johnnie.' It was pure jungle. And I have to say I was at home in it. It came to me naturally to live in this way, and I was the same as the others. Although I was a year younger than them I was tall for my age, and I liked fighting, in fact I liked it very much; also I was reasonably quick-witted; so I was able to hold my own. I was not a leader, at least not at first, just a normally-functioning member of the pack.

The one and only taboo among us boys was that it was wrong to hit a girl. How we got this taboo, and why we observed it in the absolute way we did, I don't know, but we did. It meant there were two completely different subcultures, the boys and the girls. The separation was made easier by the fact that the boys did not want to have anything to do with the girls anyway: we thought girls were silly. Although my class was mixed, there was only one girl that I even remember, Pat Beazley: dark-haired, with a fringe and dark eyes. I still recall the brightness of her eyes. She was an intelligent person, I think, and she certainly had a personality. I have memories of liking her, but I do not think she ever played with us.

On their various routes to school the boys would meet up with one another in the surrounding streets, and games would get going already, and fights. These would carry on into the school playground, where we would run wild until a teacher came out and rang a hand-bell for us to stop talking and form up into our classes. This we would do, still in the playground, at prescribed positions; then on command we would troop into the building to our classrooms. In the middle of the morning, and again in mid-afternoon, there would be what we called playtime for the whole school, when we were all let out into the playground and allowed to run wild again.

We had an immense variety of playground games, but they mostly involved chasing and fighting. My favourite was called Release. We would pick two teams, one for defence and one for attack, and the defenders had to capture the attackers. If two defenders came for you, so long as you had both hands tightly clasped on the crown of your head you could not be captured; the best thing was to roll up into a ball, and then it might take even more than two to straighten you out and tear your hands off your head. One of them would tap your exposed head three times while saying: 'One, two, three on the crowner!' and you were a prisoner, and had to go and stand quietly in the corner of the playground, where two brick walls made a right-angle. This corner was guarded by members of the defending team. So long as they formed a continuous chain, linking hands and touching both walls, thus enclosing their prisoners in the corner, you were not allowed to go free. You could not free yourself, you had to wait for your comrades to free you. If there was only one prisoner, there needed to be only one guardian, touching both walls

45

with the tips of his fingers; but as the number of prisoners grew, so the number of guardians had to grow. The rest of their team would be out trying to capture more people, but since it took at least two to capture one there had always to be some in the attacking team who were unmarked. These would be plotting to release their captured comrades. They did this by concerted charges into the corner, charges whose aim was to break the chain of linked hands between the guardians, at which the prisoners were allowed to run free. The attackers' problem was to penetrate the defenders' corner without getting captured themselves. If they succeeded they would shout 'Release!', and the prisoners could all break out. Then the defenders had to start all over again trying to capture the attackers – though during the break-out itself they usually managed to recapture one or two.

Playing Release gave me what I am tempted to call a sense of release, a sense of happiness and fulfilment. It filled my whole body, and was so deep it was aesthetic – a profound feeling of inner harmony, of being at one with everything. At that age nothing else had given me that sensation, and I loved the game with a devoted love. I was constantly initiating it. I always wanted to be in the attacking team, because for me the moments of supreme bliss came when I rushed across the playground from a distance in a surprise assault and hurled my body into the wall of guardians, and was able to shout 'Release!', at which I and my released comrades all scattered out of the corner into freedom.

Because we played these games on asphalt every day we were fairly well covered with cuts and bruises most of the time, especially on our knees. These were our most exposed spot, because we wore short trousers (kept up by a belt) and long woollen socks to just below the kneecap, so the knees themselves were naked. Mine soon had, and still have, a full decoration of scar tissue. Talking of dress, few boys wore jackets or caps until they went to junior school, and none wore full-length trousers (which were always kept up by braces) until they went to senior school. At the infant school, before graduating into jackets, we wore woollen jerseys with long sleeves. In our first year we had to walk around with a handkerchief pinned to our chest by a giant safety pin, so that the handkerchief was always to hand and we could not lose it. During this year we were known to everyone in the school as 'the babies' class', or simply as 'the babies', and we would even say of ourselves: 'I'm in the babies.' In the afternoon we would lie down on beds in the assembly hall with the blinds drawn. But after that first year there was no more bed, and we were deemed capable of keeping a handkerchief in our pocket – though we were still required to have one, because in the smog-polluted London of those days, perpetually running noses were the lot of undernourished children, which many of my classmates were. This gave rise to what was a standard phrase for the children of the poor, 'snotty-nosed kids'. I was not undernourished myself, but I was a fairly snotty-nosed kid, and to this day I have an uncomfortable feeling that there is something missing if I do not have a handkerchief in my pocket. If I realise I have left home without one I go into a shop and buy one.

Our chief experience of the teachers was of receiving from them a continuous flow of light and perfunctory assault. They saw their main task as keeping order, and thought hitting us the only way of doing it. In Miss Wynter's case, if you did anything you were not supposed to do she would tell you to stop, and then, if you did not stop, she would dart over to your desk, and with a practised gesture grab you by the wrist with one hand while the other pushed up your sleeve, slapped you smartly three times on your bare forearm, and then pulled the sleeve down. It was all over in five seconds: *slap! slap! slap!* She spent half her time darting around the classroom doing this. We saw it as her chief occupation. If you had asked me: 'What does your teacher do?', I would have answered in all seriousness: 'Give us smacks.' They came my way several times a day for talking. Apparently, as a child, I was for ever talking, and this was always getting me into trouble. I do not remember talking all the time, but I do remember being told all the time that I was talking all the time, and being unceasingly punished for it. Much of the punishment took me by surprise, so I must have talked a lot without realising I was doing it.

Because we were constantly being smacked by the teachers, often without understanding why, we took it in our stride as part of the way things were. It was nothing compared with the bumps, bruises and cuts that we inflicted on one another in our fights, or incurred voluntarily in our games, and those injuries were nearly always forgotten before bedtime. In any case most of us were hit at home by our parents as a normal thing. For all of us, physical violence was a part of everyday life, not only the standard sanction of anyone in authority but also the standard arbiter of differences and disputes among ourselves – probably the only one we could envisage, certainly the only one we took seriously. I remember being astounded when my parents asked me over dinner one day: 'Do you ever get smacked by the teacher?' The question in itself was a warning to be economical with the truth, so I told them that I was, well, yes, now and then, occasionally smacked by the teacher. Instead of expressing the sympathy with me, and the disapproval of the teacher, that I naturally expected to follow this disclosure, my parents went into hostile-questioning mode, and wanted to know what I did that incurred these punishments. Before I knew where I was I was being told off all over again for things I had already been hit for at school. It seemed to me monstrous that I should be punished twice for the same offence. Never again did I make the mistake of telling my parents the truth in answer to such a question. This conversation must have taken place before my mother started letting me go to school alone, because it was after it, and when she was standing waiting to meet me on the corner of Gopsall Street and Pitfield Street, that she would call out to me every day as I approached her: 'Any smacks?' and I would call back, 'No.' This must have been a self-amused joke on her part, but that thought did not occur to me, and soon I was pre-empting her by shouting as soon as I got within earshot: 'No smacks.'

Occasionally there were other punishments at school besides hitting. One was to make a child stay in the classroom during play-time, or hold him back for a while when the others went home. Miss Wynter once did this to me and then forgot I was there. The other children all went off while I had to stay sitting silently at my desk, watching as she cleared up her things and started to put on her overcoat. At the place in her coat where other people's had a link button on the inside, in the lining, hers had ribbons, which she tied into a bow before buttoning up the outside. Then, to my surprise, without looking at me and telling me I could go, she walked across to the door and went out through it, turned round, and locked it behind her. The door, like the wall against the corridor, was full of big glass panels, so I could see her still, but I made no attempt to signal to her, still less to call out. I assumed that this was the punishment, being locked up in the classroom by myself. My eyes followed her through the glass panels as she disappeared down the corridor.

For what seemed an age I sat there gloomily. Then I was suddenly overwhelmed by a feeling of having been abandoned, and I started to cry, in fact to howl. This went on for a long time, until I heard a banging against one of the glass panels and looked up; and who of all people should be standing there but my mother. She had become alarmed at my failure to turn up at home, and had walked towards the school expecting to meet me on the way, and had found the whole building empty, but had managed to get in – and then heard me yowling. She found a caretaker, who came and unlocked the classroom door and let me out. I rem-ember knowing afterwards that my mother had made a great fuss with the headmistress about me being locked up alone in an empty school, and I think Miss Wynter must have got into some sort of trouble about it, because on two or three subsequent occasions she scolded me for not having spoken up as she was leaving the room. This only caused a feeling of injustice inside me. How could I possibly have been expected to question what a teacher was doing? How would I have dared?

The only teacher apart from Miss Wynter who ever took us for a lesson was the headmistress, Miss Norman – I expect she filled in when any member of her staff was indisposed. She was a short, chunkily built woman with straight dark hair, and glasses astride a powerful nose. Her way of keeping order was with a ruler: she had a boxwood ruler permanently grasped in one hand, and any child who transgressed was given a lightning rap on the knuckles. Although she was small and old she could reach your knuckles from an incredible distance. Each time she took us she would tell us off for the way we spoke, which was the bugbear of her life, and any lesson with her always turned into a lesson on pronunciation. We mustn't say 'cross', which we all did, we must say 'crawss'. We mustn't say 'off', we must say 'awf'. She had a special thing about our 'often', which according to her was a double disaster: not only must we pronounce the first bit 'awf', we mustn't pronounce the 't' at all, so we had to say 'orphan'. In Hoxton this was like baling out the Atlantic Ocean with a teaspoon. In any case my grandparents said 'awf' and 'crawss', and I didn't want to talk like them, I wanted to talk like my father, who said 'off' and 'cross'. I still say 'off' and 'cross'; though after getting a set of painfully bruised knuckles for pronouncing the 't' in 'often' I stopped doing that.

The only other teacher I ever spoke to at Gopsall Street was Miss Poole, who had taught my father, and would occasionally ask me how he was. The impossible fact that she had taught my father – how could anyone conceivably have been his teacher? – made her seem unimaginably old, and she was indeed a generation older than the other teachers: I realise now that she was in her fifties. She was a motherly woman with white hair and a kindly face, and unlike Miss Wynter was liked by the children she taught. She always referred to my father as Freddie Magee, which I never heard anyone else do. Although it was *lèse-majesté*, it conjured up for me a living picture of my father as a child of my own age standing there in my place in Gopsall Street School talking up at Miss Poole.

What the teachers actually banged into us with all their thumping was the three Rs. In my case I am not sure whether I learnt to read at school or at home – I seem to remember doing both, and it may have been fifty–fifty. It was certainly at school that I learnt to add and subtract, and probably to count in a systematic way. Besides the three Rs there was something called raffia work: I was not sure what that was, even while I was doing it. But not fully understanding what I was doing was a common state of affairs with me, especially if it had anything to do with words. For example, the whole class learnt to chant together by heart some words beginning: 'What shall I call my dear little dormouse? His eyes are small but his tail is enormous . . .', and not only did I have no idea what a dormouse was, it was not until I happened to see the words in print years later that I realised that this was a poem (by A. A. Milne); and that 'call' rhymed with 'small', and 'dormouse' was jokily rhyming with 'e-nor-mouse'. All this passed me by when I was actually learning it; and although I was dimly aware at the time of not knowing what all this was about I was not troubled by that, not in this case more than any other: I did not know what most things meant, and the feeling was one that accompanied me a lot of the time. I had it at its most intense when adults were talking to one another in my presence, which was naturally an everyday occurrence: I could hear perfectly well what they were saying, but usually I had no idea what it meant, and this gave me a distant but uncomfortable feeling of being shut out of something important. I wanted to understand. And this desire to understand grew until it became very strong, though it never occurred to me to think of the classroom as a place where I was likely to acquire such understanding.

We did a few other things like singing, and drawing with coloured crayons, and building things with wooden bricks. But far and away the most important, if only because it was the one interesting thing I did in the classroom that I did not do at home, was writing. It is possible that I learnt to read at home, but certainly I learnt to write at school. We were taught an old-fashioned copper-plate twirl, which we wrote laboriously in our crude infant hands, either with our tongues sticking out of the corners of our mouths or biting a lip or two. I found it extraordinarily interesting; the differing heights of the letters, the fact that a capital sometimes looked so unlike the ordinary-sized letter that was the same letter; and pleasing things like the fact that to get a capital 'f' you made a capital 't' and then just put a little line through it, thus magically transforming it to an 'f'.

It was explained to us that we were being taught first to print words with separate letters, and when we had learnt this we would be taught to join the letters up, thus turning it into grown-up writing; and that once we had learnt to do grown-up writing we would never return to printing. This gave me a precipitate desire to do grown-up writing. I started covering page after page with joined-up squiggle, fluent but meaningless. When people asked me what I was doing I said I was writing a book. And when people asked me what I was going to do when I grew up I said I was going to write books. This intention stayed with me for quite a long while, as ambitions went, though by the time I actually learnt to write I had given it up, because I wanted to be a cowboy, and did not see how you could write while riding a horse.

CHAPTER FIVE

In a world where nobody had a refrigerator, and few women had jobs, and most families sat down together for their main meal in the middle of the day, most women's task every morning was to go shopping for food that was fresh that day, and then cook it and serve it. And, of course, before supermarkets, each kind of commodity had to be bought in a different shop, or at a different stall. This made shopping time-consuming, but it also made it a woman's chief way of meeting other people. Just as a man had the mates he met every day at work, so a woman had friends whom she would meet every day out shopping. It was the normal thing to see women standing about having what seemed like endlessly long conversations in shops, or on the pavement outside them, or a few paces away from a stall where they had just bumped into one another. Just as I thought that what teachers did was hit you, so I thought that what women did was talk.

For this kind of shopping, most communities were served by a market of open-air stalls, usually surrounded by shops. In small towns it would typically take the form of a market square, but in London, where squares were not usually available for these purposes, open-air markets grew up along certain streets, which then became the focal points of activity for whole neighbourhoods and gave them their character. Some of these street markets became famous, and the street I was born in, Hoxton Street, was one of them. Nearly all have now died, and the few that survive function usually on only a single day of the week; the scrappy little market that meets now in Hoxton Street on a Saturday is the merest ghost of its former self. Until the 1940s, when markets in general were devastated by the rationing of food and clothes, and most women got jobs – followed by the '50s, when most families acquired refrigerators – street markets were in full cry all day every day of the week, except for Sunday. At the crack of each dawn the retailers would get that day's supplies fresh from the wholesale markets – Smithfield for meat, Billingsgate for fish, Covent Garden for vegetables, fruit and flowers; and there were others. Prices fluctuated day by day. At six in the morning a street trader would be haggling as a buyer with the wholesalers in Covent Garden, and at nine o'clock he would be selling competitively himself in a local retail market. The shoppers, most of whom were poor by today's standards, were picky and choosy, and many bought whatever was cheapest. The word would go round: 'Cabbages are very reasonable today' . . . 'So-and-so has got a lot of herring.' Prices would change during the course of a day. Towards the close of trading, when retailers began to knock down their remaining stock cheaply to get rid of it – they would not be able to sell it next day – a new kind of shopper appeared in the market: the very poor, the very old, the very mean, or just people who were free to shop at whatever time they chose. When the traders actually closed down and started clearing away, the scavengers would come out – the poorest of all, derelicts and the mentally peculiar, and children – to ransack the detritus left on the ground round the stalls, secure in the knowledge that there would be at least some squashed fruit and vegetables, some cardboard boxes, and bits from broken wooden boxes that would help to make a fire.

A market was a world, with a distinctive character of its own, teeming with humanity at every age, from hordes of children to the very old, and at every level of prosperity from the moneyed trader to the famished wraith. All imaginable kinds of goods were on sale, and thousands of people mingled together every day. Monday was always busy, because there had been no shopping on Sunday, and some people still had plenty of wages left over from Saturday; mid-week would be quieter, though still busy by the standards of other places; Friday and Saturday, the days when people with jobs were paid, were busy again, above all Saturday, when a lot of men were off work in the afternoon, and the children were free from school all day, and the women had to prepare for Sunday, and it was the only day when the whole family could go together. On Saturday the crowd in the market was like the gathering at a sporting event – not a football match, where everyone is moving in the same direction, but a crowded racecourse, with the punters scurrying criss-cross past one another in all directions simultaneously.

The shoppers themselves needed servicing, of course, so vendors moved among them on foot selling food and drink; some of the stalls, too, sold soft drinks or cans of hot tea, and there were fast-food stalls where people stood and ate. Those sold mostly shellfish from the Thames estuary: cockles and mussels, winkles, prawns and shrimp, oysters and crab, all spiced up with salt, vinegar and pepper, to which the customers helped themselves from huge metal canisters on the stall. Also scattered along both sides of the street, in amongst shops of other kinds, were cafés and pubs, eel-and-pie shops, fish and chip shops, sausage and mash shops. Mingling with the crowd and living off it were beggars and tipsters, pickpockets and policemen, some people being slipped illegal bets, others carrying placards warning of the wrath to come. The sound of it all was multi-layered: a background noise of hundreds of people talking at once in the open air, over which individual voices were heard calling out to one another, and on top of all that, overriding everything else, the air-splitting cries of the stall-keepers, all shouting at once, each trying to draw attention to his particular goods by shouting either his wares or his prices, the jokers also joshing with the passers-by or with neighbouring stall-keepers. The ever-jostling crowd filled the whole width of the street wall-to-wall for well over half a mile, swarming contradictorily in both directions, pouring all over the roadway as well as along both pavements, and bunching up into knots round particular stalls, knots which sometimes caused obstructions to the rest of the crowd. Few vehicles would attempt to pass through this, and those that did were unpopular: they had to inch their way through, while the irate shoppers, especially the mums who were wheeling infants or holding them by the hand, would shout abuse at the drivers – now and then one would deliberately scratch the side of a van, or give the passing flank of a horse a vindictive jab. At the rare sign of any more widespread and lasting trouble, mounted policemen would appear on their spectacular horses, and begin to move gently in amongst the crowd, calming it down, exchanging pleasantries with the traders, or with men in the crowd they recognised, and letting the women and children pat their horses.

For all the chaos and crowdedness, the endless movement, the colour and the noise, it was a world that everyone in it was familiar with and felt at home in. To many of them it may have seemed that all human life was here – even those who were very poor were surrounded by people they knew, and an atmosphere of plenty. On any normal day the market was a friendly place, lively and cheerful. This made it positively enlivening, because of the stimulation to which everyone in it was subjected from all sides. Individuals at home who were down in the dumps, or bored, or lonely, or upset about something, would wander along to the market just for the distraction of it, to be taken out of themselves and cheered up, and to see a few faces they recognised.

The sheer multiplicity of life in Hoxton Street as it was before the Second World War is something I cannot adequately describe in words, for I was already familiar with it before I had any words that could describe it. It was something I surfaced into consciousness knowing. From before I was old enough to be wheeled around in a push-chair – which means from before any continuous memories begin – I was used to being in amongst it in somebody's care; and from about four or five I was used to being in it alone.

When we turned left out of our shop there were only shops for the first few yards, then the road widened out and the market began. The first street vendor you came to was a small, bony woman on the other side, standing on the edge of the pavement outside St Anne's church, opposite the Keppel. She did not even have a stall, but sold her goods directly off the kerbstone. The stalls began immediately after her, but hers was the first voice you heard, shouting in a strident tone: '*Come along, ladies, green or white!*' Because of the curve in the street you heard her before you saw her. She was white-faced and hungry-looking, always wearing a light-brown overcoat. What she sold was hearthstone, used by people to whiten their front doorsteps and clean out their fireplaces; and on the kerb beside her was a pile of green and white hearthstone bricks. She would arrive there every morning with as many of these as she could carry, and if she sold them all she cleared off early and did not come back. It was normal to see her standing there with only three or four left to sell. If she got down to one she would shout over and over again: '*Only one left! Only one left!*' and sell it off cheaply so she could go home. I once saw her offer the last one at half-price to a passer-by who shook her head and said she had spent all her money in the market, whereat the woman gave it to her for nothing. Next to her was the first stall, also kept by a woman (most of the stall-holders were men), wrapped in several layers of textiles and wool, a roly-poly figure with brown hair pulled straight back, black outer clothes and a money apron – there was something fierce about the way she thrust money into its kangaroo pouch. She sold fruit and flowers with the cry: '*Iddy piddy, fresh and nice!*' When I imitated this at home my family denied that she could actually be shouting '*Iddy piddy*', no matter if that was what it sounded like, so we went and listened to her together, and it was what she was saying. Children used to try to steal fruit from her stall, if only because it was the first one you came to if you approached the market from our end; but she was one of the hardest of all the stall-keepers to steal from – not that any of them was easy – and not many of the children got away with it. Any of them seen by her to be lurking with intent were sworn off savagely, with a brutal invective that made no allowance for their years. Some of the children were so frightened of her that they did not dare to chance their arm. Others had a go, but would scapa the moment she spotted them.

From her onwards the stalls were packed along both gutters side by side, with just enough space between each for one person to pass between the pavement and the roadway. There were more than two hundred of them altogether: stalls selling fresh fish (though not fresh meat: this was because of the law, I think), tinned food, groceries, tobacco, snuff, confectionery, new clothes, carpets, furniture, kitchenware, electrical goods (many of them not in working order), toiletries, cosmetics, magazines, junk. Almost everything could be bought either new or second-hand – one stall sold nothing but second-hand boots, another nothing but second-hand hats. Every stall had its cry, usually praising its own wares: '*Lovely carpets, nice rugs!*' This would be repeated over and over again, often with '*Come on!*' between repetitions. Sometimes there was praise without identification – '*All good quality!*' was the most familiar example – and you had to look to see what it was that was all good quality. Less often, a price would be mentioned. '*Any hat you like for sixpence!*' . . . . '*All shoes, two bob a pair!*' Each stall-holder was striving to be heard above the others, and the cacophony was indescribable.

Although there was every kind of stall there were more selling fruit and vegetables than any other single kind. Because these were the most numerous they were also the most competitive, and their owners would not only shout their prices but would often mention the price before the goods. So it would be '*Tuppence a pound pears!*' If they were selling two fruits at the same price, so that the purchaser could mix them in any proportion she wanted, they would signal this by shouting, '*Apples a pound pears!*' This last was the commonest single cry in the market. Apples and pears were the nearest thing to a staple food that local people had – the poor would come to the market at the end of the day to buy them for almost nothing. If on any day there was some item that was especially cheap the traders would keep repeating the word 'today' in their shout . . . '*Cauliflower today so-much! Come on ladies! Today it's only so-much! Only so-much, cauliflower! Just for today!*' Although the shout might differ from day to day, on any given day they would stand there and shout the same words over and over again, all morning and all afternoon. (And some of them were the same every day.) My friends the Tillsons ran a stall outside their main shop only on Saturdays, and this was worked by a young woman I knew called Ena (who had a Monday-to-Friday job elsewhere): she would stand there all day shouting: '*Penny a quarter! Penny a quarter! Penny a quarter!*', keeping the world informed that all the different sweets on her stall could be bought in any combination at a quarter of a pound for a penny. If you pushed a little further up through the crowd you would see, on the other side, an old bloke with gingery hair who wore a long, thin, ochre-coloured coat, sitting there all day on a high wooden stool shouting: '*Savaloys! Savaloys! Savaloys!*' He was there every day, shouting one word all day, with never a rest and hardly a pause for breath. Even as a child I sometimes wondered what was going on in the minds of people doing this, and tried to imagine myself doing it, and couldn't.

Not all the traders prompted such thoughts, though. Near the far end of the market there was one I envied, and I used to stand there for long periods watching him, listening with fascination. He was broad-faced and stubbily built, obviously Jewish, no longer young, with a bald front to his head and a stance like a boxer. While he was talking he would pace forward aggressively, then retreat, and then go forward again. He sold confectionery, a fact of compelling interest to me in itself, only instead of selling it item by item in the normal way he made up separate lots of it to the accompaniment of an uninterrupted spiel, and sold it off by Dutch auction, each lot different. He was so quick and amusing in his banter with the crowd that he always had a laughing audience round his stall.

I do not recall his jokes now, but the working parts of his patter, presented here without the humour that gave them life, and condensed, would go something like this. 'Now here [holding it up] is a half-pound bar of Cadbury's brazil nut chocolate. The best quality chocolate you can get anywhere today. Beautiful great brazil nuts. Whole. And a whole half pound. Now you all know how much that costs [waving it about]. It costs so-and-so. But I'm not only going to give you that, I'm going to give you another half-pound of something else to go with it, a half a pound of [picking up another packet] liquorish allsorts. And these aren't just any sort of allsort, they're Bassett's. You all know Bassett's [waving it around, showing it off]. They're the king of allsorts, the only real sort of allsort. Now I'm going to let you have the two of these together [bringing them together in his two hands with a great smack]. And even then it's not all. The lucky person who gets this lot is going to get something else as well. I'm going to throw in a tube of those new Smarties we keep hearing about. Now there's something to keep your kids happy. Here we are [picking up the Smarties and adding them to the pack]. All good stuff. First-class quality confectionery. Famous makes. You know me, I never give you rubbish. Go into any shop here in Hoxton and ask for these, and they'll cost you at least so-much all together, probably more. Just work it out for yourselves. You don't need me to tell you. But I'm not going to ask you for so-much. I'm not even going to ask you for so-much-less. All I'm going to ask you to give me here today is such-and-such. There you are. You can have all this lot for only such-and-such.' And he would look round expectantly and wait. If he had no takers, at the point when the silence might have started to become an embarrassed one for the crowd (instinctive timing was crucial to his art) he'd say: 'Well, look, I'll tell you what I'll do. I'm already offering this to you for a price you can't find anywhere else, but I'll throw something else in on top of it. As well as all this you can have a Mars bar. [Adding the Mars bar.] What about that?' Looking round, apparently sure of himself this time. Still no takers. 'All right, then, a Mars bar *and* a Milky Way.' Pause. 'Come on, then. You can't do better than that, you know you can't.' Pause. 'Blimey, you're a right lot, you are. What are you trying to do – drive me to the workhouse? I can't afford to give away any more than this. But I tell you what. I'll do you a favour. I'll take less for it. You can have it all for such-and-such.'

And on he would go, with never a loss for a word. He did a tremendous trade, selling big handfuls of confectionery at a time, the whole thing moving very much faster than this account of it suggests. He never sold anything singly, and nothing was ever straightforwardly priced. Looking back, I feel fairly sure that his goods must have been stolen from some regular source, and that this was why he was selling them so cheaply, and that he sold them in lots because he wanted to get rid of them fast, and also because he made more money this way than he would have got from a fence, who would have given him roughly a quarter of what the fence could get for them. For that matter, he looked as if he enjoyed doing it – he was a natural performer. From him I learnt about the recognised makes of confectionery that were too expensive for me to buy but which I expected to grow into being able to afford. The sweet shops in which I spent my ha'pennies and pennies sold rubbish by comparison. I also became familiar with his methods. He always built the price up step by step to something that was a lot more than he was going to ask, and then made a great show of coming down from that. And this coming down was the part of his spiel that I always most enjoyed, a sort of grand finale beginning with some such words, ringingly delivered, as: 'I'm not asking so-and-so!' Dramatic pause. 'I'm not even asking such-and-such!' Even more dramatic pause. 'All I'm asking is a mere this-much.' And then came the moment of suspense – will anyone take it at this price or not – will he have to come down even more? It was as good as a play.

One way and another there was plenty of drama in the market. An escapologist performed there regularly, and I watched him many times without being able to figure out how he did it. In addition to the man who was doing the act there was his partner who did all the talking, whose job it was to get as much money as possible into the hat before putting his mate standing there in chains, handcuffs and leg-irons into the sack. Sometimes I would get fed up with the delay, and move off; but more often I stayed. Quite often, too, there was a man on a one-wheeled bicycle, but he didn't seem to do much. Frequently a new act would appear and then never be seen again: once, to my amazement, I saw a fire-eater, and I thought he was wonderful, and longed for him to come back, but he never did – or, if he did, I never saw him or heard about him. There were always a lot of people playing musical instruments – beggars, really, but some of them quite good. And there were public speakers. The crowd would stream past the religious ones without taking any notice of them, and this gave them the appearance of being mad, standing there ranting to themselves. But the political ones could usually drum up an audience, if only a small one, and sometimes I would find myself standing listening to one of them with interest in spite of the fact that I did not understand what he was talking about. In circumstances like those, in fact in any crowd, I would often get interest as much out of watching the people in the audience as the performer – their faces, the variety of things they were wearing, their body language, for instance the way so often they visibly had to gear themselves up to ask a question. Sometimes there were peculiar goings-on in a crowd, transactions taking place, undertone conversations. A crowd had an internal life of its own, its own rules of behaviour.

The favourite pitch for most of the turns was on the crown of the road where the roadway was at its widest. I thought of this as the centre-point of the market, but seeing it now I realise that it was very much at our end, only a couple of hundred yards from my front door. At that point there were green-railinged entrances to underground public lavatories, and because of the iron railings in the middle of the road neither shoppers nor vehicles could pass there, so a kind of natural clearing was created. Also, an oblong area surrounding the lavatory entrances had been built up to the height of a kerb, creating a plinth-like surface that could be used as a dais or platform. And of course the lavatories were always busy, with people making their way to and from them, so it was a focal point anyway, and therefore a good place for collecting an audience. Incidentally, my parents did not like me using these lavatories, and tried to discourage me, but I did not understand why, so I ignored their prohibition and used them frequently.

Not everybody working in the market was out in the open. The shops were busy too, and in bad weather they could be a lot busier than the stalls. They were more expensive, and their goods were thought to be a couple of notches higher in quality. 'Quality' was a word that was in constant use in the market, as if it were what people were really buying and selling. If a shop also ran a stall at the kerb outside, it would sell its cheaper merchandise from the stall and the better stuff in the shop. For instance, a family named Brooks ran the best flower shop in the market, outside which they ran a fruit stall.

My mother used to buy her vegetables, fruit and flowers from the stalls, and sometimes fish too, but most other things in the shops. Her butcher was Gunner's, where there were always two queues, one at each counter – one for meat, the other for sausages and offal. (Tripe was a great delicacy, much displayed around Hoxton, sometimes in the windows of poky little shops that were scarcely shops at all; but I found the look of it disgusting, and have never been able to put it in my mouth. Fortunately my mother never gave it to us. I think my father disliked it.) In the butcher's shop, or any other for that matter, my mother watched the weighing like a buzzard. I was with her in Gunner's on an occasion when the man flung some sausages down on the scales and then swiped them up and was already putting them into her basket when she said in her coldest voice: 'I'd like you to weigh those again, please.' He tried to bluster his way out of it, but she was not to be budged, even though there was an impatient queue building up behind her; so he weighed them again, and found them a whole sausage short. Grumbling rather than apologising, he gave her another, and she marched out of the shop in grim-faced triumph, a feeling which I at her side shared in a more positive spirit. On the way home she indignantly told everyone we met how the man had tried to swindle her in Gunner's, and how you couldn't allow people to get away with that sort of thing when you were, as she put it, 'paying tip-top price for sausages'. *Tip-Top* was the name of a comic I was reading at the time, and I had no idea the words meant anything, and was intrigued to hear her use them. I was also intrigued by her repeated demonstrations of how, if you threw something down on a scale, the impact made the needle go past the real weight.

For groceries there were two shops she liked to patronise as well as the Co-op, one called Home & Colonial, the other Sainsbury's (next to Boots, which I thought a marvellous name). I preferred Sainsbury's because of the things you saw people doing there. The assistants all wore straw hats, and I loved to see one of them take two grooved wooden paddles to an immense block of butter and slash a great chunk out of it, and then slap the chunk around between the paddles, weighing it every few seconds and knocking bits off the edges until it was a dapper little squared-off half-pound – it gave me satisfaction to see the neatly-shaped bricklet emerging from the chaos. There were all kinds of butter with different flags sticking out of them, salted and unsalted, English, Dutch, Danish, French, Irish and New Zealand, some almost white, others a pungent yellow. There were rows of cheeses in a wider variety of colours – yellow, red and blue – and of shapes – barrels, blocks, bricks, tiles. I liked to see a man take one of the tubbier barrels from a shelf and put it under the wire cutter, and slice parts of it off, weigh the slice, cut off some more, weigh it again, add a separate bit to the scale . . . I was fascinated by the way a wire no thicker than a hair could cut something so huge and solid into pieces. I was even more fascinated by the bacon-slicer, but was made to watch it from well away, because my mother was afraid to let me stand near it, fearing, correctly, that I might poke it with my finger to see what would happen. I used to stand there wondering how thin the slices could get without disappearing altogether, realising that no matter how thin they got they could always get thinner, so you would never get down to nothing. Was there a thinnest possible? How could there be? Yet how could there not be? . . . My mother thought Sainsbury's the best-quality shop in the market, and to my eye even its frontage reflected its grandeur – not the thin painted wood and plain glass of the others but chunky, thick, engraved glass and heavy dark wood. It was, I think, the grandest place I knew. When you went in you knew you were somewhere special.

A shop I enjoyed going into even more, though, was Binysh's, a haberdasher's further up on the opposite side. This was a much bigger shop than others, bigger even than ours, for it was three knocked into one. It was an amazing world in which money and bills whizzed around on overhead wires, pinging bells. Sadly, my mother went there only occasionally, but when she did I was enthralled. There were lots of counters served by grandmotherly women, and when my mother gave money to one of them the woman would make out a bill, unscrew a metal cylinder the size of a hand grenade, put the money and the bill into the cylinder, hook it on to a wire over her head, pull a cord, there would be a loud *ping!* from an electric bell, and the cylinder would rocket away overhead to the other side of the shop, to a woman sitting at a cash register. This woman would pluck the cylinder from the air, unscrew it, take out the money and the bill, put the change and the receipt back in, and with another loud *ping!* send it rocketing back to where we were standing. I could have watched it all day. It gave me the same sort of pleasure as watching electric toy trains (which I always longed for but never possessed) only more so, because it was 'real', grown-up, and on what seemed an enormous scale. Whenever I heard my mother say she was going to Binysh's I asked if I could come too. Although it was the biggest shop in Hoxton Street, and always full of people, I seemed to be the only male who was ever in it, and I thought of it as a world full of women, and not only women but old ones, which made me feel like an alien creature on a visit.

For me, however, in spite of all competition, the shop of shops was Burchell's, the toy shop. This was Aladdin's cave, a paradise in which everything shone. I could never walk past it without stopping to look in its window, so at any given moment I could have told my parents in detail what it had in stock and how much each item cost, and which of them I wanted most. It was quite a big shop, and so had quite a big window, with dolls in it for girls, and fluffy toys for children younger than me, but also lots of things for me too, especially weapons like catapults and pea-shooters, and best of all penknives, and toy guns of many kinds – whole cowboy sets (hat and gun) and policeman sets (helmet, handcuffs and truncheon). There were things to play with out of doors, like kites, bows and arrows with their targets, hoops and spinning tops; and things to play with everywhere, like spillikens, yo-yos, marbles, fivestones and dice; and things to play with indoors, like dart-boards, shove ha'penny, skittles, quoits, dominoes, toy musical instruments, even real musical instruments, such as Jews' harps, tin whistles and kazoos. There were board games of every sort, and equipment for indoor sports such as boxing, table tennis and billiards, and for outdoor sports too – roller-skates, cricket bats, hockey sticks, footballs, tennis balls, even a bicycle. It was a window into heaven.

My longings as I gazed at these numinous objects were unbounded. But there were multiple ceilings on what I could actually hope to get, which was not very much. I learnt what the limitations were that I had to live with. I knew I would get one big thing on my birthday and one big thing at Christmas, but never any big thing in between, though I might hope for one or two of the small things. A lot of the items, especially of the sports equipment, were, as my parents would say, 'too old' for me. But the best of what was not 'too old' was 'too dear'. To get some-thing I really wanted for my next big present I had to calculate what was attainable within these constraints; if I asked for some-thing that wasn't I got an unrelated present that was something I didn't want at all. I received many promises for doubtfully exis-tent futures – 'You can have it when you're eight' – but by the time these futures arrived I had usually changed my mind. It was all very tricky, like deciding whether to stick or twist at pontoon: experience taught you that you were likely to lose either way. I never did get the things I wanted most of all, which were an electric train and a bicycle, but a fair proportion of the other things managed to come my way over the years. The smallest and cheapest of them, such as fivestones and tops, had a way of turning up in Christmas stockings.

Some of the shop-fronts in the main body of Hoxton Street were not part of the market's noisy outgoing life: English's, for example, the undertakers who buried my father and my grandfather – no one wanted to shop there; and the pawnbrokers, almost next door to it, where my parents pawned their rings when they were desperate – no one wanted to be seen going in or out of there either. The large grim grey-black façade of St Leonard's Hospital, formerly a workhouse, ran alongside the widest section of the street. But the life of the market swarmed past the doors of all these places and ignored them. People went to them when they had to, but discreetly, and avoided talking about it.

St Leonard's Hospital has such a revealing history that it is worth saying a little about it. There have been several workhouses in Hoxton for the desperately poor. They housed people of all ages – men unable to cope alone, unmarried mothers, the physically handicapped, and whole families that contained these – but most of all they were a knacker's yard for the old. Anyone ageing and destitute was likely to end up in one. When whole Victorian families lived penniless in one room, and the local infant mortality rate was 46 per cent (which is what it was in Hoxton in 1858, less than twenty years before my grandparents were born there), a sick old relative would probably be every bit as well looked after in the workhouse as at home, horrific though workhouse conditions were, and so was likely to be packed off to one by his grown-up children, especially if they had children of their own and only one bed. So an almost universal terror among the poor was that

of 'ending up in the workhouse', and it was where a high proportion of those who lived long enough did end up.

The first workhouse on the site of St Leonard's was completed
in 1777. A parliamentary report published in 1848 revealed that
by that year it contained more than 1000 people, 150 of whom
were chronically ill, though not separated from the others. This
led to the old workhouse being demolished and a new one created,
on a tremendous scale, a whole street long and four tall storeys
high. It had accommodation for 1200 inmates, including separate accommodation for the sick, and stretched all the way from
Hoxton Street to Kingsland Road, with what looked like a main-
entrance frontage on each. The sheer bulk of it still makes one
gasp to look at. It is an architectural phenomenon, though scarcely
one that elevates the spirit. As care of the sick became better
organised inside it, it became more and more like a hospital. The
transition was gradual. Not until the year of my birth, 1930, did
the pure workhouse side of it close down and the whole place
become St Leonard's Hospital. From then until the 1980s it was
Hoxton's general hospital, so throughout my childhood it was the
place you were most likely to be taken to if you were ill.

There was one other building in Hoxton Street that was out of
all proportion in size to the rest, though on nothing like that
scale. It was the Britannia, a vast Victorian theatre seating 3000
people which had earlier, before remodelling, seated 4000. It had
been built on the site of an Elizabethan tavern called the Pimlico;
the street alongside it was Pimlico Walk, and that whole area was
known to us locally as Pimlico. Apparently 'Pimlico' had originally been the name of a drink, but then got launched as a place-
name by the tavern. The Pimlico in Hoxton was mentioned in a
sixteenth-century dancing-and-drinking song that became widely
popular, and it was from this that an entire district of what was
later to become London, near Victoria, got its name. As a small
child I was unable to pronounce it properly, and used to say

'Plimlico' – which then became a family joke, so all the members of my family said 'Plimlico'. A few years later I was surprised to discover that a whole other area of London, as big as Hoxton itself, had this name. To this day I occasionally think of that too as Plimlico.

The massive dark hulk of the Britannia was referred to as 'the old Brit', or just 'the Brit'. It had become famous well back in the nineteenth century. Dickens visited it more than once in the 1850s. The descriptions he left of it, and even more so of its audiences, in the fourth chapter of *The Uncommercial Traveller* under the title 'Two Views of a Cheap Theatre', are so vivid they are worth quoting at length.

What Theatre? Her Majesty's? Far better. Royal Italian Opera? Far better. Infinitely superior to the latter for hearing in; infinitely superior to both for seeing in. To every part of this Theatre, spacious fireproof ways of ingress and egress. For every part of it, convenient places of refreshment and retiring rooms. Everything to eat and drink carefully supervised as to quality and sold at an appointed price; respectable female attendants ready for the commonest women in the audience . . . Magnificently lighted by a firmament of sparkling chandeliers, the building was ventilated to perfection. My sense of smell, without being particularly delicate, has been so offended in some of the commoner places of public resort that I have often been obliged to leave them when I have made an uncommercial journey expressly to look on. The air of this Theatre was fresh, cool, and wholesome. To help towards this end, very sensible precautions had been used, ingeniously combining the experience of hospitals and railway stations. Asphalt pavements substituted for wooden floors, honest bare walls of glazed brick and tile – even at the back of the boxes – for plaster and paper, no benches stuffed, and no carpeting or baize used; a cool material with a light glazed surface being the covering of the seats . . . The stage itself, and all its appurtenances of machinery, cellarage, height and breadth, are on a scale more like the Scala at Milan, or the San Carlo at Naples, or the Grand Opera at Paris, than any notion that a stranger would be likely to form of the Britannia Theatre at Hoxton . . . As the spectators at this theatre, for a reason I will presently show, were the object of my journey, I entered on the play of the night as one of the two thousand and odd hundreds by looking about me at my neighbours . . . Besides prowlers and idlers, we were mechanics, dock-labourers, costermongers, petty tradesmen, small clerks, milliners, stay-makers, shoe-binders, shop-workers, poor workers in a hundred highways and byways. Many of us – on the whole, the majority – were not at all clean, and not at all choice in our lives or conversation. But we had all come together in a place where our convenience was well consulted, and where we were well looked after, to enjoy an evening's entertainment in common . . . we were closely attentive, and kept excellent order . . . Between the pieces we almost all of us went out and refreshed. Many of us went to the length of drinking beer at the bar of the neighbouring public-house, some of us drank spirits, crowds of us had sandwiches and ginger-beer at the refreshment-bars established for us in the Theatre. The sandwich – as substantial as was consistent with portability, and as cheap as possible – we hailed as one of our greatest institutions. It forced its way among us at all stages of the entertainment, and we were always delighted to see it . . .

Of the Brit as it was a generation or two later – in the Hoxton in which my grandparents grew up and were young theatre-going adults – *The Oxford Companion to the Theatre* writes: 'It was a unique institution; authors wrote exclusively for it, actors joined the company as young men and remained until old age. It was supported mainly by the people of the surrounding district, who loved the theatre and revered its manageress, who played in the annual pantomime (which always ran until Easter) until she was in her 70s.'

At that time the locality possessed at least one other theatre of spectacular proportions and design, the Grecian Theatre in the Hoxton section of City Road. This was decorated with the stages that had been used for William IV's coronation in Westminster Abbey. In 1873 it was described as still being a 'stupendous edifice'. For many generations the area had numerous theatres in operation – full-scale theatres as well as music halls and penny gaffes – but during the first few years of my life most of them were converted into cinemas to exhibit the newly-invented talking pictures that had suddenly become all the rage. People who persisted in wanting live theatre – and there were a lot of them – had to take a bus-ride to the theatres of the West End, where they helped to fill the pits and galleries, as of course many had always done. The audiences for theatre in London have always included Londoners from every section of society. Shakespeare's groundlings were hardly genteel.

At the time when my memories begin, the theatre in neighbouring Pitfield Street, which had been another of those that were well known in the nineteenth century, had been converted and was now called the Hoxton Cinema. I saw Chaplin's *Modern Times* there with my mother in 1936 or '37, and went frequently. By this time the Brit had ceased to function as a full-time theatre, but was too big to fill every day as a cinema, so it languished: it still had one-off stage shows, and ran films occasionally; and it always had a matinée film show for children on Saturdays – the so-called 'tuppenny rush'. All these were things I went to. But you never knew when there was going to be something on at the Brit and when there wasn't, which was unsatisfactory, so it played only a sporadic part in my calculations. However, Hoxton Street's other theatre had survived as a music hall, and for an opposite version of the same reason, namely that it was too small to be run economically as a cinema. Near the middle of the street, on the same side as our shop, it was a plain but charming little theatre that had been known in the nineteenth century as McDonald's Music Hall, and by the time I came on the scene was called Hoxton Hall. The Quakers took it over as a meeting house in the late nineteenth century, and by the mid-'30s it was the focal point of the temperance movement in Hoxton. They cleverly took the view that the way to put their message across was to stage music hall shows, and deliver homilies on temperance during the intervals to an audience that had no bar to go to. As a result, Hoxton Hall was again functioning as a music hall during my childhood. I went to many shows there, from as early as I can remember, and it was there that I learnt the old music hall songs. It is still there, but as a community centre now, though still partially used as a theatre. The Brit, on the other hand, got a direct hit in the blitz, and was destroyed.

Beyond the Brit, Hoxton Street closed in to a long bottleneck corresponding to the narrow way at our end, only longer: here again there were no stalls but only shops. Foyles is said to have started there, and grown in premises elsewhere to be the biggest bookshop in the world. A shop I remember, Pollock's, sold toy theatres and stiff paper cut-outs from which you could build your own. For these its pitch was 'Penny Plain, Tuppence Coloured', a phrase that has gone into the language with Pollock's referred to as its source. As a boy my father bought many playthings there, and he retained a special affection for the shop, and knew the man who ran it. But like Foyles, it eventually moved to the West End.

The whole area was one in which live theatre and everything

to do with it had been part of people's lives for many generations before the advent of cinema, and was still loved and pursued
by a large number. In a quiet square near Pollock's called Hoxton
Market a public statue was set up in 1994 inscribed: 'To commem-
orate the traditions of Theatre and Music Hall in Hoxton and
Shoreditch'. London's very first theatre – called, appropriately
enough, The Theatre – was built in the sixteenth century only a
couple of hundred yards away; and also the second, The Curtain;
both of them in what is now Curtain Road, which on a map looks
like a continuation of Hoxton Street. The area was still famous
for its theatre three hundred years later. Stephen Inwood's *A
History of London* describes (p. 659) 'a period of intensive building
between 1828 and 1842, in which the number of theatres and
saloon theatres (based on public houses) in London was doubled
to about twenty-six. These included four in the East End (the
Garrick, the City of London, the Effingham and the Pavilion)
and four in the increasingly shabby and crowded suburbs of
Hoxton and Shoreditch, where London's first theatres had been
built in the 1570s. This was roughly how things stood until the
late 1860s, when seven new West End theatres were built on or
near the Strand.' It was by the happiest of chances that I grew
up not only in a family but in a surrounding community in which
theatre-going had always been part of life. I get naïve pleasure
from the thought that the London theatre and I were born in
the same parish, namely the parish of St Leonard's, Shoreditch.
The church itself was known for a long time as 'the Actors'
Church', from the fact that so many of the earliest actors in
London got married and were buried there, in the sixteenth and
seventeenth centuries.

The street you have to cross from Hoxton Street to Curtain
Road is Old Street, and at that corner of Old Street stand two
institutions that in my childhood were ever-present in their influence on Hoxton life: the local police station and the magistrate's

court. Just as the words 'Fleet Street' were generally used to mean the press, so 'Old Street' was used by Hoxtonians to mean the long arm of the law: 'If you do that you'll soon find yourself in Old Street' . . . 'I wonder if they know about this in Old Street?' . . . 'Will Old Street do anything about it, do you suppose?' . . . Few expressions can more commonly have expressed people's unspoken thoughts.

CHAPTER SIX

It has long been a matter of controversy whether Hoxton should be thought of as part of the East End. Hoxtoners themselves are divided on the question. They have always had a sense of their own identity, and of Hoxton's being a distinctive place; and I have to say that I grew up thinking that there was an East End and a West End and that Hoxton was different from either of them, being on the northern edge of the City. My impression is that the majority of Hoxtoners when I was there thought of the East End as continuous with Hoxton but starting where we finished, a neighbouring territory. The most immediate bit of it spread southwards beside the City through Spitalfields and Whitechapel, and out eastwards to Stepney; and while nearly all of this lay to the east of the City of London, Hoxton was on the City's northern border. According to this perspective, there was Hoxton, and then there was the East End, with the meeting of Kingsland Road and Old Street as the dividing point. As if to endorse that view of the matter the Eastern districts of London's postal service began with the other side of Kingsland Road. Hoxton was in N.1. The postal address of my birthplace, where I lived throughout the period covered by this book, was 276–8 Hoxton Street, London N.1.

Even on this reckoning, though, Hoxton was indeed continuous with the East End; and there can be no doubt that a number of Hoxtonians thought of themselves as part of it. People from elsewhere talked nearly always as if Hoxton belonged to the East

End – as if, travelling from more westerly parts of London and then through Islington, Hoxton was the first part of the East End you came to – the westernmost part of the East End, so to speak. This view was powerfully reinforced by Hoxton's reputation for low life, a reputation which was at its apogee when I was a child. Its notorious combination of crime and poverty made it, people thought, archetypally East End.

When I moved into a wider world I grew accustomed to people describing me as coming from the East End, although it had not occurred to me up to that point to think of myself as doing so. I soon decided to accept the description rather than launch each time into a distinction-drawing homily that had neither interest nor significance for most of the people I was talking to. Today, I am inclined even myself to say that I come from the East End, especially now that the borough of Shoreditch has been abolished, and Hoxton, having lost most of its traditional character, is not as familiar to people by name as it used to be. If I say nowadays that I come from Hoxton it is not infrequently met with the question 'Where's that?' In any case, it has now been lumped in with Hackney, the poorest of all the boroughs today, though it was not part of Hackney when I lived there. It is N. 1. still, with Islington. When I was a child, Islington was almost as poor as Hoxton, and we thought of it as an area continuous with our own, much like it in character. Now, of course, it is fashionable. And Hoxton is becoming fashionable too. But its former associations have not entirely disappeared. Recently a fellow-member of the Garrick Club, explaining to me how Caruso had grown up in the poorest surroundings imaginable, described him as coming from 'the Hoxton of Naples'. This phrase delighted me, and I had pleasure in telling him that I came from the Hoxton of London.

Like most of the areas of London that truly have, or had, a distinctive character, Hoxton existed separately for hundreds of years as a village. It is mentioned in Domesday Book, and seems to have come into existence long before then as a settlement that grew up in the angle where two Roman roads met, the roads now called Kingsland Road and Old Street. These remain two of the boundaries that define it, the third being, more roughly and recently, the Regent's Canal that squiggles round in a quarter-circle in that part of its course. Hoxton comes wholly within the parish of St Leonard's, referred to by the locals as Shoreditch Church, and more widely known as such through two lines in one of Britain's most popular nursery songs: 'When I grow rich/say the bells of Shoreditch'. This church, a couple of hundred yards from one end of Hoxton Street, has always functioned as the main church for Hoxton's special occasions. For many generations, including the period embraced by my familial memories, Hoxton was part of the London Borough of Shoreditch, and its local government headquarters was Shoreditch Town Hall, almost opposite the end of Hoxton Street in Old Street. The most exact definition of Hoxton I can think of is 'that part of the old borough of Shoreditch that lies north of Old Street and west of Kingsland Road'.

All this is on the northern edge of the City of London. From the end of Pitfield Street to the City's boundary at Moorgate is only a few hundred yards; and only a few hundred yards more to the City's central point, the Bank of England. It is this fact of being adjacent to the City, more than any other single factor, that has determined Hoxton's development over the centuries.

In the late Middle Ages Hoxton was an attractive village in the countryside that lay immediately outside the City's gates – Moorgate and Bishopsgate – and as such was a favoured destination for country walks. References to it at that time were often idyllic in tone. Then it became an easily accessible place where London's legal and other restrictions could be evaded. This was the chief reason why London's first theatres were built where they were – they were just outside the City's jurisdiction. Becoming as it then did a focal point for London's first 'show-business' world, Hoxton became also notorious for its drinking and carousing – as a popular poem published in 1609 expressed it, ''Tis a mad world in Hogsdon.' Later the same century, and throughout the following century, freedom from the City's restrictions made Hoxton one of the centres of activity for religious dissenters – Wesley's home and chapel are in City Road just round the corner from Pitfield Street, as is also the grave of George Fox, the leading Quaker. Today, again, it is Hoxton's proximity to the City that is lifting the area out of the squalor that engulfed it in the nineteenth century – the fact that yuppies can buy property there cheaply, and gentrify it, and thus provide themselves with homes from which they can walk to jobs in the City.

Because London's first two theatres were built in Shoreditch, and these were the only theatres when Shakespeare arrived in London from Stratford-on-Avon, it has always been assumed that his earliest London work and lodgings must have been there, and several traditional stories exist to that effect. *Romeo and Juliet* is known to have had its first performance there, and the district was certainly at that time the area most inhabited by actors. Burbage is buried at Shoreditch Church, as was the most famous of all court jesters to Henry VIII, Will Somers, in 1569; and as was to be also Gabriel Spencer, the actor killed by Ben Jonson in a duel in 1598. This duel took place in what was then called Hoxton Fields and is now Hoxton Square. Jonson escaped hanging only by pleading benefit of clergy, and was branded on the thumb as a felon, imprisoned, and had his goods confiscated.

During the seventeenth and eighteenth centuries prosperous City merchants built houses for themselves in this district because it was so easily within walking distance of the City, and took scarcely any time at all by horse or carriage. What transformed it, socially, so drastically downwards, to the point of degradation, was the population explosion that came about in London as a result of the Industrial Revolution. The crucial result of this for London was not that it became a centre of manufacturing industry – it did of course do that, though nearly all the industry was small-scale – but that it became the supreme centre for the trade that was demanded and created by industry, in fact the biggest trade centre in the world. As part of this development, East London's dockyards were the largest and busiest in the world, and through them poured ever-increasing numbers of immigrants into an ever more rapidly expanding London. At the same time the English rural poor were swarming into London in search of the new jobs being created. It all happened so fast, and on such a scale, that immense areas beyond the gates of the old city were swallowed up into London before even the most rudimentary social amenities could be created to keep up with them. The new urban poor lived by their tens of thousands in such areas as Hoxton and the rest of Shoreditch, and because of that the prosperous moved away – westwards, because of the prevailing winds, so as to escape from the air pollution now being created by the smoke of burning coal pouring out of hundreds of thousands of chimneys.

London fog, so horrendous that it became notorious all over the world, was man-made, and was smog. The new poor lived in it, and spread with it eastwards, bringing into being London's infamous East End, a world of increasingly grimy and overcrowded streets and alleyways. In what had previously been prosperous areas, like Hoxton, they moved into the vacated houses of the well-to-do, sometimes a family to a room, so that a house that had been home to one family would now hold several – but still have only one water pump, if any, and a system of sewage disposal hopelessly inadequate to the demands now made on it. Remorseless landlords packed families into these tenements and made fortunes, but the living-conditions were so appalling that such districts became a national scandal. One detail that made an impression on most social observers was the number of people living in basements and cellars, with which the houses had been so amply provided for servants and storage. Shoreditch in general and Hoxton in particular became (according to which basis of calculation is used) either the most poverty-stricken or the second most poverty-stricken area not only in London but in the country. It was because of this that its name came to be used in speech and writing to represent the ultimate in social degradation, the poorest, most criminal, most uncivilised corner of Britain. The acquaintance of mine who talked about the Hoxton of Naples was using it in that sense, which early in the last century was quite common in the conversation of people who had never themselves set foot in Hoxton: the name had become a symbol. At the turn of the century it was cropping up as such in popular literature. In one of P. G. Wodehouse's earliest books an author's works are described as being read everywhere where the English language is spoken and in Hoxton. In the opening scene of Bernard Shaw's *Pygmalion* Professor Higgins illustrates his skill by instantly identifying a cockney from his speech as being from Hoxton. In the Bulldog Drummond books Hoxton is perpetually referred to as the archetypal low-class criminal area. It meant something by now to the general reading public, and they took the name up from such sources and used it themselves.

In areas like the real Hoxton the laws of the rest of society ran incompletely. It was only in the nineteenth century that a police force was created at all, partly in response to such social conditions; but the very extent of these conditions made such areas impossible to police adequately, and there were some which not even the police cared to penetrate. Not surprisingly, the police came to view the job as primarily one of containment. Their chief concern was to see that the wild life in these urban jungles did not become a menace to society as a whole. To this end they came down crushingly on any crimes against respectable citizens from outside, including therefore crimes against house and business property in the slum areas themselves; but apart from that it was only the most flagrant of violent crime that they treated as of pressing concern. The everyday crime that was part of normal life among the overcrowded poor was not something they could realistically regard as within their control – the pilfering and petty thieving that went on all the time, the violence within families behind closed doors that was the rule rather than the exception, the drunkenness, the prostitution. In such an enormous world as the slums of East London, in which it was common for a whole family to sleep in one bed if it was lucky enough to have a bed, such crimes as incest and the abuse of children were beyond all possibility of detection. If circumstances forced the police to take notice of something, they did, but otherwise they let it be. Among the ranks of professional criminals there were plenty who would do almost anything for money, and so were willing to be paid informers, and it was these who kept the police informed about the identities and whereabouts of the criminals they most needed to apprehend, and also kept the police abreast of forthcoming developments. Very little serious crime was solved by detection, nearly all by paid information. This meant that for policemen to do their job it was essential for them to have highly venal relationships, secret and illegal relationships of trust, with criminals. At best, corruption among the police became endemic, and at worst the police themselves became part of organised crime.

In areas like these, poverty and crime were organically interrelated. Because of the overcrowding, and the absence of any large-scale employer except for the docks, there was a permanent shortage of jobs; and people without jobs were forced – simply to get by – to be always on the lookout for short-term opportunities of getting small amounts of money, whether by little bits of work, odd-jobbing, doing favours, stealing, or receiving payment for criminal activities. As they often said cheerfully: 'Anything for a few bob.' Tolerable-looking females had special opportunities for earning money, and perhaps for helping the rest of their family; and many of these were lured away to the West End, and a life of quite likely eventual disaster, though occasional fortune.

For many, if not for most such people, everyday life included a certain amount of petty crime as a matter of course. In these circumstances, few were inclined to be judgemental. Even so, the most important social distinction between individuals, and the only one most people came up against themselves, was between the 'respectable' and the 'rough', between those who strove to get and keep work, staying out of debt and above all out of prison, not committing crimes, bringing up their sons honestly and their daughters chastely, and generally maintaining their self-respect, and those who tried to live without working, always on the lookout for tricks and fiddles, anything for a few bob, but usually broke; pawning clothes, bedding or furniture when desperate, sending children to school without shoes or breakfast, doing moonlight flits when they could not pay the rent, in and out of petty crime and in and out of prison. The population consisted just about equally of both types. Most often the difference went by families – were those people over the road rough or were they respectable? Quite often one side of a street would be rough, or would be thought rough, the other respectable. There were whole rough streets like Wilmer Gardens, and rough areas, like the Nile (as it used to be known – Nile Street and its surroundings).

The outlook of the respectable was based ultimately on a sense of human dignity which they clung to at all costs as their one and only precious possession. Independence was its touchstone. They considered it shameful to be beholden to anyone, to accept gifts or charity, to borrow and not repay (or even simply to borrow). They would do any work, however menial, obnoxious or badly paid rather than be dependent on others, or rather than see their children go to school unshod or badly clothed. Face was all-important – you kept your good name, your honour. In today's

Europe something of the same ethos is still to be found in areas of the greatest social deprivation, for instance parts of Sicily. Such people are in danger of being, as they were in Hoxton, only too often regarded as mugs by the others, the wide-boys, the roughs, and looked on as people who accept unacceptable conditions, who work like slaves but are still poor at the end of it and spend their lives taking orders from others, missing out on all the good things of life. For individuals of spirit and intelligence there might seem at least as much to be said for being rough as for being respectable, and so a high proportion of the ablest in Hoxton ended up on the wrong side of the law. The life of the respectable poor was essentially a life of repression, a great deal of it self-repression, and was no life for anyone with drive and ambition unless he were dedicatedly self-disciplined.

An ever-present fact of life for most people in those circumstances was the sheer stress of it. The extreme overcrowding alone was stress-inducing, and on top of that there were unsocial hours of physical labour, often mindless labour in primitive conditions, bad-quality food and clothing, bad-quality housing and heating, poor sanitation, little or no medical attention, no holidays, searing money troubles, the crushing burden of family responsibilities in circumstances always harsh and difficult. Life was just plain grim, and most of its victims were trapped in it. Serious illnesses among them were common. The average expectation of life was several years less than it was for the rest of society. Breakdowns were familiar news, and so were suicides. The great escape route that lay to everybody's hand was alcohol. People drank to escape, to tranquillise themselves, to forget, to get out of it all. Drunkenness to the point of alcoholism was common among both sexes, especially as people got older and felt themselves less able to cope: but of course those who spent a lot of money on drink made their other problems worse, and just added a drink problem on top of them. It was a downwardly spiralling form of self-destruction, and many families were devastated by it.

For all the inhabitants of this world, rough and respectable alike, there were only a small number of genuine escape routes. For reasons of education and social class the professions were barred to them regardless of their personality, ability or intelligence. There were one or two possible careers in which their lack of education and class was not so much of a handicap, notably sport and show-business – and these were activities in which the poor took a vivid interest anyway – so quite a number of individuals tried to travel along those roads. But to succeed in that way you needed a highly specialised talent. Otherwise the only ways of making significant amounts of money, and thus breaking through to autonomy and freedom, were business and crime. And for all the reasons I have suggested, it was not always easy to draw a clear distinction between the two.

When the British Empire was at its zenith, preening itself on being the greatest empire the world had ever seen, conditions like this existed on an immense scale at the very heart of it, in its capital city. This fact became a matter of widespread concern. In the second half of the nineteenth century a great movement of social rescue arose, directed towards the East End: philanthropists built hostels for women; public kitchens were opened where undernourished children could get free dinners; huge churches were built, and Christian missions; organisations like the Salvation Army and the Quakers founded their centres and halls; the temperance movement launched its crusades against drunkenness among the poor. These things sprang up on all sides, and the visible signs of them were everywhere; but to the bafflement of their well-intentioned paymasters they remained like bubbles on the surface of the East End's life, becoming just one more new and familiar feature of that life, taken for granted by everyone and not altering the basic situation. The problems were on too vast a scale to be solved in this way. They involved a population of a couple of million people in an area of many square miles. It was not to be until the better part of another hundred years had passed that they were removed. What finally did for them was the bloodless revolution brought about in Britain by the Second World War and its aftermath. It was change in the surrounding society that destroyed that world.

But in the meantime, this was the world into which both of my father's parents were born in the 1870s (the decade that also saw the introduction of universal education). The two of them entered this world a couple of hundred yards on either side of where I entered it myself, and I knew both of them well throughout my formative years – I was in my thirties when my grandmother died. My father, too, was born only a few streets away, and his two sisters a few yards from where I was; so our combined family memories of the village that was Hoxton go back from the time of my present writing for something like 120 years. During that period there can have been few families more deeply rooted in Hoxton than ours, or – because of our larger-than-average shop in its main street – more widely known to the people there.

CHAPTER SEVEN

When I was in my fifties a friend who was a professional genealogist – he lived in the Royal College of Arms and was listed in
the London telephone directory as Dragon Rouge Pursuivant –
offered to trace my ancestry. He said he wanted a change from
upper-class families who always turned out to be related to one
another and kept sending him back to the same sources. He
wanted to try his hand at something entirely different.

He found himself able to trace the main line back to the first
years of the nineteenth century. Throughout the time since then
the Magees (I am speaking only of my direct ancestors) had lived
in the same general district of London just north of the City. For
much of the period a swath of that area that included Hoxton
had counted, for purposes of public record, as Clerkenwell (when
I was a boy the telephone we acquired in our shop was given a
Clerkenwell number, so something of that classification remained
even then) and in that broad sense of 'Clerkenwell' my family is
known to have lived in Clerkenwell for two hundred years or
more. For generations they had lived in what is still known as
Clerkenwell, and from there had moved – not far – into Hoxton.
The oldest male Magees were christened, in alternate generations,
Felix and John, and were skilled craftsmen: one a shoe-maker,
another a glove-maker, another a jewel-worker. I had heard already
from my grandfather about his father Felix, who was a designer
of wallpaper – for which there was great demand in the Victorian

era. My grandfather was himself a John, but used his other name, Edgar. I do not know what he christened his firstborn son, who died in infancy: perhaps Felix.

There is something frustrating about investigating your ancestors if nothing is known about them other than what can be gleaned from certificates of birth, marriage and death, because all you end up with is a list of names, dates and occupations: you know nothing about them as people, their lives, what they were like as human beings; and you have no way of finding out. As far back as the church records go in my case they were Church of England records. My genealogist friend warned me against making any inferences much further back that were based on the spelling of my name, because until a certain period there was no such thing as standard spelling of names. He told me of a family called Jones who had always taken it for granted that their ancestry was Welsh, when in fact the name had earlier been Janes and had come from Cornwall. The probability was, he said, that someone with the name Magee had come over to England from Ireland in the eighteenth century; but that was not certain. My family name, he said, could at one time have been Maggs or Magnus, Mager or Mauger – Mauger, he told me, was in fact Germanic, and the British surname Major had been misleadingly derived from it.

I found this aspect of what he told me enlightening, and it changed my assumptions about my ancestry. When strangers first told me my name was Irish I had been surprised, and even more so when they told me that *I* must be Irish. My family had no sense of being Irish, none at all, though there had been a bone-marrow feeling of belonging to London. I looked the name up in a dictionary of surnames, and sure enough the dictionary did say it was Irish – and, what is more, Roman Catholic Irish, from County Antrim. This surprised me again, because in my family there was no ancestral memory of anyone having been Catholic, not even a lapsed Catholic. Yet without much reflection I had accepted these things as probable facts about my family. The big influx of Irish into East London had occurred at the time of the Great Famine in Ireland, 1848–9: poverty-stricken Irishmen had been herded on to the boats like cattle, and poured out into the docks of Glasgow, Liverpool and London. So I assumed that this was how my forebears had come to Hoxton: they had got there from the East London dock area, and the one who had actually got off the boat had been, presumably, my grandfather's grandfather.

Now, I learnt, all this was a self-created myth. None of it had happened. I understood why no one in my family had ever re-flected any echo of anything Irish, or hinted at lapsed-Catholicism in our ancestral past. It explained what had perplexed me most of all in this connection: I knew that my grandfather had never in his life been a believing Christian, and that he had still been in his teens when he met my grandmother in a Protestant mission hall: how had he become so completely detached from a Catholic background in so short a time? All this was now explained. However, just as I am used to letting it go when people refer to me as coming from the East End, so I also let it go when people refer to me as Irish. To be perpetually correcting others on such points becomes crotchety as well as boring, and in any case smacks of protesting too much, and so tends to be counter-productive: many are the people inclined to take denial of such a thing as that one is from the East End, or Irish, as confirmation that one is.

People have an illogical attitude to the relationship between names and ancestry. Suppose, for example, that I have my name because a direct ancestor who bore it moved to London from Ireland more than two hundred years ago. I must necessarily have hundreds of other ancestors in the same degree of ancestry, or closer, but with other names; and I am as much the descendant of each one of them as I am of him; so the part of me that is him is a fraction of one over hundreds. The others could have been anything. Among such a large number there are quite likely to have been foreigners, especially in London. To think merely of Clerkenwell, it was always teeming with immigrants; at one time it had a notable Huguenot population, so I might easily, through wives, have not just one but several Huguenot ancestors. But even if that were known to be the case, it would not occur to anybody today to say I was French. On the other hand, if my name were known to be, as it could be, an anglicised spelling of the name of a single Huguenot called Maguy, an existent French name which is pronounced in the same way as mine, then there would be people who referred to me as French. We are victims of word-magic here: we tend to associate a person's identity with his name, in a way that is at odds with the genetic facts of the situation, and may also, as in this case, be unrelated to a well-founded sense of their own identity that individuals and families have.

Whatever the nature of the mists that my grandfather's remote ancestry was lost in, the woman he married was plain English all the way back. She was born Lily Cox, in Penn Street, which now you can actually see from where I was born. Her father had grown up in Manchester, in a middle-class family connected with brewing, and he had been to a decent school, one of the bluecoat schools, and then become a stonemason. But he had fallen in love with a strikingly beautiful factory girl, or perhaps brewery girl, who was illiterate. His parents, aghast, threatened that if he married her they would have nothing to do with her, or with him. He married her, and his parents kept their word. The couple made their home in London, had two children, and were happy – until he was killed, still young, in an accident at work. It has to be remembered that we are talking of the 1880s, long before the Welfare State. A charity tried to help the young widow and her children, and a clergyman went to Manchester to see the dead man's family and ask for their help; but they adamantly refused even to see their daughter-in-law or her children. These ended up in circumstances of the uttermost poverty. Because of her illiteracy, the young Mrs Cox could get only the lowest-paid work, and this she did, for instance scrubbing people's front steps before daylight in the depths of winter; and she needed to do long hours of it in order to scrape together enough money for herself and her children to get by on. Without making a song and dance about it she kept her self-respect; but my grandmother, who adored her, found their lives traumatising, not least because of what she saw her mother going through.

When my grandmother was in her eighties and I in my late twenties she made a passing reference in conversation with me to the grinding poverty in which she had spent her childhood, and I stopped her and asked her if she would tell me about it. Her reaction took me wholly by surprise. Not only did her mouth and lower jaw snap tight like a trap, her entire face did. Then she said, in a strained, unnaturally quiet voice: 'No, Bryan, I won't tell you about it.' I was derailed by this, and did not immediately know what to say, and must have shown my confusion, because she went on: 'Don't worry, I don't mind you asking. But I don't want to talk about it. I've never talked about it to anyone, not even your grandfather. And I'm not going to talk about it to you.' It had scarred her for life. And she was not a delicate flower, but an unusually tough, determined character, not to say hard and obdurate. It gives an insight into conditions in which millions of people in Britain, including many of above average intelligence and ability, have lived in the past, indeed until recently.

As I write these words, the older of my grandmother's two daughters, Peggy, is alive and well, and in her nineties. She tells me of how, for many years as a child, she was taken on weekly visits to her grandma, who by then was living alone in Spitalfields and keeping herself by working at home on the making of artificial flowers for hats. Peggy loved her more than anyone else in the world. She was, apparently, a person of unselfconscious good nature, a wholly unsentimental sweetness, and for Peggy the greatest of treats was to be allowed to stay with her overnight. No doubt it was a case of grandma acting as a baby-sitter on Saturday nights. It was obvious, apparently, that she had been a rare beauty when young, and she was still beautiful, and much loved. When she died at seventy her death seemed to Peggy not right, and she resented the way the grown-ups assured one another that it had to be accepted because seventy was 'a good age'.

Of my grandmother's life between the childhood of which she would never speak and her marriage to my grandfather I know little, but I doubt whether there is all that much to know. She went to school, and was fully literate, as were all the members of my family that I knew. She worked hard in an overdriven way, determined to raise herself out of the poverty in which she had grown up, and not to have a life like her mother's. She became a seamstress, worked all the hours God sent, saved fanatically, and soon, while still very young, opened a little rented shop in which she sold clothes for women and children. Her experience as a seamstress had taught her not only about quality of workmanship but also where the best value was to be found among suppliers, while she herself could carry out alterations and repairs, and make whole garments to special order. She took it for granted that she had to work unremittingly to make her shop a success. She was a hard bargainer, but she gave value for money, and tried to sell only well-made clothes. No rubbish. She had plenty of low cunning, but retained direct, simple notions of right and wrong, good and bad, and lived by them, come what may, unshakeable, genuinely shocked by any untruthfulness or wrongdoing. But although she was honest and truthful she was also stony and narrow. Her business prospered.

My grandfather, who rented a shop next door to hers, arrived there by a different route. He had grown up in a family in which drink was the problem. His father, Felix the wallpaper designer, was always in demand for well-paid work but kept spending all his money on drink. He had a wife and five children who half the time were penniless and desperate because of this. He would disappear on benders for several days at a time without their having the slightest idea where he was, until he was carried back to them by his friends insensible with drink. After he had dried out he was able to get work again and earn money, but then he would go off again on the next bender. My grandfather, the oldest child, grew up detesting the havoc this was making of all their lives. As most people did in those days, he left school and started work at the age of thirteen, while continuing to live with his parents. With his first earnings he was able to buy himself some decent clothes for the first time. But one day he returned home from work to find that his father had pawned his clothes and disappeared with the money, leaving him the pawn tickets so that he could get his clothes back. He walked out of the house there and then, and never again lived there, nor did he ever again have anything to do with his father, though he continued to help his mother and her other children.

He worked at various jobs. I know that at one time he worked in a sweet factory. Whenever I as a child offered him a boiled sweet he would always insist on picking out a translucent, light-coloured one, and would get serious about refusing if I tried to press on him one of the fuller-flavoured dark ones that were my favourites. On a couple of occasions he made mysterious, inexplicit jokes about what he had seen the lads in the factory putting into the dark-coloured sweets: whatever it was, it had given him a lifelong determination never to eat one.

His decisive career-move came when he got a job on a second-hand clothes stall in Hoxton Street market, run by a Mr and Mrs Tubb. He had to pull the barrow morning and evening when the stall was set up and dismantled, and that could not have been easy for him, for he was physically small and frail. But he became interested in the clothes themselves, and in the buying and pricing of them; and he learnt how to sell them; and he also learnt the dos and don'ts of running a small business. He developed an unusual degree of expertise and assurance in these things, based on genuine interest. Years later, decades after he had ceased to have anything to do with second-hand clothes, he remarked that he would never be in need of a job, because if he lost every penny he possessed he could go straight out and start earning his living in the second-hand clothes market, where he knew exactly what he was doing.

The Tubbs did well, and decided to take two steps up-market by exchanging their stall for a shop and by selling new clothes only. They took my grandfather with them, for they regarded him as having contributed to their success. He lived over their shop and learnt their new business. Then Mr Tubb was taken seriously ill for a long time, and my grandfather found himself running the shop, again successfully. Then one day he was taken ill himself and had to spend three days in bed. When he returned to work, and was paid by Mrs Tubb at the end of the week, he found himself docked three days' wages for the time he had been off sick – and on wages like his he was already living from hand to mouth. He was thunderstruck. After all he had done for the Tubbs he realised that their attitude to him was exploitative: they had made use of him without seeing him as a human being like themselves. As when his father pawned his clothes, he walked out immediately.

What he then did was to set up a shop of his own. He had no money, but there was a shop standing empty a few doors away, owned by somebody he knew, Mr Pemberton, the keeper of the paper shop. So he went to Pemberton and asked if he could lease the shop that was currently earning nothing anyway, and delay starting to pay rent on it for three months, after which he would make up the arrears. At the same time he considered which of the suppliers to whom he was already well known personally would be willing to give him long terms of credit. Meanwhile the Tubbs went to Pemberton and urged him to take three months rent from them, in advance, to keep the shop empty. But he told them he had given his word to my grandfather, and as far as he was concerned that was the end of the matter. So with no money my grandfather opened a shop of his own. He had to borrow for his living expenses, and his first couple of years were high-risk and hard going; but he managed to get himself up and running. The business always thereafter had its downs as well as ups, partly because of the Depression but chiefly because of my grandfather's love of betting on the horses: there were several times when he was in serious financial trouble, in fact stony-broke; but the shop as a business was always well run, and in spite of the way his betting habits put it so often at risk it never went under, but prospered modestly over the years. Perhaps for him that too was a form of gambling: if it was, he emerged from it a winner. But there were times when it was touch and go.

At what stage in the development of these parallel stories my grandparents married I do not know. In both cases they rented only their shop itself at first, not the rooms above it. My father was born in 1901 in a rented room a few streets away, in what was then Culford Road and is now Lawford Road. Peggy, six years his junior, was born in a room over Tubbs' shop, where my grandparents must therefore have been living in 1907. Their youngest child, Hilda, was born in 1914 in the room over my grandmother's shop, so by then my grandmother, if not necessarily yet my grandfather, was renting the rooms over her shop in addition to the shop itself, and the family was living there. Eventually there came a time when my grandparents were able to buy the whole of both premises, rooms as well as shops.

Peggy tells me that up to that time the cellar under my grandfather's shop had been let separately to a man known as Charlie.

He entered and left his cellar through a trapdoor in the middle of the shop. He did not live there but spent all the hours of daylight huddled up tight against a basement window under an iron grille in the pavement, over which people walked past one of our shop windows. All day, every day, he sat there making sieves. When my grandfather became his landlord he told Charlie – regretfully, and holding out money – that he would have to leave, because it was not really acceptable to have to keep making the customers in the shop stand to one side so that an unexplained figure could come up through the floorboards. Charlie was indignant. The cellar had been his all his adult life, he said, and was ideal for his purposes – where else was he going to find such perfect premises at so low a rent? He offered to pay more. But my grandfather was adamant, though no doubt also generous. By the time I came on the scene the cellar was our coal cellar, kept filled through a manhole in the street outside. I was forbidden to go into it because it made my clothes black; but because of the huge piles of coal I loved playing there, on the rare occasions when I got the chance.

My grandparents' first child, a boy, died in infancy and was never thereafter mentioned, with the result that even his brother and sisters did not know he had existed. My father, the second child, assumed all his life that he was the first. At the time of my father's birth my grandfather was friendly with the husband of his favourite sister, a Swede called Knut who was working in London for a Scandinavian fur company. Apparently the two of them went out and about everywhere together. So when my father was born he was christened Frederick Knut Magee. As a name, people thought this foreign and therefore funny, and teased him about it. There also happened to be at that time a slang word for a young dandy which was pronounced 'nut' though spelt 'knut', and when my father went to school there was a music-hall song with the refrain 'I'm Gilbert the filbert, the knut' – which of course was chanted at him by the other boys. He tried anglicising the name to Canute, but people thought that even funnier. On my birth certificate he appears as Frederick Canute Magee, but shortly after that he disowned his second name altogether and ceased to use it even on official documents – so he became, in full, Frederick Magee. He was known all his life as Fred.

The sister he acquired after six years was christened Lily, the same name as her mother. She too disliked her name, and in young adulthood became the Peggy I have mentioned. Then after another seven years a fourth and last child was born unexpectedly. My grandfather, determined in advance that it should be a boy, referred to it ahead of time as Bill, a name he never abandoned. She was christened Hilda, however, and that was what everyone except my grandfather called her. At the age of sixteen she became my only godparent.

My father's early childhood was in many ways like mine. He lived in the same rooms over the same shops, and went as an infant to Gopsall Street School. But he was physically more ill-treated by his mother than I was: she sometimes beat him savagely about the face and head. He never said anything about it to me, but Peggy tells me that there would be times when his collar was torn and sticking out, and his face and hair blotched with blood from where my grandmother had dragged him around and hit him. It seems to have given him a deep-seated need for her approval, which became a hang-up for him in later life – he was otherwise a person of secure independence of mind. Even as a boy he was conspicuously intelligent, with a confident and likeable personality. It was taken for granted at his school that he would pass what was then referred to as the Scholarship (what came in later years to be known as the Eleven Plus) and win a place at a grammar school. But he failed. The headmaster was incensed. My father had been such a certainty to pass that the headmaster believed he could only have failed on purpose, and hauled him up in front of the school and gave him a public dressing-down – which remained one of his most unpleasant memories all his life.

This kept him on course to leave school and start work at the age of thirteen, and he did. But there was one particular might-have-been that is worth recounting because it casts light on how the family at that time appeared to others, and also shows how my kind of life-path might have been followed, more surprisingly, by my father. The family was beginning, in its small way, to be looked on as unusual. Starting from absolutely nothing it had acquired a shop that was two or three times the size of others, and had gained a reputation for selling only good stuff, and at a reasonable price. Yet my grandfather, far from being the familiar Victorian type of disciplined, earnest and self-improving working man who becomes an employer, was a sport-loving, theatre-going, whisky-drinking, card-playing and altogether life-relishing enjoyer, who was known to be constantly in hock to the bookies, but was amusing even about that. It was in this spirit that he had had all his children taught to play musical instruments – and they seemed to be turning out as a fairly bright bunch of kids. The key to him was that he was a life-lover who was also an inveterate gambler, but he had been quick-witted and lucky enough – so far, at least, and in spite of his own worst efforts – to hold things together and keep his show on the road. Perhaps the most remarkable thing about him, given his experience of life and his circumstances, was that he was spontaneously and almost recklessly generous. In the eyes of others this was his most conspicuous characteristic: he was kind. He was far from being a soft touch – if anyone was alert to the ways of the world it was him, and he found no difficulty at all in saying No, and being as firm as any situation required him to be; but if there was someone he knew who genuinely needed help which he was able to give, he gave it. My grandmother upbraided him endlessly for this, but then she upbraided him for everything – his drinking, his gambling, his sitting up late into the night playing cards – and he was unperturbed by it. He went his own way, and she was never able to make him do otherwise, though I suspect her restraints on him were indispensable to his survival and success. He just gave money to people without telling her, or, indeed, telling anyone. There was nothing sugary about any of this; he was a dry character, and his sense of humour was unsentimental and disabused; nor was he concerned to win anybody's approval. He just took a matter-of-fact attitude towards helping people, as if it were like changing a fuse. Without realising it, he became the most liked and respected person in the immediate neighbourhood.

Suppliers who visited our shop from outside Hoxton tended to see him and his family as standing out a little from their surroundings, and to find them interesting, and enjoy talking to them, getting to know them. The maker of the best-quality clothes my grandfather sold was a firm belonging to a family called London. Their main factory was in London, but they lived in Brighton. A second-generation heir, Jack London, was now running the business. (I met him many years later, and found him unfussily delightful, not unlike my grandfather.) When my father failed the Scholarship, Jack London declared that it would be a crime for such an intelligent boy to be denied a good education. He took it on himself to open discussions about this with my grandparents, as a result of which it was arranged that when my father left the state system at thirteen he would go as a boarder to Brighton College, a minor but good-quality public school in Brighton that did not take pupils until they were thirteen anyway. Whether Jack arranged for this to be paid for by a trust, a charity, or other organisation with which he had some connection, or whether he intended to pay for it himself, or somehow get it charged to his business, I do not know. His family may already have been benefactors of the school, and he may already have been on the lookout for clever kids to send there: whatever the background, the arrangements were put in place. And then, only a few weeks before my father was due to go to Brighton College – he had been born in December 1901 – the First World War broke out. It is amazing to think that if it had not done so when it did, he would have had a public school education. In pre-First World War Britain that would have been almost unimaginable for someone from his background. As it was, his parents were frightened at the prospect of his living on the south coast, which everyone expected to be bombed; and confronted by all the uncertainties of war they felt they had better keep him at home with them. So he left school altogether and started work in the shop. In those days fourteen was in theory the minimum school-leaving age, but children were allowed to leave before their fourteenth birthday if they could produce evidence that they had a secure job to go to. The law was well intentioned in this respect: it meant that in a time of widespread unemployment a school-leaver would not be forced to pass up a valuable opportunity for the sake of a few weeks at school.

My grandfather was already doing well enough to employ an assistant, so now there were three of them working in the shop. From the start my father was trained in a co-managerial role, the assumption being that one day the shop would be his. Because he was seventeen when the war ended he did not have to serve in it, and in fact he worked in the shop until the end of his life. He never found it fulfilling, but the family connection attached him to it more closely than he would otherwise have been, and he developed the view that the real point and value of life were to be sought by him outside work. He and his father were especially close. Physically they were unlike: my father grew to be six feet tall, and was well built. But they were both intelligent, with a wide range of interests, many of these in the same things. Above all, they were both enjoyers. Their chief concerns had nothing to do with rising socially in the world, an empty notion for both of them: it was to enjoy their lives. They loved horse-racing, and betting in almost any form. Every day they took successive editions of the evening papers to keep abreast of the racing results, and of sport generally. They took particular interest in football, cricket and boxing, and went constantly to sporting events of many different kinds. From Liverpool Street station, which they could bus to in a couple of minutes from Kingsland Road, or even walk to, they caught trains to Newmarket. The Oval was only seven stops on the tube from Old Street, without changing. The nearest football team was Arsenal, which between the wars was persistently at the top of the league. The next nearest was Spurs. They attended championship boxing matches, which in the 1920s moved quite close, to nearby Harringay. There was greyhound-racing all over London. They worked much longer hours in the shop than most people would nowadays, because it was open from nine till eight, and again on Sunday mornings; and there was as yet no early closing day apart from Sunday; but they knew from experience when the quiet periods were likely to be, and with three of them available it was frequently possible to arrange for one to slip off to the races, or some other sporting event, especially as they felt in their hearts that doing so was of greater value and importance than running the shop.

My grandfather, unlike my father, was an active participant in sport. He had been a cyclist at a time when cycling was all the rage; and as someone small and light he successfully coxed a boat on the River Lea – he got two silver medals with his name on for this, of which I now have one and my sister the other. But somewhere along the line he contracted a double hernia, probably pulling heavy barrows, so by the time I knew him he had given up sport. He and my father both liked indoor games, which for them meant chiefly cards and billiards. Card-playing was almost a part of their daily lives, being the most popular of all pastimes among their friends and neighbours. As for billiards, in those days there were billiard halls all over London: many pubs had tables, as did every good club and hotel, and many private houses; so that this beautiful game, which has now almost died out, was played everywhere. My father loved it, and was quite good at it: he never made a hundred break, which he daydreamt of doing, but he made several in the sixties and seventies, which was not bad for an amateur. The world he and his father inhabited was one in which bets took place on everything, so they played all these games with side-bets as a matter of course; and they would also bet against one another on the sporting events they attended.

The other great interest they shared was the theatre. They had grown up surrounded by theatres, including two in their own street, and for more than was provided locally they had only to go to the West End. Hoxton's location in inner London meant that all London venues, whether for theatre or sport, were within easy reach by bus or tube. To enable themselves to go to as many things as possible – and because the only times they had much money were when they had had a big win – they sat in the cheapest or next-to-cheapest seats, which in theatres gave them a choice between the pit, the gallery and the upper circle. The pit and the gallery were usually the same price, the pit being at the back of the stalls. (Theatres have since upgraded their pits to stalls, thus overnight making the cheapest seats some of the dearest.) When my father and grandfather were together they sat in the gallery, because my grandfather, being so small, could seldom see the stage from the pit. But of course they did not go to everything together; they often went with friends of their own generation, or my grandfather with my grandmother, or my father with a girl-friend. For quite a while my father went out with a girl from Vooghts, one of two daughters of the woman with the tongue. This girl was greatly liked by everyone, or so I am told, and after my father married my mother people went on saying for years what a pity it was that he hadn't married the Vooght girl.

My father's greatest love, perhaps after horse-racing, was music, but this was something his father did not share. He early on became an enthusiastic concert- and opera-goer. Monday has always been the quietest day in the London theatre, and today some theatres close on Mondays while others charge lower prices; but between the wars both these customs were much more widespread: nearly all theatres either closed or charged lower prices. For the inter-war seasons of opera and ballet at Covent Garden, seasons that now seem drastically short, my father and a fellow-enthusiast called Fred Griffin would each buy a subscription ticket for all the Mondays, thereby getting a double discount, and they would go together every Monday night regardless of what was on. They would queue early to get these tickets, and invariably sat in the same seats in the amphitheatre slips (which I sometimes, out of pure sentimentality, chose myself during the years immediately after my father's death in 1947).

I knew Fred Griffin; and I also knew another friend of my father's who went with him to a lot of musical events, a man who played the trombone in a Salvation Army band. I addressed him as Mr Fawkes, but everybody else called him Chopper because of his profile. He loved not only orchestral music but band music too, and took my father to a lot of it, not least because it was free – he knew every venue in London where you could hear a good band for nothing. I remember being a very small boy with the two of them at a band concert in which a man played a saw with a violin bow, and this seemed to me miraculous. It sounded like the way I thought angels were supposed to sound when they sang.

My father was with Chopper when he met my mother. It was in one of the West End theatres, the Garrick in Charing Cross Road, in the very early 1920s. The two men were sitting in the pit behind two girls, and the girl in front of my father was wearing an immense hat, very fashionable at the time. All women wore hats then in public places, and would often keep them on even in the theatre. (This was still true in my own earliest theatre-going days, and most theatres displayed notices asking women to remove their hats.) When the curtain went up, my father found he was unable to see the stage. After a few moments he leaned forward and asked in a whisper if the girl would mind taking her hat off so that he could see. She minded very much, and refused. At that time she wore her hair down to her waist, and on this occasion it had been taken up carefully into her hat, where it was being held in place by hatpins; so to take the hat off she would have had to take the hatpins out, and her hair would cascade down around her. My father was unwilling to take No for an answer, and a long, acrimonious altercation took place in the dark. When the lights went up at the first interval they talked again, and the two young men invited the two young women to the bar for a drink. Among the many consequences of this was me.

CHAPTER EIGHT

My mother was not a Londoner, she came from Newcastle-on-Tyne. A few years before she met my father she had been one of those teenage girls you can see to this day arriving alone at King's Cross station from the North determined to make a life for themselves in London. Because she had, in effect, run away from home she was on distant terms with her family, though she kept in touch with them. I never knew them well, in fact never had any sense of them as being my family, and almost never thought of them. When I was very small she took me and my sister once on a visit to Newcastle so that they could see us, and I have some memories of that; but I have not been there since, until the writing of this book made me curious to see it; and I never met most of those people again, though there were a couple who dropped in on us subsequently in London.

My mother's childhood had been ruined, she told me, by violent and perpetual conflict between her parents over what religion their six children were to be brought up in. Father was determined that they should be Catholics, mother that they should not. As the battle-line surged a long way forward, then a long way back, the children were dragged out of one set of schools and packed off to another. This made both school and home life intolerable, for the rows at home were often physically violent. From the earliest age my mother developed a 'plague on both your houses' attitude towards her parents, and while still a child she swore to herself that if ever she had a family of her own there would be no mention of religion in her household. She wished it to have no place in her life. And she kept her word. Without being aware of it at the time, I grew up in a family for which religion played no part, and was never referred to. I have been abidingly grateful for that: the development of so many people, in the past perhaps more than now, has been deformed either by their having been indoctrinated with religion when small or by their having reacted against such indoctrination. At least I have been free of those two things.

It is ironic that the Irish and Catholic connections that people so often attribute to me because of the name Magee, although nowhere ascertainable in the history of my father's family, are immediately there in my mother's. She had dissociated herself from them before I was born, but her maiden name was Lynch, and her father was a Roman Catholic who had come to Newcastle-on-Tyne from Ireland. He got work as a school caretaker, and married a Protestant Englishwoman. If my mother is to be believed, he was in real life the drunken Irishman of caricature, frequently coming home drunk and beating his wife and children. She grew up fearing and detesting him. She told me that one day when she was fourteen, shortly after having left school, she was already in bed when he came home drunk and started beating her mother. When the children intervened he beat them too. She ran out of the house in her nightdress, with bare feet on the cobblestones. A neighbour took her in, but the next day she refused to go home; and it was then that she took the decision to clear out altogether and make a new life for herself. Whether she came to London immediately I am not quite sure, but I think she did.

She had four brothers and one sister. The oldest of the six was her sister Nora, who married a coal-miner whom I learnt to call Uncle Ned. They lived in one of the satellite towns that are nearly but not quite Newcastle, and we stayed with them for part of our visit. I found Nora forbidding, but I liked Ned – a warm, humorous man. He took me down a coal-mine, which I found thrilling. His coal-miner friends were black all over, face and all, and treated me in a joshing, noisy, kindly way, and I thought them rough and wonderful. At first, when the cage, which had no sides, just dropped down the pit-shaft in free fall, I was terrified; but Ned reassured me: 'It has to go as fast as this because it's a mile down.' After that instant of panic I felt all right again, and then I loved it. In the short time I was with Ned he taught me all sorts of things. 'Never forget,' he said, 'that one Englishman is worth ten foreigners.' I accepted this as being some sort of fact, like twelve inches make a foot. Every time he put a glass to his lips he said: 'Down the Pope,' and I asked him what the Pope was, and he gave me some sort of explanation – I wish I could remember it. I became enormously fond of him; but I never saw him again, or Nora. They had a son, Eddie, who became a policeman and dropped in on us once or twice when he was on holiday in London. But he was nearer my sister's age than mine, and I don't think he noticed me. All I remember is thinking that Eddie Monday (as I imagined it to be spelt – it was really Mundy) was a funny name. Much better, I thought, to be Eddie Saturday.

Of my mother's four brothers only one was in Newcastle while we were there, and that was the youngest, Fred. He was unemployed, living on the dole. Because of this my mother openly declared contempt for him, repeatedly saying that anyone could get a job if he really tried, and that Fred was just a layabout, a parasite. Not once, I think, did she refer to him without describing him as lazy. Of her other brothers, Len had a job with a tea company in Ceylon; Dennis was in the navy, abroad most of the time; and Clem was a private in the Coldstream Guards in London. (I realise now that this collection of occupations says something revealing about the British working class in the age of empire.) I have only one memory of seeing Dennis, a fleeting and hazy visual image of a man in a sailor's uniform; I particularly liked his hat. Although Clem was in London we rarely saw him, though he did occasionally turn up at our home and ask if he could sleep for a night or two on our living-room floor. On some of these visits he took me and my sister out, usually to a matinée at a West End theatre – I think it was with him that I saw *Where the Rainbow Ends*, a great favourite with children between the wars. On one occasion he took us to the Natural History Museum. That remains one of the experiences of my life that had the greatest impact on me at the time. The skeletons of the dinosaurs were the most spectacular and amazing things I had ever seen. Because I was so small they appeared impossibly immense: and to think that these had been live animals that ruled the earth for millions of years before there had been any people at all! I was wonder-struck by them, and for weeks afterwards I could not get them out of my mind. I even dreamt about them. Clem's visits were something I always enjoyed, but they were not frequent; and he was a shy man anyway, so I never really felt I had got to know him. Eventually he married and stopped coming to see us.

My memories of being taken by my mother to see (or rather to be looked at by) her family in Newcastle are patchy. Her mother was by that time an alcoholic, so it was a question of catching her at the right time, and I doubt whether we did: I saw her only once, and she seemed to take no notice of me at all. I also saw my mother's father only once. All I remember of him is a big, round, sweaty and bright red face and a physically alarming manner: he was someone I was afraid to go near, and I remember that some sort of social embarrassment was caused by this. I had difficulty in understanding what people were saying a good deal of the time, because they spoke with such thick Geordie accents. My mother had lost hers in London, so it was something I had never heard before. To this day I find it the only accent in England that I some-times cannot understand. There were other communication difficulties too. Wanting an ice-cream in a cafeteria, I asked for 'a wafer', because, where I came from, if you asked for ice-cream they said 'Cone or wafer?', so you just said 'wafer' in the first place. Here they gave me, literally, a wafer. I was nonplussed by this. When I spoke up I was told off for not having asked in the first place for 'an ice-cream sandwich', a term I had never heard. I felt doubly hard done by, because an ice-cream was self-evidently not a sandwich. Of the city itself all I remember is the Tyne Bridge and Grey's Monument, and an impression of the whole place as being either black or dark grey, and somehow oppressive. It seemed to me a strange town – chiefly, I suppose, because it was strange to me, and this was because it was not London. I was much struck by the way everybody we met quizzed us about London as if that were a strange place. This was not really comprehensible to me. Already, I think, I was beginning to equate real reality with London.

When my mother left Newcastle I think she must have re-invented herself to some extent, as people do when they are consciously trying to make a new life for themselves. In Newcastle she had been Sheila, but when she entered her teens the maga-zine most popular with her peer group ran a serial called *Sheila of the Shadows*, and this got attached to her as a nickname, which she disliked. She wanted to shed it, so on arriving in London she used her other name. On my birth certificate it appears as Kathleen, but on equally official documents it is Cathleen, and I believe it is the latter spelling that is strictly speaking correct, if such a concept applies. Oddly, she herself used both spellings, even both initials, sometimes signing herself S. C. Magee and sometimes S. K. Magee. (It was standard in those days for people to use ini-tials in a signature.) This means, by arcane coincidence, that my mother and father both had second initials which they themselves varied between K and C. In my world my mother was known to everyone as Cath, or Kath, which people spelt as they liked. When we visited Newcastle it was disorienting for me to hear everyone call her Sheila.

In London, then, she adopted a different name, and shed her Newcastle accent. Exceptionally, this loss of accent was total – no trace of it was left in her voice when I knew her. With a thick Geordie accent she must have found that she had to talk differently simply to be understood; but beyond such basics as that I think the change was almost certainly unconscious for the most part (and this in turn would mean it must have happened when she was very young), because there was nothing self-conscious about the way she spoke. It was with a generalised version of a London accent – London without being cockney. Actually, I do not think people noticed the way she spoke: it sounded sort of neutral. If she arrived in London at the age of fourteen this could easily have been how she was speaking by the age of sixteen or seventeen.

Another reason why I think she most likely came to London at fourteen is that she worked as a butcher's-boy for quite a time, living in Islington and walking every day to and from her job in Whitechapel, since she did not earn enough money to pay bus fares. It was only from the ages of fourteen to sixteen that butcher's boys were employed. And Islington begins at King's Cross, which was her point of arrival in London. So it all fits in.

Whenever she was asked in my hearing what she had done before she married, her reply was that she had been a waitress. For some time she worked in Lyons' original tea shop at 213 Piccadilly, where the waitresses were some sort of special feature – they were known as 'Nippies', and so widely did this term come to be used, and only with reference to Lyons, that the firm registered it in 1924. (There was an allusion to it when, during the Second World War, women conductors were employed for the first time on London's buses and were known by everybody as 'Clippies'.)

At around the time when my mother met my father she was sharing rooms in Islington with two other working girls, one of whom, Ada, had a boyfriend who was a motorbike-policeman, Tom Western. Ada married Tom and had a son called Gerald, and as a child I knew them all; but decades later, after the deaths of Ada and my father, my mother married Tom Western; so I was all along destined to become Tom's stepson and Gerald's step-brother. However, I was to have no inkling of these developments until, many years later, they happened.

My mother was, to say the least of it, a difficult person, and the truth is that most people found her impossible to get on with. The main causes may not be far to seek – her violent and deprived childhood, and then being thrown into the deep end of life on her own resources in London while she was still really a child. On the surface she was tough and determined, and an effective coper, but hidden underneath was a terror of being overwhelmed by her circumstances. She thought and behaved as if the whole world were trying to do her down all the time, and no one could be trusted an inch, and she had to fight for her interests unceasingly, regardless of anybody else's. This caused her to behave in a distrustfully hostile way towards everybody, and with an almost total lack of consideration, a closed absorption in the protection of herself. She had little or no sense of responsibility to others, and also (on her own admission, I subsequently learnt) little or no affection. She was almost strangely without affect: she simply did not care about other people, and her responses to whatever happened to her were purely practical, cold, prudential. She was as near to being a person without feelings as I have come across outside institutions that cater for disturbed personalities – except that there was always, under that cold exterior, an almost uncontainable anxiety about her own situation, which caused her to explode in eruptions of resentful anger in which she would suddenly leap into a tight-lipped, white-faced fury, quivering with tension, and sometimes given to physical violence. And there was never much warning when it was coming.

However, along with that she was, in many people's eyes, beautiful. So when she was young she was the sort of woman whom some men are powerfully attracted to and then find nothing but trouble. This was my unfortunate father's experience. He once said to my grown-up sister, his eyes becoming suddenly brilliant: 'She was a *cracker* when I married her!' His own sister, my aunt Peggy, believed there was nothing more to their relationship than a sexual attraction that would have blown over in the natural course of events, and if only he had been left alone about it he would not have married her. The trouble was that his family took against her, too strongly and too openly. His mother in particular nagged my father about getting involved with that terrible woman. So fiercely and remorselessly did she nag him that, in Peggy's words, 'she made his life a misery' and 'he was afraid to come home'. Peggy is insistent that it was my grandmother's fault that the marriage took place at all: her behaviour was impossible, and it drove my father into marrying to get away from it. And of course there were, as a consequence, the worst possible relationships between my mother and her in-laws from the beginning.

Blazing rows were normal in my family as I knew it, and ordinary life in the home was one in which the most violent hostilities seethed unspoken under the surface. My sister's earliest memory is of my mother throwing most of the crockery at my father in our kitchen, and of him backing up against the wall, into a corner, raising his hand to protect his face. (It was that raising of the hand, she says, that upset her most.) One of my own earliest memories is of my mother, also in the kitchen, threatening to stab my father with a carving knife. She was holding it fiercely in a stabbing grip, her knuckles tight and white, while she was obviously having trouble restraining herself. It was clear she wanted to do it, and I thought it was about to happen. I think it nearly did.

Before my parents married, my grandparents had already moved their living-quarters away from the shop; so the rooms above it were available for my parents to make their home in, which they did from the beginning. This had come about because my grandparents had decided to go in for pub management in combination with shopkeeping, though actually the first pub they ran was not one in which they lived. For a long time the shop had barely been producing enough income to keep a family of five, in addition to paying the wages of an assistant, so my grandparents decided to diversify, to leave my father and the assistant to run the shop while they took over the management of a small pub nearby. This, the Tiger, was very close, down by the canal, beside or near the Gainsborough film studio. Peggy tells me that as a girl she was thrilled one day to meet Clive Brook, a famous star of the time. The studio building is still there, but the pub has gone. The Tiger was tiny, a local snug, most of its trade a by-product of the fact that two illegal bookmakers used it as their centre of operations. Even so, running it for two or three years taught my grandparents how to run a pub, and made them ready to take on a bigger, more income-producing one. This, which they were no doubt encouraged to take, and fixed up with by the brewers, was miles away, in the unknown remoteness of South London – the Duchess of York, in Battersea Park Road. This time they actually went and lived there, as indeed they had to. It is there still, a substantial Victorian pub, almost a museum piece, with the date 1883 in the brickwork.

The period during which my family ran the Duchess of York was not happy. In taking it on they had gone too much from one extreme to another, from a pub that was too small for their needs to one that was too large for their resources. Having the shop in Hoxton to run as well as a pub too far away, they were overstretched. When my father shut up shop at eight o'clock in the evening, after an eleven-hour day, he would take the bus (two buses) to Battersea and help out in the pub till late at night. His two sisters were also roped in. But a big Battersea pub in those days was not a salubrious home environment for two young women. They all became strained, unhappy, edgy. Tempers frayed. Relationships deteriorated. This was the family situation into which I was born in 1930. Altogether it was spread over a number of years; but it came to an end before my memories begin.

When the national economy began to pick up after the Depression, in the early '30s, my grandfather, having made good money out of the Battersea pub, took the decision to give up being a publican and return to the shop. Contributory to this was the fact that the whole family had discovered that it disliked having to be in South London. It has always been a much remarked-on fact that when North Londoners go south of the river they feel as if they are in a foreign country; and if they go intending to live there they usually, eventually, come back. I have to say that something like this applies to me. I have London in the marrow of my bones, and an inexpressible, almost immoderate love of it, but I have never felt South London to be a part of it. South London is for the most part a recently created dormitory, brought into being in only the last two centuries by the railways. Real London is nearly all north of the river: not only the whole, almost, of historic London but London as an exciting city to live in today, and the worlds of government and administration, the arts, the university, entertainment, the City, the various headquarters of all the professions, even such things as good hotels and good shopping. South London is foreign to all this. At no time in my life would I have dreamt of living there.

My grandparents returned from Battersea to N.1., but not quite to Hoxton. They wanted to be nearby, in an area with which they had been familiar all their lives, but they were now able to afford better living conditions; and the big-windowed, high-ceilinged rooms over their Victorian pub had accustomed them to more space and light. So they rented a house in Southgate Road, a whole house, with a garden. Their side of the road was in Islington, the other in Hackney – our end of Hoxton filled the corner of Shoreditch where the three boroughs met. They were now back to within a ten-minute walk of the Tiger, and within a quarter of an hour or twenty minutes of the shop – half that if they took a tram part of the way – in an area where they knew every street. Life was back to normal, and able to go on as before, only better.

While they were looking for and securing the house in Southgate Road, and to help them move into it, they rented rooms close by in Balmes Road. This was only a temporary arrangement, but it is worth mentioning because Balmes Road has left its mark on the English language through the word 'balmy' as an expression for 'mad'. This came about because for many years it was the location of a well-known, down-market lunatic asylum. I believe it was the one Mary Lamb used to spend time in periodically. When her brother Charles Lamb went mad, which he did only once, and for a short while, he spent the time in an asylum in Hoxton Street itself.

It was my grandparents' long, financially successful but emotionally dissatisfying detour through a career in pub-keeping that resulted in my birthplace and childhood home being where they were, in the rooms my grandparents had previously occupied behind and over their combined shops. There had been a period before my father married when he slept above the shop alone at night. I am not sure how long this went on, I think quite a while, and I know he hated it. Perhaps the shop had been burgled when its premises became unoccupied at nights. In Hoxton that would be so likely as to be a near certainty. The shops in Hoxton Street were burgled so persistently that insurance companies either refused to insure them or demanded premiums calculated to be prohibitive. However the arrangement began, my father was pressured by his parents to sleep on the premises as a deterrent to burglars. To defend himself (and their shop) they gave him a gun, an automatic pistol kept loaded. He viewed with absolute horror the prospect of shooting anyone; and because an attempted burglary was so probable the whole experience made him seriously disturbed. For the rest of his life he looked back on it with revulsion. I am quietly certain that it was a contributory factor to his decision to get married, so that he would no longer be alone at the shop at night. Even when he did marry, though, and had a wife there to live with him, the gun remained. He showed it to me when I was a little boy, knowing it would fascinate me, which it did, but he took great care that I never knew where it was kept.

When my parents married, their roles settled into the standard ones for their time and place. My mother gave up her job and devoted herself full-time to looking after home and husband, doing all the housework and preparing three meals a day, for which she went out shopping at least once a day and usually twice. My father opened the shop at nine, after which his father would arrive from Southgate Road, and the two of them would be there all day together, serving the customers or, during lulls, chattering to one another or to the neighbouring shopkeepers, and betting on the horses. In no circumstances would the shop ever be left empty. At least one of them was always there. My mother served my grandfather with a separate midday meal after the family dinner, when my father was back in the shop. Closing time was eight o'clock on weekdays and nine on Saturdays, so they had a long day during which they were on their feet for most of the time, and it was physically tiring. It never entered my father's head that in addition to this he should contribute to the housework, or the shopping, or the cooking. The separation of roles was complete, and was something I grew up taking for granted. The nearest my father ever came to cooking at any time in his life was the making of a pot of tea; and that happened not very often. Luckily for him, my mother was an excellent cook. She had learnt something about it in a semi-professional way during her waitressing days. Her range was a lot wider than that of most domestic cooks, and she was resourceful in her use of materials. Not only was the food good to eat, it was good to look at. My father's mother, on the other hand, on whose cooking he had subsisted until his marriage, was without competition the worst cook I have ever encountered. In that respect, at least, getting married brought an improvement.

A couple of years after they married, my sister Joan was born, in 1926. Then, in 1930, came me. It can have been only a year or two after this that my grandfather came back to work in the shop, for I cannot remember him not having been there. His return constituted something of a problem for my father, who had been running the shop for some years now and doing so successfully. Devoted to his father though he was, it was difficult for him to step down into being number two again, especially now that he was older, and married with two children. He pressed to be allowed to start another shop at the other end of Hoxton, a lock-up shop that he would run from the main one, his own sideshow. My grandfather was dubious about the idea, but my father kept on at him until he agreed. It turned out to be another case of overstretch. The national economy might be coming out of recession but it had a long way still to go; and in any case my father was unable to be in two places at once. The venture failed, and lost a lot of money, all of it being my grandfather's. It caused a great deal of acrimony in the family, and this is something I do remember, or half remember: the after-effects of it were going on at the time I was emerging into conscious life, and I picked up on the fact that there was some particular ill-feeling going around within the family that was focused on a big thing that had happened recently, though I did not understand what it was.

Another way in which that episode was to have a knock-on effect in my life was that my father, having burnt his fingers badly in an enterprise undertaken entirely on his own initiative and insistence – and so soon after the family's unhappy experiment with the Duchess of York – never again (perhaps partly also because of the Second World War) considered trying to move out of his position in his father's shop. He accepted that he was there for life, working for his father until his father died, whereupon the shop would be his, and he would carry on working in it. For some reason, though, he never seems to have supposed that the shop would be mine. And nor did I. As a child I was stuffed to the gills with daydreams about what I was going to be when I grew up – a cowboy, an airman, an explorer; it changed every few months, but whatever it was it always involved my going out into the big wide world. I loved Hoxton, and it was all I knew, but as far back as I can remember I thought there was a world outside it into which I would go when I was big enough; so I always assumed that I would not be living in Hoxton when I was grown-up. My father always assumed that too.

CHAPTER NINE

While I was being born my head was tightly squeezed, and when I was then shown to my mother it had the shape of a flattened lemon, straight-sided and startlingly high-domed – completely deformed-looking, she said. Her immediate thought was: 'I've given birth to an idiot.' And her immediate feelings were of outright rejection. 'Take it away. I don't want to have anything to do with it.' She told me this several times during my childhood. Within a matter of days, apparently, my head resumed what turned out to be its normal shape. But her feelings never took on those of a normal mother. She no more felt any affection for me than she did for anyone else. She had married for security, but children disrupted everything. She wished she had never had any – the phrases 'I wish I'd never had any kids' and 'I can't think why I ever had any kids' came over and over again from her lips. She resented the two of us for being a nuisance, for making demands on her, for getting in the way – in reality, of course, for existing. Whenever either of us asked for anything, however necessary or untroublesome, she would turn a forbidding face towards us, and her harshness of manner would say unmistakably: 'You again? What is it this time?'

My sister suffered more than I from this. Even if Joan had not received any love from our mother she had at least been the exclusive recipient of all the maternal attention that there was going until I came along. Textbooks about child development stress the fact that when a second child is born, the first, having been the sole object of parental attention and love up to that point, is at a stroke no longer so, and no longer even receives equal attention, because the parents make a fuss of the new-born baby – or, even if they don't, the baby makes more demands on them that have to be met. So the first child feels that all the love and attention have suddenly been taken away from it: its parents seem not to love it any more, and all because of the new-born baby, whose arrival it fiercely resents. This hostility of the first child towards the second can be extreme: there are well-authenticated stories about it trying to put the baby on the fire, or in the dustbin. This reaction is in the logic of the situation, and fully understandable. My sister had it to an extreme degree. I think it was because she was in truth not loved by our mother anyway, and as she grew older was beginning to become conscious of the fact, perhaps at about the time when I came along, when she was three and a half. She supposed that all the love and attention were now being diverted to me, and that this was the reason why she herself was unloved, when in fact I was no more receiving affection than she was. Many years later my mother confided to someone, who after her death told me, that she had never felt the slightest affection for either of us. And we were always only too aware of that from direct experience. As a small girl my sister was too young to understand the situation, or to understand the misleading nature of her own emotional reactions towards it; and so it became engraved on her mind and her feelings that I was the reason why she was not getting her due. Her attitude towards me became, fundamentally, one of resentment. She got into a habit of inventing private explanations for herself along such lines for each individual unhappiness, and then seeing these as being the facts of the situation.

So I emerged into consciousness, from before I can remember, with a mother and an only sibling both of whom, for quite different reasons, resented me for existing, wished I did not, and made this clear to me in the way they behaved towards me, and in things they said. My way of coping with this – quite uncalculated, of course, at that age, and indeed unaware – was to live life away from them to as great a degree as circumstances allowed, simply not be with them if I could help it. Because Joan was significantly older than me I doubt whether she wanted to be with me much anyway. My earliest memories of my feelings towards my mother were of trying to avoid her, trying to keep out of her way, suddenly falling silent when she appeared, hoping not to be noticed in case she should tell me off or give me a slap in the face for some reason I did not understand. I was afraid of making demands of any kind on her attention, because I knew they would be met with glaring hostility, no matter what they were. From the earliest age I tried to manage without her, never calling her in if I could possibly avoid it, but trying to do things for myself, preferably with other children. When she told me to go out and stay out, and not come back until it got dark, it was what I wanted to hear. I grew up away from her, in so far as I could, and was happy to do so. People who knew us all say that I appeared to be an open, sunny child, seemingly happy most of the time – by contrast with my sister, who seemed to be unhappy most of the time, and was either withdrawn into herself or complaining, protesting or crying. And that is also how I remember it. Although I had a relationship with my mother that did me a certain amount of psycho-emotional harm that made itself felt later in life, I did not have an unhappy childhood. On the contrary, I found life enthralling, and took intense pleasure and interest most of the time in most of what was going on around me. I loved being. Only I had somehow to keep the fact of my existence from my mother.

Sometimes her resentment of my existence took violent form. For instance, as a small child I used to wear leggings in cold weather, and one day when she got them out from the previous winter and sat me on the kitchen table to button them on to me she found I had grown too big to wear them any more. For a long time she struggled with the buttons with ever-increasing frustration, until finally her temper broke and she shook me for a long while with frightening violence, shouting into my face: 'Do you think I'm made of money?' My feeling in these situations, apart from terror, was of total helplessness. I was completely at the mercy of this raging giant. And I could not stop myself growing. There was nothing whatever that I could do about it, in spite of the fact that she kept getting furious and shouting at me for doing it – more or less every time she found I had grown out of something to wear. There used to be an American phrase: 'Pardon me for living'; and towards my mother I felt in a very deep way what that phrase is intended to express. When she was around, I, who loved life so much, wanted to disappear and not be. A feeling of radical insecurity about my own existence, a feeling of not daring to exist, became central to my personality.

Another thing that greatly influenced my feelings towards my mother was that she made a habit of hitting me in the face. What I objected to was not being hit in the face *as such*: I was used to that: every day I was hit in the face by boys. But then I hit them back, whereas hitting my mother back was out of the question for me, I am not sure why. When other adults hit me – teachers, or occasionally my father – they did so on my hand, or my arm, or my bottom: only my mother, among adults, hit me in the face. It was always a single stinging blow with her open hand, fierce, jabbing, jolting, always sudden, sometimes out of the blue. She never beat me black and blue, or drew blood, or tore my clothes, and she probably hit me only once every few weeks; but even as a child I found the fact that it was always straight into my open face a personal violation. In a way that I understood emotionally, I knew it to be a repudiation of me. And I felt it to be vicious, spiteful.

What made all the difference in the world to my happiness as a child (and no doubt my mental health too) was that I loved my father, and also my grandfather, and knew that they loved me. And both of them were there all day every day on the other side of the kitchen door. Both were people of unusual warmth. Just being with them gave me a satisfied feeling inside, as if their warmth had passed into me. It gave me whatever feelings of security I had. They seemed, as I did, to delight in my existence: they took obvious pleasure in being with me, talking with me, telling me things, showing me things. I was endlessly curious, as if interested in everything; and every day there was something new; and whatever I noticed, or whatever I was told, I seemed to take in and remember. This afforded them ever fresh delight, while I, of course, regarded them as omniscient, and would stand there riveted with fascination at whatever they were telling me. On the whole they were good judges of what this ought to be, and a lot of elementary understanding of life and the world got fed into me in those earliest years, worldly wisdom of a rudimentary but important kind. Sometimes they amused themselves as well as me by telling me anecdotes, jokes, riddles, playing word games; but when they were being serious, which was probably most of the time, they talked to me not about abstract or theoretical things but about whatever was going on in their lives. They would tell me about the things they were selling in the shop, or horse-racing and the various other sports, or what one of them had just seen at the theatre, or what was currently in the newspapers, or about the people in the surrounding shops, or what was happening up in the market – in other words they talked to me about whatever was immediately on their minds. Most of it was about people, but in the course of it they would explain to me what pubs were, or churches, or pawnbrokers, or factories, or other of the places I could see around me; and then again what the people in them did, and how they worked. If one had just eaten a good meal in a restaurant – or a bad one for that matter – he would describe it to me, and explain what a restaurant was, and tell me where this restaurant was, and what it was like compared with other restaurants. Looking back I can see that what they were very often doing was reliving, and re-enjoying, the things in their current lives that most interested them, by recreating them for me in words; and that this was to some extent an escape from boredom for them, an escape from the tedium of having to pay for these things by working in the shop. I was a diversion for them. But I was also a good audience. To me everything they said was vivid and real. It was the life of the grown-ups, and what is more the most important of all the grown-ups. This was the Big Wide World they were telling me about, and I was agog for it. And the fact that it was they who were telling me about it put it before me as a warm, friendly, inviting place that would welcome me into itself.

The other person from whom I learnt what seemed an infinite amount was my sister. Although we went our separate ways during the day we shared a bed at night until I was five and she was eight. Inevitably, we never just got into bed and went to sleep, but talked and talked and talked, as children are bound to do. Often our parents would shout up the stairs: 'Stop talking, you two, and go to sleep!' Sometimes they would stomp up into the bedroom and give us a ticking-off. All this was normal, and everyone accepted it as such.

Being three and a half years older than me, Joan was at a more advanced stage of development than I at more or less everything. She was allowed to do or have all sorts of things that I was not, though I knew they were coming my way 'when you're older'. This meant that she was always currently experiencing the life that lay just ahead of me. I was perpetually curious about it. Luckily for me, she had a natural desire to talk about what she was interested in, and in me she had a captive audience. So I became the recipient of a more or less perpetual input of her experience at second hand. I found it immensely interesting – it meant something to me, engaged me, mattered to me. It was almost like a second life, with its own coherence and ongoing flow; and I felt like a participant, concerned to know what was coming next, and how this or that was going to turn out. As with everything else, her vocabulary was in advance of mine. She was continually using words I did not understand, and I would ask her what they meant, and she would tell me. She would tell me about what she was doing at school, and of course this lay ahead of me too, so it was a kind of preparation for what I was in for. I think that whenever anything that particularly interested her was taught to her she had a desire to explain it to somebody else, and again I was the person who was always there at hand for this purpose. Because of the differences in our temperaments she caused me to see matters more critically than I would otherwise have done. My natural bent was to accept everything as it was and just make the best of it, whereas hers was to feel sharply what was wrong and complain about it. So when talking to me she would criticise our parents, or the domestic arrangements, or the neighbours, or the way things were being done at school, or whatever else was impinging on her life at the time, and nearly always I could see at once the truth in what she was saying, yet it was not something that had occurred to me, or would have done so had she not said it. This had the effect of opening my eyes to many of the things that were going on around me. Even if at that point my reaction was to see what was wrong but wonder why she minded so much I was still acquiring greater perception and understanding.

Among the things she told me about were the contents of whatever books she was reading, and whatever plays and films she saw. She was, of course, old enough to be taken to the theatre and cinema before I was, so she saw all sorts of things I never did. She would describe not only the story but other things I might not have noticed, such as what clothes the actors were wearing, and would retail it so involvingly that I have remembered some of it all my life. This has the odd consequence that I have all these years had what are sometimes surprisingly detailed mental pictures of the contents of plays and films of sixty-five years ago that I never saw. On the whole this information has proved to be reliable, so Joan must have been an accurate reporter. Another reason why I remember so much of it is that there was an edge, a hunger, in my reactions; I wanted to see these things for myself, and it seemed to me unfair that she was allowed to see them and I wasn't. When eventually I was allowed to go, it had the added attraction for me of the previously withheld; and, what is more, by then I knew quite a bit about the actors and the theatres. I fell on it all with sharpened curiosity, and consumed it with double relish.

It was to theatre and cinema that this vividness chiefly applied, rather than to books – mainly, I think, because going to them was an outing that others were having and I was being denied, but also because I had no interest in books but was addicted to comics, the visual side of which meant an enormous amount to me. Joan, unlike me, read books from an early age. And they meant an immense amount to her, perhaps more than anything else. Her inner life may not have been as vivid as mine but it was more passionate. With me, everything I saw and everything that happened to me cut into my awareness, and bit into my mind with such razor-edged sharpness that it came to within a hair's breadth of hurting. I was on the edge of being over-stimulated all the time, and could only just bear it, yet loved it. Joan lived less in terms of this sort of pellucid perception and more in terms of emotional response. She felt deeply – and much of the time unhappily – in reaction to whatever was happening to her. So this was how she responded to what she read – not with my self-forgetful perception but with the most extreme subjectivity, through her own overwhelmingly powerful feelings for, with and against the characters she was reading about. She would sit reading a book with tears pouring down her face, sobbing noisily; and if one of the grown-ups came by and said: 'Why don't you stop reading that book if it's upsetting you so much?' she would reply – with difficulty, through her gulps – 'But I don't want to stop. It's lovely. I've *got* to read it.' One of her most often quoted remarks was: 'I'm enjoying it *so* much. It's *terribly* sad.' Although this sort of reaction was different from mine I had no difficulty in understanding it, and was puzzled by the grown-ups, who seemed uncomprehending about it. But in any event Joan's experiences all got passed on to me in bed at night, with the result that I knew the contents of a whole range of books – especially the so-called children's classics, but by no means only those – years before I read them myself, if I ever did.

Occasionally Joan and I would quarrel in bed, and fight; I remember once biting her savagely in the back. Perhaps surprisingly, we never played sex games, though she did explain sex to me. What got her started on this was that she wanted to tell me the dirty jokes she was picking up at school, and this meant of course that at first she needed to explain them to me. But I got it into my head that the so-called facts of life were something we had to pretend to believe for purposes of making certain kinds of joke, just as later we pretend to believe that Scotsmen are mean and Irishmen stupid – we know they aren't in fact, but unless we pretend there's no joke, so it's fun to pretend. It was not until I was nine that I realised that grown-ups did in fact do these un-believable things. Between the ages of something like three and nine I knew about them in the abstract, and had a big repertoire of jokes about them, but did not realise that they happened.

Our conversations at night were usually highly animated, either with much giggling and shouting or a sort of hissing intensity in the darkness. Yet, for all this animation, when it came to next morning I could never remember them ending. Unless our parents made us shut up I was never consciously aware of stopping talking and settling down to sleep. All I remember was our talk bowling along at full tilt and then – chop! – it was morning again and I was waking up to a new day. How was this possible? We couldn't have fallen asleep in mid-sentence. Actually there must have come a time every night at which we stopped talking and turned over to go to sleep, and yet I could never remember it. I found this so perplexing that I got quite worried about it. I voiced my puzzlement to Joan. She dismissed it completely out of hand. 'Of course you don't remember going to sleep,' she said. 'Nobody does.' And I thought: 'How does she know? She hasn't gone round asking people. All this means is *she* doesn't remember.' But that magnified the puzzle. If neither of us could remember going to sleep, why couldn't we? It was something we did every night. This baffled me for years, and it was not until I was grown-up that I gained a full understanding of the solution to the problem.

It was chiefly for reasons to do with sex, but also partly to reduce the amount of disturbance at night, that our parents decided eventually that Joan and I should sleep in separate rooms. She being older, and a girl, was to have a room to herself, the one we had shared, and I was to sleep in the living-room. For this purpose a divan was bought and placed against the wall immediately to the left of the living-room door, to function as a settee during the day and a bed at night. My clothes went on being kept in my sister's room, because there was nowhere else to put them.

Psychologically, the change was a milestone in my life. I felt as if I had begun to be a separate person. There was something about my new situation that I deeply liked. I had never before spent periods of so many hours alone, least of all at night, or in the dark, but now that I was doing it, and every day, I found it surprisingly satisfying. I was free to lie in bed and think about whatever I liked for as long as I liked without any interruption or distraction. However, my responses must have been more complicated than I was aware of, because although I did not connect the two things it was at this time that I started to have nightmares. Sometimes I would walk in my sleep. I went downstairs asleep once or twice, and my parents led me back up to my bed and told me about it the next morning. More often I would believe myself to be struggling frustratedly to get out of the room through the door, which I was bafflingly unable to open, when in fact I was standing jammed into a corner of the room, trying impossibly to move further forward into it, until I woke up and found myself there, and took myself back to bed. I had what I suppose were standard nightmares – being chased by someone petrifying who was about to pounce on me, or else my feet were so heavy I was unable to lift them enough to run away, or my escape was blocked by a blank wall. Sometimes I woke up shouting. Some of these dreams were among the most vivid I have ever had, and I still remember them. But the most disturbing of all the nightmares were not visual, they were purely emotional. Fast asleep, and without any accompanying visual element, I would be engulfed and overwhelmed by unbearable emotion. The key feeling was not terror, it was grief. Although I was asleep, my whole being would be taken over by a supercharged sense of loss, limitless loss, as if all the sorrow in the world were mine and irreparable, a cosmic bereavement that was for ever impossible to rectify. I would lie in bed convulsed with sobbing, moaning, groaning, gulping, crying my eyes out, and yet all the time I was asleep. The predominant element in the experience was its oceanic quality, its all-engulfingness and boundlessness.

When my parents heard me downstairs my mother would advocate taking no notice, just leaving me until I exhausted myself and went on sleeping quietly, but my father would come up and wake me and sit on my bed comforting me. He assumed I must be going through some terrible unhappiness, and he was concerned to know what the cause of it was. Gently, sympathetically, he would probe me with kindly questions. But to 'What's wrong?' my answer always was 'Nothing's wrong'; and to 'But you must be upset about *something*' the answer was 'No, I'm not upset about anything.' And I meant it, I was sincere. I was entirely without conscious awareness that at the deepest levels of my self I felt bereft. I was just having a bad dream, that was all. I realised that to him it seemed self-evident that I was upset about something and was refusing to say what it was. There seemed no way I could convince him otherwise. What his private conjecture about the cause of it was I have no idea: in fact I suspect, calling to mind his worried face, that he could not think of one either.

There was a sense in which the living-room was 'my' room now, and I took possession of it in a new way – the pictures on the walls, the books in the shelves, were all in my domain. I was incapable of reading any of the books, but I became familiar with each one of them as a separate object, its colour, cover, lettering, binding, and all their differing degrees of thinness and fatness. Two were fatter than the others by an order of magnitude. When I asked what these were I was told that the mauve one was a dictionary and the black one an encyclopaedia. When I asked what *those* were I was told that every word that existed was in the mauve one and everything else to know was in the black one. Everything? I asked. Yes, everything: if it wasn't in the encyclopaedia it wasn't true. This caused me to look on this big fat friendly book with awe. Occasionally I would take it off the shelf and flick over a few pages, as if looking at them would cause me to know everything, but when I tried to read the entries I was unable to make head or tail of them. However, this reinforced my conviction that it was serious and grown-up and important. If I caught my father taking the book down and looking up something in it I would watch him closely to observe what difference it made to him, but I never spotted it.

Not the least reason why I loved the room as I did was that it was lighter and brighter than the one I had shared with my sister.

That was always dark and gloomy – because it faced north-east, I now realise – whereas this one, which faced south-west, was light and cheerful quite a bit of the time. It was better lit in any case, and was also much bigger. And whereas the other one contained almost nothing but a bed and a chair, with only a wall cupboard to put clothes in, this one was full of interesting things, many of them brightly coloured, and some enormously comfortable, such as the sofa and the armchairs, which I would bounce about on a lot when I was alone.

I would be woken by my mother at around a quarter to eight, whenever the way was clear for me to wash at the kitchen sink. She would spring the roller-blind up while she was telling me to get out of bed, and when I was on my feet (by which time she would be out of the room) the first thing I did was look out of the window at Goorwich's clock to see what the time was. I began to notice that the better I felt the later the clock would say. Best of all were non-school days. The time I got up on those days was a question of what time my mother felt like giving me breakfast; and since she usually acted on the principle that the less she saw of me the better, she would often leave me to sleep until I awoke and appeared downstairs under my own steam. Those were blissful mornings. Even as memories they purr. Super-sumptuous were the days when the living-room needed to be prepared for a special occasion such as Christmas. Without waking me she would come into the room and lay and light a fire, to make it all cosy in advance of the guests' arrival and to leave herself free to think about the cooking, so I would wake up in a brightly coloured room as warm as toast, with an open coal-fire blazing in the wall opposite my eyes. Revelling in the luxury of not having to snatch at something warm the instant I came out from under the blankets I would step across the floor in my pyjamas, and stand on the rug in front of the fire to take in the heat through the soles of my feet. As a child I had unusually prehensile toes – it was a party trick of mine to pick up coins from a bare wooden or linoleum floor with my toes, and I could do it with farthings, and the little silver threepenny bits that people called Joeys – and I would stand there for a long time wriggling my toes in amongst the long black curly hairs of the rug, deliciously drinking in the warmth of it.

There was one night in that room, after a Christmas party, when I came across a port bottle in the corner behind one of the armchairs, open but a third full. I took a swig, and found it disconcertingly powerful, yet unimaginably gorgeous. I took another swig and instantly found myself coughing and spluttering, and feeling as if a fire had broken out behind my nose. I said nothing to anyone about it, but left the bottle in its position for the grownups to find if they should happen to – I did not dare to let it look as if I had discovered it without saying so – but they failed to find it in time, and I helped myself to a swig a night until there was nothing left. I knew that for a bottle to be found in a corner behind an armchair would be regarded as natural, and that if it was empty no one would associate its emptiness with me.

The fact that I was now sleeping in a different room from Joan meant that we no longer had to go to bed at the same time. It became an individual matter, about which we could negotiate, or make a deal or a fuss, or resist, separately. Occasionally, not often, I would be read to, and that was something I loved. The book which had far and away the greatest impact on me this way was Lewis Carroll's *Through the Looking Glass*. We did not possess *Alice's Adventures in Wonderland*, so not until years later did I know that book, and when I did it seemed to me not as good. *Through the Looking Glass* exercised an imagination-seizing power on my mind, not least through its illustrations. I loved it; and yet everything to do with it has ever since been associated for me with the deepest melancholy, because it was in connection with it that I discovered that I had to die.

The opening poem, which was read to me by my mother, contains the lines

> We are but older children, dear,
> Who fret to find our bedtime near.

I did not understand what this meant, so I asked my mother. When she had explained it I asked: 'Do all grown-ups die?'

'Yes, I'm afraid they do.'

'And do they always not like it?'

'I don't think anyone likes it. I don't think anyone wants to die. Not usually.'

'Will you die?'

'Yes, I'm afraid I will, eventually. But I hope not for a long time yet. So there's no need for you to worry about it. It's not something that's going to happen for a long time.'

'Will Daddy die?'

'Yes.'

'Will Grandad die?'

'Yes. Everybody dies. In the end.'

'Will I die?'

'Yes, you will, I'm afraid. But it won't be for a long, long, long, long time. It would be silly for you to start worrying about it now. There's lots of time before you need to think about it.'

But that's what I started to do. I had never thought about it before, but I was now overwhelmed by the realisation that eventually, inevitably, I was going to die. I felt the most powerful objection to it, a bodily feeling of rejection across my chest and the full length of both my arms and legs. I believe this was a biological reaction, animal resistance. I didn't want to die. But the more I reflected on it, the more I realised that I was going to whether I wanted to or not. And then I started to feel sorry for myself. I was swept by a sense of unutterable sadness, real grief, true mourning for myself. I was confronting the loss of everything. And there was nothing I could do about it. Tears came into my eyes every time I thought about it.

I went through a period, not actually all that long, when it was the chief thing I thought about: *Through the Looking Glass* was read to me one chapter at a time, and by no means every night, so the two periods probably coincided. When we reached the final reading, which was given to me by my father, its last line exploded like the second barrel of a shotgun.

Life, what is it but a dream?

The end. Silence from my father. Long silence. Never had I been flooded with such sadness as at that moment. The thought, the very thought, of life being nothing but a dream was more than I could bear. It was worse than having to die, because it meant you had never lived. Everything was nothing. Even this now was nothing. Scarcely able to get the words out, I said croakingly to my father: 'Is that true, Dad? Is life only a dream?'

'No. No, it's real, son. Life is real. This is just a way of talking, that's all.'

I was almost reassured, because my father could be trusted. And if life was only a dream then he would be only a dream; and I knew him to be the most substantial thing there was. So it couldn't be true. And yet . . . and yet . . . somewhere down in the depths of my psyche a possibility had been touched on. The idea of it was sad beyond endurance. And even if it wasn't true that life was only a dream I still had to die. I experienced not fear of death but bereavement, illimitable sorrow at the evanescence of life. In an inwardly appalled way I began to cry silently. My father looked at me with astonishment.

'What are you crying for?'

'Nothing.'

'You must be crying for something. What is it?'

'I don't want to go to bed.' I seized on this because I knew I would have to go to bed now that the reading was over, and there had been occasions when I had cried in protest at having to go to bed.

'No, it isn't that,' he said. I was disconcerted that he should be so undeceived. I had expected him to believe me.

'Tell me, really,' he said. 'What is it?'

'Yes, it is that I don't want to go to bed,' I said, though this time I could hear myself that I was being unconvincing; while the words 'I don't want to go to bed' were coming out of my mouth I heard an inner voice saying: 'I don't want to die.'

My father looked at me with undisguised disbelief, then hesitated, then appeared to make a decision, and said softly, with affectionate irony: 'All right, then, you can slip off to bed.' And slip off was what I did, scuttling away with wordless relief, not realising how this exposed me.

It turned out that the idea of death was something I discovered but then got used to. For a time I thought about death obsessively, and always with this immense sadness; but after a while I got so used to it that I no longer felt sad about it. And from then on, thinking about it began to feel like an over-familiar and stale activity, and I started to tell myself that I had no need to go on doing it, because I had done it enough already. There would be no need to do it any more until I became so old that it was of pressing importance – and that was not going to be for donkeys' years.

CHAPTER TEN

When I was six an earthquake shook the grown-up world around me. Everyone was talking about it for months. It was to do with arrests, a big trial, and prison sentences. Usually these things were talked about only within the four walls of home, and then in hushed voices, not in front of the children, out of fear of what they might say in the hearing of others. But now it was different: grown-ups were coming out with it in the open – 'Have you heard?' . . . 'Is it true they've arrested So-and-so?' . . . 'His girlfriend says he was with her, but even the police know he wasn't.' . . . in the street, on the pavements outside the shops, in the market, regardless of who heard, children or anybody. It was as if war had broken out and the adults forgot themselves in the public emergency.

Children, however young, nearly always understand not just more than the grown-ups give them credit for but a lot more, and this was already true of me with regard to criminal affairs. The reason, of course, was that I found them so interesting: I loved hearing real-life stories about cops and robbers; and the hushed secrecy with which the grown-ups usually discussed them tuned my antennae all the finer for picking them up. I probably pieced some of the stories together over a far longer period than now seems to me the case in retrospect: all I remember now is the story. But I knew early on about Screwneck Webb, who lived, or had, in Wilmer Gardens: I had seen my father explaining the reason for his nickname by poking his head forward sideways at a funny angle; and I loved to hear about how one day when he was beating his wife her screams had been so terrible that the neighbours were afraid he might be killing her, so they called the police; but when the police arrived and tried to arrest him he knocked the helmet off one of them, at which his wife immediately slipped off one of her shoes and started bashing the policeman over his bare head with her metal heel. It was the sort of story that could easily have appeared in one of my comics, except that comics were seldom as good. There were other nice stories, too, about Screwneck – and some not so nice, like him being given a terrible hiding in the back of a police van by several policemen at once, which seemed unfair. The grown-ups were continually bandying this sort of thing around among themselves, about people they all knew, often chortling away as they did so but sometimes looking grave and shouting in hoarse whispers.

The most bloodcurdling story that I managed to piece together – the most extreme, and perhaps for that reason the most unforgettable – was about someone who everybody seemed to know already as a tremendous character called Jimmy Spinks. During a row with his girlfriend he had grabbed a heavy mirror off the wall and smashed her over the head with it and killed her, and her blood had splashed all over him. In a drunken panic, his first thought was to get away from the scene, so he ran out of the house and tried to get on a bus. When the bus conductor saw this wild-looking man, obviously drunk and covered with blood, stumbling to get his feet up on the platform, he refused to let him on, and pushed him away, and the bus pulled off without him. Several passengers saw this scene, which would not have been easily forgettable, so putting together a case against Jimmy was essentially a matter of establishing the identification: was the blood-covered man that all these people saw Jimmy Spinks? None of the witnesses could say. Confronted with Jimmy, not a single one of them could remember. Not even the bus conductor was able to recall. So there turned out to be no witnesses after all. And there turned out to be no other way, either, in which he could be linked to the crime. Friends of his swore that he was with them somewhere else. And it was suggested that there were plenty of people who might want to wreak a personal revenge on him by doing his girlfriend in. Why on earth would he want to kill his own girlfriend? So he got away, literally, with murder. I reckoned this a first-rate story. But I could not quite make out why my grandmother went on about Jimmy's family, and how awful it must be for them. Why them? And what about the girl's family? They never got so much as a mention. When my grandmother said, with uncharacteristic but obviously felt sympathy: 'Poor Grandma Spinks! They were always such a respectable family. How must she feel about them having turned out somebody like him after all these years?' it came as a revelation to me that grown-up men could have grandmothers, especially if they were murderers.

Jimmy Spinks turned out to be a leading character in the entirely different story that set Hoxton by the ears in 1936. I was not aware of having seen him up to that time, though I was to see him often in later years, but already he was vividly alive in my mind as a larger-than-life person. When in 1936 he and his leading associates were sent to prison for long periods of penal servitude it was the end of an era, and the beginning of the end for the Hoxton of popular legend, Hoxton as the biggest centre of large-scale but low-life crime. No one was in a position to realise this at the time, but few of the key villains were to come out of prison again before Hoxton started to be demolished by German bombs, a process that was then to be completed by slum-clearance programmes under the post-war Labour Government – and by then the old Hoxton had gone for ever.

So this was the most decisive event in the inter-war history of

Hoxton, the Hoxton of my childhood. But for it to be understood, a little background is necessary.

At the time when my grandparents were just becoming teenagers a magisterial – and today still cited – study, *Life and Labour of the People of London* by Charles Booth, was published, in 1889–90. In it Booth wrote: 'Hoxton is the leading criminal quarter of London, and indeed of all England.' What had thus distinguished Hoxton was not only the amount of crime but the fact that it was so highly organised, some of it with a degree of sophistication. For example, when it came to the sale of stolen goods the cream of the trade from the whole of London found its way to Hoxton. The fences there were at the very top end of the market. Most of them were apparently respectable citizens who ran a small and honest business unconnected with the stolen goods that they traded in, except that it provided them with storage space, means of transport, and a way of laundering money. Some of the more specialised fences were not businessmen but skilled craftsmen, and in those cases their skill was likely to be directly connected with the goods they traded in – for instance, there were some expert jewel-cutters among them, people at the top of that craft as well. It made for a clever criminal community. Often the fences would themselves organise the theft of the goods they knew to be in demand, so they would have burglars on their payroll, and were likely to want only the most reliable and tight-lipped of these working for them – those, again, at the top of their trade. Also, the fences were always in need of protection, because they were constantly in possession of either stocks of valuable goods or the cash to pay for them; and most of the people who knew this were criminals themselves, many of them violent. If fences were attacked, robbed, double-crossed or even merely threatened, they were the last people who could go to the police and ask for protection; so it was mandatory for them to arrange for their own protection. For this they needed heavies than whom there were not going to be many heavier. In this way what might loosely and informally be called gangs would come into existence, based on division of function. They were never as tightly organised or clear-cut as in fiction – real-life gangs do not have lists of members, rule-books or permanent premises – but the citizens in the surrounding community knew pretty well who was working with whom, and what they were up to, and kept out of their way. The locals, provided they kept their mouths shut, had nothing to fear from them, partly because most of the locals had nothing to steal anyway, but also because the criminals were usually careful to adhere to their well-known maxim, 'Never shit on your own doorstep'. They took pains to keep their assaults on the law-abiding community away from the areas in which their own wives did the shopping and their children went to school. Nearly all the local violence – and there was a lot of it, much of it extreme – went on among the criminals themselves, and was to do with disputes over territory, the breaking of deals, the punishing of informers, and the paying off of personal scores.

Organised crime comes most fully into its own when an activity is made illegal that millions of people are prepared to go on pursuing and paying for. The criminals seize control of the illegal trade, and are then in their element, with a field of operation as wide as society itself. As I write, this is what is happening with the supply and sale of illegal drugs: it has given rise to the largest-scale organised crime there has ever been, global in its operations. As for the past, the most notorious gangsterism that there has ever been flourished in the United States between the First World War and the middle 1930s, and was created largely by Prohibition, the attempt on the part of the Federal Government to outlaw the sale of alcoholic drinks. By 1930 more than half of all cases heard in the Federal Courts were for violations of the liquor laws; and the gangsterism growing up on the basis of

Prohibition was on the way to becoming a part of world mythology.

In Britain during the first half of the twentieth century the legal prohibition that brought a similar harvest to the criminal community was the outlawing of cash betting on horse-racing except at the racecourse itself. At first sight, it may not be obvious why the consequences of this should be so momentous. They were made so by the fact that in inter-war Britain literally millions of men and women were in the habit of placing illegal bets regularly, large numbers of them every day. The British are often said to be the people in the world most addicted to gambling, and this was an example of it.

It was legal to gamble on credit off-course, but not in cash. My father and grandfather, for example, both had credit accounts with bookmakers with whom they were in daily communication through the shop's telephone, so their betting was legal. But in those days, as now, gambling debts were not legally recoverable: their payment depended solely on the loser's willingness to pay – or his fear of the extra-legal consequences of not paying. That is why gambling debts were always known as 'debts of honour'. In these circumstances even the most up-market and respectable of all bookmakers, Ladbrokes, estimated in the early 1920s that something like an eighth of the money owing to them was never paid. And the great majority of people were not at all as well-off as most of Ladbroke's clients. So what proportion of *them* could be relied on to pay, not just on one occasion but regularly, debts that the law did not require them to pay? Most people were quite unable to find a bookmaker who would let them bet on credit: it had to be cash or nothing for most clients, as far as the bookmakers were concerned. In any case, in those days, not many of the population had telephones. So an illegal network of bookies' runners grew up, men who would loiter at street corners, usually to be found at the same pitch, surreptitiously taking bets. And in every place of work, every office and every factory, every street, and every in-group of friends, there would be somebody who knew somebody who knew how to place a bet. Britain became a nation of illegal gamblers. In most areas the police, genuinely unable to control this nationwide activity, and far less to suppress it, behaved in accordance with the logic of the situation and went on the take from the bookmakers; and because they had to be seen to be taking action against this illegal activity that was going on everywhere they kept up a perpetual flow of arrests of lawbreakers who did not pay them (which meant, of course, that the police force was itself a nationwide protection racket).

From a history of gangsterism in London published by Faber & Faber in 1993, *Smash and Grab*, by Robert Murphy, I fillet the following more specific description of the situation (pp. 28–9):

After the 1906 Street Betting Act was passed, any person loitering for the purposes of taking or making bets could be fined £10 for a first offence, £20 for a second, and £50 or six months' imprisonment for a third. Not until the Betting and Gaming Act 1960 was passed was the working man legally permitted to place bets off the racecourse . . . Ways were devised of avoiding the penalties and street betting became a ubiquitous part of working-class life in the first half of the twentieth century . . . Off the streets, in pubs, barbers, newsagents, small general stores, someone could generally be found to take a bet and bookies staked out regular pitches outside factory gates and employment exchanges. Big industrial enterprises – shipyards, steelworks, mills and factories – had secret networks of touts and sub-touts . . . Illegal gambling became a huge industry in Britain in the interwar years and it was hardly surprising that such a profitable industry should invite the attention of protection gangs. (Estimates put its annual turnover at somewhere between

£350 million and £450 million, a figure larger than that of
any other industry except the building trade.) Between 1918
and 1956 the underworld was dominated by the race gang
bosses . . . .

And that is how it came about that – just as, during the same
period, the largest-scale organised crime in the United States had
a symbiotic relationship with the liquor industry – the largest-scale
organised crime in Britain had a symbiotic relationship with horse-
racing.

Once the gangs had got their sucking pads into the betting
industry they started crooking the results of some of the races,
usually by either bribing or terrorising jockeys and trainers. But
this was not their chief activity on the racecourses. It was only at
the racetracks themselves that bookmakers were legally allowed
to take bets in cash; so it was there that the bookies pitched their
stands, rows upon rows of them, all shouting the odds: with their
gaping giant leather bags into which they tossed the cash as it was
handed up to them by the punters, and their blackboards and
clerks and tic-tac men, they were the most colourful sight on the
racecourse, rivalling even the horses. Every day they were wherever the racing was, the same people. And there were a lot of
important racecourses. Most of these, of their nature, are set in
relatively isolated surroundings, either in or on the edge of open
country; so there, in the middle of nowhere, were the bookies
with their bags of cash at the end of each day's racing; and there
also were the race gangs. In these circumstances it was impossible
for the bookies to operate without paying protection money. In
return for this, not only were they left alone to make more money
for the extortionists but these were pleased to oblige them by
acting on their behalf as debt-enforcers.

Until the beginning of the '20s this whole situation was
controlled by the same gang at all the important racecourses, a

gang based in Birmingham and led by a man called Billy Kimber. Its members were always referred to as the Birmingham boys (or lads, or gang, or mob) though in fact there were two parts of London from which it drew significant numbers, these being Hoxton and the Elephant and Castle. However, with the ending of the First World War a rival gang emerged on the scene, based in Clerkenwell and run by five brothers called Sabini. The two gangs fought it out for a few years, sometimes in pitched battles – which occasionally contained an element of black farce, as when the Birmingham gang ambushed a charabanc on its way to Epsom for the 1921 Derby and laid out all the passengers with coshes, bricks and iron bars, believing them to be the Sabini gang, only to discover afterwards that they had got the wrong bus. As this story illustrates, the Birmingham boys tended to adopt an uncomplicatedly British approach to things, an approach that was currently sustaining a great empire. The Sabini brothers, on the other hand, made use of foreign guile. They hit on the simple but brilliant idea of planning pitched battles and then informing the police about them in advance, in return for an undertaking that when the police swooped in on the mêlée unexpectedly they would arrest only members of the Birmingham gang, most of whom they were already acquainted with. They had wanted for years to clean up the Birmingham gang, and were prepared to accept the Sabini brothers as allies in the process. After they had broken up a number of battles, Billy Kimber found that half his most valuable henchmen were in prison, doing five-year stretches, while the Sabini gang had lost none of its members at all. He was outclassed; and eventually he came to terms in which he agreed to withdraw to Birmingham and confine his operations to the Midlands and the North, and leave, to the Sabinis, London and the south of England. He was to find, though, that even when he gave way to the Sabinis they remained dangerous – at the end of one of their truce meetings he was shot and left for dead, though in fact he recovered.

The withdrawal of the Birmingham gang to Birmingham took place in 1924. But of course this involved abandoning their cohorts in Hoxton and the Elephant and Castle, who were thus left to their own devices; and as a direct result of this these now became two small but autonomous gangs, looked on with extreme disfavour by the Sabini brothers, who regarded their very existence as a breach of the agreement. So from 1924 to 1936 Hoxton was home to its own race gang. Its members went off most days by train or taxi (four of them would think nothing of taking a taxi together to Brighton) to wherever the racing was that day, just as they had long been used to doing for their former Birmingham colleagues. They also controlled most of the important rackets locally, and in particular the illegal betting. Because of ever-present dangers from the Sabini brothers in nearby Clerkenwell they recruited as many additional members as they could from neighbouring Islington, being as this was adjacent to both Clerkenwell and Hoxton. There were vicious fights between the two groups, but these usually took place on or near the racecourses, where they confronted one another almost daily in their struggles for territory and influence.

The person who emerged as the leading figure of the Hoxton gang was Jimmy Spinks. What chiefly brought him to the top was the fact that he was the outstanding bare-knuckle fighter, anywhere, of his generation, and as such the person everyone else least wanted to get into a fight with. Bare-knuckle fighting, although illegal, was widely organised, as it still is today. It takes place in secret venues, and there are two kinds of fight: 'stand up', in which you hit only with your fists, and 'all in', which means what it says. The prize money put up by the organisers is high, and the winner takes all, the loser getting nothing: this fact is crucial, its purpose being – since what the loser does take is a terrible hiding – to make fights impossible to fix. Broken bones are the rule rather than the exception, loss of sight in one eye not uncommon since gouging is part of 'all in', and death occasional. The fights arouse immense passions in the spectators, who bet large sums of money on them; and it is out of the bets as well as the entrance money that the promoters make their profits. Not only was Jimmy the greatest bare-knuckle fighter of his day but he also, from that position, organised fights between others, from which he made a lot of money. His sister in Gopsall Street was years later to have a grandson, born there after the Second World War, who grew up to become the most successful bare-knuckle fighter Britain has ever produced, Lenny McLean: his career climaxed in his flying to the United States to defeat, for a vast amount of prize money, the champion put up by the New York Mafia. So there was something in the genes, perhaps, or possibly the blood.

I did not, myself, see Jimmy Spinks until I was about eleven, when he came out of prison during the war. The authorities made no attempt to call him into the armed forces – wisely, since they would not have been able to control him – and he was left at liberty to build up his share of the black market in addition to resuming his former activities. To this day I do not think I have seen anyone else who, when normally clothed, conveyed an impression of such strength. He was balanced like a bull, with his huge weight all in the form of hard muscle up around his shoulders, and high across his chest and upper arms, so that he was a massive man without being either tall or fat. My eye noted, having been educated in a shop that sold men's clothes, that his were exceedingly expensive and beautifully made, with nothing the least bit flash or spivvy about them. He wore them well, too, moving easily for his weight. Penal servitude had kept him fit. Now that he was a free man again he exuded wealth and power. But what left the sharpest impression on everyone who saw him was the number of razor scars on his face – you would not have thought it possible to get so many scars on to one face. There were two or three big ones, but when you examined him up close you saw that the entire face was a mass of fine scar-lines, dozens of them, some no more than a millimetre apart, criss-crossing in every direction. It looked, as somebody said once, like the map of the London Underground. His face had been slashed to ribbons not merely on one occasion but several times.

People who inferred from his appearance that he would not be intelligent made a mistake for which some of them paid dearly; and they would perhaps not have made it if they had paid as much attention to his eyes as to his scar tissue. He had plenty of cunning, was alert to everything going on around him that concerned him, was good at predicting how individuals would behave, and was not easy to deceive. He also had the sense and self-confidence not to run the Hoxton gang as a dictator, which it was within his power to do, thereby subjecting its operations to the limitations of his own understanding, but led it as first among equals, encouraging his most useful colleagues to make their own contributions. And for a dozen years, the years between 1924 and 1936, it prospered.

The other time-honoured criminal activities of Hoxton went on prospering too, at the same time, especially the traffic in stolen goods; but there was no way in which the fences and the race gang caused problems for one another, so they lived harmoniously together. One thing they had in common was that their most important and lucrative crimes were committed outside Hoxton, and this helped with local relations. Nearly all the crime that took place within Hoxton consisted either of theft or of violence between individuals. As a boy I often saw men fighting in the streets, sometimes savagely, and I always stopped and watched, because I enjoyed it.

Apart from this occasional street-fighting the casual visitor to Hoxton in those days would have seen little sign of criminality, except for the bookies' runners loitering on the street corners.

What would have presented itself to his eye would have been an inner-London village crowded with horses and carts as well as people, all of whose activities seemed to be focused on the teeming open-air market in its long main street. But, because it was a village in which everybody knew, or knew about, everybody else, the locals were aware of what was going on, and knew what some of their neighbours were getting up to elsewhere. And of course the market was a live network of gossip in which news travelled at incredible speed, as it does in a Middle East *souk*.

In the first days of the Hoxton race gang's independence they tried putting the bite on traders in Hoxton Street, but they quickly gave this up: it caused bad blood locally among too many people who knew one another, in return for pickings that – by the standards of the betting industry, the racetracks, and bare-knuckle fighting – were too small to make enough difference. Again there was sometimes an element of farce in it. When they tried it on my grandparents, my grandmother threatened to have a word with Jimmy Spinks's mother, and the matter was dropped. Occasionally after that a few freelance toughs would have a go at my grandfather, but he always responded with fearless refusal, saying (and meaning it) that he would sooner go out of business altogether than pay protection money. This seems to have non-plussed the toughs. At least, they never wrecked the shop. That may also have had something to do with the fact that my family were known and respected by the organised criminal community, many of whom got their suits made to measure through our shop simply because it was the best men's clothing shop in Hoxton. (They always, I remember, had unusual pocket requirements.) This put them on friendly terms with my father and grandfather, whom many of them had known and liked over many years. So any freelance extortionists who smashed the place up would, I expect, have been made to regret it; and this fact was possibly conveyed to them.

Once the local criminals had dropped their attempts to squeeze the local traders – which they quickly saw to be a mistake on their part, and declared to be a misunderstanding on the traders' – they left the local community in peace; and from then on, as individuals, they were able to have normal relationships with the people around them, often friendly ones, as with us. I was taught that you never talked out of doors about what any of them did, or about the clothes they ordered, or showed in front of them that you knew; and you never asked questions. My father would identify them for me by saying: 'He's one of the boys' (or 'lads'). Generally this was a purely factual observation; but he felt a sour contempt for those of them whose job it was to exact terror or revenge, and these he would identify by saying, with a tiny curl of the lip or nostril: 'He's one of the hounds.'

He could never bring himself to serve such people in the shop, though he would turn them away with, if necessary, inexhaustible politeness: 'I'm sorry, we don't have it' . . . 'Yes, I know there's one in the window, but it's a different size, and I'm afraid we haven't got it in your size' . . . 'No, alas, we can't order it for you. I don't think they're making them any more. But if you're quick you may find it in another shop' . . . and so on and so forth. Once, not understanding what he was up to, I nearly blurted out the fact that we did have what the customer was asking for, but my father saw it coming and headed me off. When the man had gone he turned to me and said: 'With someone like that, *whatever* he wants, we haven't got it. If he pointed straight at something and said he wanted it I'd say we were keeping it for another customer who'd already paid for it. I won't have people like that in the shop.'

Some of the traders tried to keep on the right side of the leading villains by letting them take goods without paying, but we never did. Both of my grandparents, like my father only more so, were tough-minded people who were not to be intimidated: they had all been born and lived their whole lives in Hoxton, and had grown up with criminals, been to school with them, knew their sisters and their mothers, and were on terms of easy independence with them, a kind of straight-talking, no-nonsense friendliness. They knew most of the tricks that these people got up to, and made it clear that they were not having any themselves; and they got themselves accepted on that basis. In any case, traders who did allow themselves to be put upon were put upon. The best fish and chip shop owner got so fed up with Jimmy Spinks dropping in and demanding an extra-big portion of the most expensive fish with his chips and then walking out without paying that he stood his ground one day and demanded payment – whereupon Jimmy, to teach him a lesson, seized the shop's cat up off the counter and threw it into the deep-fryer.

Jimmy Spinks and some of his colleagues were, I guess, psychopathic in their use of extreme violence. However, they went to serious lengths not to kill anyone, because in those days this meant that if they were caught and found guilty they would be hanged. As well-known violent criminals they would have little chance of reprieve, and even that would mean life imprisonment for them. So they did not carry, or even possess, guns, and they regarded people who did as stupid, or crazy, a danger to themselves and everybody else – although they did, nevertheless, occasionally make use of such people. Knives were held to be almost as dangerous as guns: it was too easy to kill somebody with one even when you hadn't intended to. The weapons they used were carefully chosen and used in such a way as to do grievous bodily harm without killing. Their favourite was the open razor, and its use was to disfigure: that was really the point, you made a mess of the other bloke's face. The key to their selection of the razor as their weapon of choice was that it could slash but not stab, and however wildly you slashed at someone it was only by the most outside and unlucky chance that you could kill him, or even blind him, whereas you could hardly fail to slash his face, or his hands, and had a good chance of lopping off a piece of an ear, or nose, or a bit of finger. So it inflicted just about the maximum nastiness with the minimum risk of killing. To this it added the great advantage of being terrifying: most people were more panicky if threatened with a cut-throat razor than if threatened with a cosh, which was the other popular weapon. A few professionals preferred the iron bar to the cosh, but if you used one you had to be careful not to hit anyone over the head with it, but to confine yourself to breaking bones below the neck – preferably the arms and legs, which was a very practical thing to do to anyone you wanted to put out of action. It was much too dangerous to hit someone over the head with any kind of hard weapon that exerted leverage: the best thing there was a brick, or, better, half a brick, which would knock people out but almost certainly not kill them.

There were graded punishments and disincentives to rivals within the criminal world. On the first occasion you were given just a normal beating up, and on the second you might be beaten seriously badly. But on the second you could also (and on the third certainly) be 'cut'. Several men would hold you down while one of them elaborately carved your face with a razor. If the offence was that of informing, they had an especially long cut deep down into the upper lip which, when the scar tissue formed and pulled the lip upward, had the effect of leaving the mouth permanently open. Once the lads had truly got hold of you, you knew you would be cut far worse if you struggled violently, so you lay still and let them get on with it, perhaps trying to distract yourself by making a concentrated effort to remember their faces. There was scarcely a significant figure in any of the racecourse gangs who did not have razor scars on his face; but even this had its uses to them: it showed the people from whom they were demanding money that they were in the business seriously.

Because razors were frightening, and were meant to be

frightening, their users carried them in a way that left them slightly visible, folded into the outside breast pocket, with just the tip of the metal hinge showing. From there, practised hands could whip them out in a single movement, the same hand unfolding them in the process. If challenged by an authority-figure about their possession, villains would say they were expecting to stay away from home overnight. Because the race-course gangs became especially notorious for their use of this weapon they came to be known to the general public, no doubt through the press, as 'razor gangs', and their activities on the racecourses became a national scandal. Special squads of race-course police were organised to deal with them, but had only partial success.

It was the increasing frustration and desperation of the police that gave the Sabini brothers the idea of repeating against the Hoxton gang the tactic they had employed so successfully against the Birmingham gang. They organised a pitched battle to take place at Brighton racecourse in June 1936; and, in the setting up of it, so skilled was their use of underhand diplomacy, especially in the handling of informers and double-agents between gangs, that they ensured that all the most important villains of Hoxton and Islington would be turning out against them. And then they contacted the police, and made a deal with them. The result was that when the police, secretly positioned and lying in wait, swooped in on the battle, the members of the Sabini gang were allowed to melt into thin air, leaving the police to round up all the members of the Hoxton gang, now caught red-handed using their weapons against other citizens – who naturally had fled the scene. The weapons were described by the detective Edward Greene, who later became well known as head of the Flying Squad: 'hatchets and hammers, knuckle-dusters and two-foot iron bars. One man had a length of inch-square rubber and another man's club looked like the half-shaft of a car wrapped in newspaper.'

The judge was determined to make an example of these villains, and show the law to be serious about wiping out gang warfare from Britain's racecourses. He sentenced sixteen of the Hoxton gang to forty-three and a half years of penal servitude between them. Jimmy Spinks, their leader, got five years. And in those days penal servitude meant living in brutally harsh conditions, and doing long, punishing hours of mind-numbing physical labour – not watching television and taking degrees from the Open University. This outcome was to the satisfaction of both sides in the alliance between the police and the Sabini brothers: gang warfare came permanently to an end on the racecourses, and the Sabini brothers were left in undisputed control of the rackets. People down in the Elephant and Castle felt themselves to have had a narrow escape, and either threw their lot in with the winning side while the going was good or confined themselves henceforward to their cabbage patch. None of them gave the Sabinis any more trouble.

A remote and unexpected side-effect of this historic battle was that Jimmy Spinks left his fingerprints on a page of English literature. The so-called Battle of Brighton, and the ensuing trial, received sensational coverage in the national press, and this gave Graham Greene many of the basic ideas for his novel *Brighton Rock*. In particular, Greene is known to have read carefully through the verbatim evidence given at the trial, as reprinted in detail in the *Brighton Argus*: he was fascinated, apparently, by the way the gangsters actually talked. Only one gang, the Hoxton gang, was on trial, and its leader was constantly being referred to by the other occupants of the dock as 'Spinky', this being what Jimmy had always been called by his mates. Graham Greene's biographer Norman Sherry considers it obvious that this is what made Greene think of giving the unusual name 'Pinkie' to his central character, who is the leader of a razor gang on Brighton racecourse. I agree that this must almost certainly be how the name itself came about, though it has to be said that the character could scarcely be more different.

The social consequences for Hoxton of the Battle of Brighton were seismic. They were also lasting and detailed. The entire leadership of the Hoxton gang had disappeared overnight, leaving their underlings to run – or fight one another for – the illegal betting industry in their own back yard, and whatever other local rackets they happened to be running at the time. After what had occurred, these underlings knew better than to poke their noses outside Hoxton into any territory that the Sabinis might consider theirs, and they confined their activities to Hoxton. But they were little people, and they quickly discovered that the local book-makers and other such interested parties, many of whom were tough customers themselves, were not frightened of them, and felt in a position to defy them, perhaps even pay other people to deal with them. Life for the petty criminals, the minions and the hangers-on – who had always been many times as numerous as the big boys now in gaol – became desperately hard. Success in their industry, as in any other, depends primarily on management. The good times had gone. Many of them submitted to the ulti-mate indignity of getting a job. Some left the area in search of better pickings elsewhere. For the surrounding community a long, slow process of change was inaugurated which was to result in Hoxton losing a lot of its traditional character and becoming more like other places.

My family's shop, like most of the local traders who sold good-quality stuff, had lost its most free-spending customers. They were young, or youngish, and nearly all had wives and children, who were now in a parlous state. The women were not used to having jobs – few women in those days were, after they got married. But they were used to having money. Part of the ethos of the crim-inal community was to be profligate spenders. The men especially were swaggeringly open-handed, ostentatiously improvident, the subtext of their behavioural language being, 'I don't need to be careful with money, I'm going to get plenty more where this came from.' Nothing like the post-war Welfare State existed, so anyone in desperate straits financially was dependent on private and voluntary help. But charitable organisations and social workers had tended to give Hoxton a wide berth in the first half of the twentieth century, because, when they did get involved, they found that the very people they were trying to help behaved criminally or even violently towards them – deceived them, robbed them, beat them up for their money – and so came to be looked on by them as incorrigibles who should be left to stew in their own juice. Such respectable charities as there were around were not enthusiastic to help the families of violent gangsters, and were in any case niggardly and patronising at the best of times. Almost any of them might give someone a single hand-out, but none would provide a regular income of the sort needed to sustain a family, even to sustain it in poverty.

My grandfather had been used all his life to seeing the destitution to which the families of men in prison could be reduced, and often they were families he knew. He cared about the children especially – I think he was moved by their innocence of any of the wrongdoing that had brought them to their plight. So in this case, as in so many others, he quietly helped. If he saw one of the mothers walking past the shop with her little boy in rags he would greet her, invite her in casually, and then say something like: 'I've been thinking, I've got these things here that I've had in the shop for a long time. I don't seem to be able to sell them. They're just sitting there, not earning me anything. But the fact is they'd look very nice on your boy here. Will you do me a favour and take them off my hands? I really need the space for other things.' If it was a girl he would poke his head into Sugars' shop next door and exchange a quiet word with them, and pay them later. If he saw a child in the street without shoes he would give the mother a note to take over to the boot shop opposite, where they would do the necessary and charge it up to him. If the woman protested or was embarrassed he would say: 'Look, I'm not giving you anything. He'll pay me when he comes out. There's no point in letting the kids go barefoot when you know he's going to pay me anyway.' And 'he' always did, apparently – or so my grand-father claimed when I asked him about it many years later. I knew him well, and I am certain his motives were not self-interested; but his behaviour had the consequence of making our family one that was much approved of by the criminal community. When the men eventually came out of prison and started to build new careers for themselves in the black market created by wartime rationing I was impressed by the way they – all of them, including Spinky – would do a little salute, forefinger to eyebrow, whenever they greeted my father or grandfather, and address them as 'Guv'nor'. After the war, and after the deaths of my father and grandfather, when the shop fell for a time into the inexperienced hands of my mother, she began to notice that it was being kept under constant surveillance by the bookies' runner on the nearest corner, and that at the least sign of trouble from a customer he would come into the shop and ask in menacing tones if every-thing was all right, and stay there until the trouble-maker had gone.

I do not believe that any members of my family were involved in serious crime – the whole ethos of the family was against it, though they were not especially judgemental, except about viol-ence. Even so, my grandfather had got up to one or two tricks when he was younger. He once sold pigeons in the animal street market that has always been held every Sunday in Club Row: they were homing pigeons, so they would return to him during the week, and he would sell them again the following Sunday. He sold the same pigeons every Sunday for a long time, until one week they did not return – his last customer must have made pigeon pie. Something else he did that has always caught my fancy is – before it was made illegal to sell things on London's underground trains – sell walking sticks on the tube.

The nearest he came to doing anything seriously amiss was on one single occasion. He was neighbour at the time to a colourful character called Billy Chandler – who, incidentally, was an outstanding example of a villain who made good and went more or less straight eventually, becoming the multi-millionaire owner of two of London's greyhound-racing tracks. There was an occasion when Billy was tipped off at the very last moment by a policeman that he was about to be raided by the police, who had just themselves received a tip-off that he was in possession of stolen goods. At no notice at all he asked my grandfather if the stuff in question could instantly and unceremoniously be dumped with him. My grandfather – seldom able to say No to a friend in perilous straits – agreed against the grain. It was obviously either that or prison for Billy. The police were at Chandler's in no time, and were nonplussed not to find anything. Instantly they dispersed to all the homes and haunts of his criminal associates, and found nothing in any of them either. My grandfather had saved Billy Chandler's bacon – but at the cost of being a knowing receiver of stolen goods. He did not like it, and he declined the money Chandler tried to pay him for doing it. He said he did not want to be asked again, and he never was.

CHAPTER ELEVEN

It was when I was about six that I started taking a general interest in what was going on around me. The Battle of Brighton, with all its consequences, was among the catalysts of this process: I listened with spellbound fascination to everything to do with it, and it was among the things that helped to give me my first primitive, subliminal awareness that what happened in the community at large had an effect on us and our lives. When my parents observed this awakening they began – with some relief, I believe – to take me with them when they went out.

Getting baby-sitters had always been a problem for them, partly a problem of money. My Aunt Peggy had been happy to do it for nothing whenever she had been free, and as far as Joan and I were concerned she was our favourite person to be baby-sat by; but she had got married when I was five, and was now rarely available. (A family photograph exists of me as a page boy at her wedding, wearing short black velvet trousers, scowling like thunder.) Apart from her there was a good-looking but weakly diffident young man whom we knew as Mr Davis, who helped out in the shop in the pre-Christmas time, or when anyone was ill or on holiday. We liked him, but he needed to be paid. I remember, too, an older man, a Mr Jacobi, a German Jewish refugee who had arrived next door and was staying temporarily with the Sugars, and was known to be penniless. But he knew no English, and Joan and I found the fact that he could not understand anything we said frightening, so we asked not to have him any more. The problem, especially of expense, got worse when my parents felt able to take Joan to something but not me. So it was a relief to them when they felt able to take me as well.

What it meant, in effect, was sport, entertainment, and outings. By the age of nine I had been to every racecourse within comfortable reach of London, and most of London's greyhound racetracks. On bank holidays we invariably went to a football match, with either Arsenal or Spurs. My father was especially keen to do this because he was permanently unable to go to football matches on Saturday afternoons, this being the shop's busiest time. On one occasion or other we did all the standard London outings: the Zoo, Madame Tussaud's, the Tower of London, Greenwich, Kew Gardens . . . my parents went back to some of these every few years, whenever the mood took them. On sunny Sunday afternoons we would often visit one of a range of parks, from Epping Forest to Richmond. The one I liked going to most was Hyde Park, partly because my father always wanted to spend time at Speakers' Corner, which I found riveting (many of the speakers being on my mental level), and also partly because I found being in the West End exciting – there was so much going on there, even on a Sunday – and we always walked around for a bit, and had something to eat somewhere. There were hardy annuals. Every Easter we went to an open-air funfair on Hampstead Heath. I found this thrilling, but even better was the World's Fair, which took place in the Agricultural Hall in Islington, and which we also went to every year. The highlight of this was the circus, and the highlight of that was the lion-taming act, which I found so exciting I could scarcely contain myself. Going to the World's Fair enthralled me so much that I would think about it from one year to the next, and keep asking when it was going to come round again.

Then there would be one-off occasions, some of them public

events. Of these, one is etched in my mind more sharply than the rest, because I got lost at it. Among the first public events of any kind that I was aware of was the death of the king, George V, in 1935. Then came the prolonged sensation surrounding the abdication of King Edward VIII, which schoolchildren invented jokes and skipping songs about (mostly about Mrs Simpson). And then Edward's self-effacing younger brother, George VI, came to the throne. My parents, not in the least monarchist in their interests normally, were curious to see what this surprise king looked like. So when his first public appearance was announced after his coronation they decided to have a look. He and his wife were to take a ride in an open carriage along a route that was to end with Birdcage Walk on their return to Buckingham Palace. So up we went to St James's Park. And so did dozens of thousands of other people. When we got there it was like being in a football crowd. I saw the king, but for me the experience was as anti-climactic as a horse-race, and in precisely the same way: after endless waiting the horses rode past, and everybody shouted at the tops of their voices, yet the whole thing lasted only a few seconds, and that was it. It was over. I was left engulfed in disappointment. I think I must have been expecting the king to be wearing glorious robes and a crown, because I felt monumentally let down by the fact that he was wearing exactly the same clothes as I had seen undertakers wear at the funerals that passed by in the road outside our shop: a black morning coat and a black topper. The shininess of the topper struck agreeably, but why on earth was he wearing those clothes? He was leaning forward in the carriage with his hat off, tipping it shyly under his nose as if saying goodbye to someone crouching invisibly at his feet. It was a cramped, embarrassed gesture, inward-turned, and I realise now that it betrayed a terrified desire to escape from the crowd; but all I could see was a nice chap with a face like Mr Davis. I couldn't see what we had come all this way for.

Perhaps my alienation from the event contributed to my getting separated from my family. St James's Park, the smallest and most charming of central London's parks, is split in two, lengthwise, by a lake, and the only way of getting from one side to the other, apart from going all the way round one end, is across a bridge in the middle. The entire crowd had been in the southern half of the park between the lake and Birdcage Walk, but once the king had gone by, half of them, including us, wanted to leave via the north, so they made for the bridge. A dangerous bottleneck developed, the bridge so jam-packed that people could scarcely move on it at all. It took us an alarmingly long time to get over it, with me being crushed and frightened in the crowd; and at the point where we burst off free on the other side I lost sight of my parents. I found myself confronting three different paths converging on the bridge, all of which were crowded, and along any of which they might have gone, no doubt assuming I was still with them. I turned left, where the crowds were thinnest, and walked along beside the lake, looking for them. But I could not see them, and was overwhelmed by a sense of having lost them.

I started to cry, and walked along crying. A motherly woman sitting on a park bench asked me what I was crying for, and when I told her, she invited me to come and stand beside her, and not wander any further away, because my family were bound to come back to this part of the park looking for me. This did not seem likely to me, and I said so; at which she said that if they did not, she would take me to my home herself, so I was not to worry. This stopped me crying. What a nice woman, I thought: it's a pity she's not my mother. She asked me if I knew my address, and when I told her she said: 'Oh, that's not at all far from me. I live near there. I'll take you home all right. It'll be no trouble at all.' I expected us to set off immediately, but she said it would be better to wait, in case my family should come looking for me – which, sure enough, at about that point, they did. There were thanks and explanations, laughter and smiles all round; and then, as I was walking off with my family, my father asked me: 'What did that woman say to you?' When I told him, he shook his head and said firmly: 'I'm sure she doesn't live anywhere near Hoxton.' This shocked me. She'd *said* she did, and what's more she was nice, and it was unlike my father to be uncharitable; yet I trusted him. Why should she have lied to me? I asked him how he knew. 'From the way she talks,' he said, 'and the way she's dressed, and the way she behaves.' I was stumped by all this. I had no idea what he was talking about. But I still assumed he must be right in some way that I did not understand. In that case, I asked him, what would have happened if he hadn't found me? 'Oh,' he said, 'she'd have got a taxi and taken you to our address. And if we hadn't been there, she'd have left you with neighbours.' To me this sounded such an exciting adventure that I felt sorry it had not happened. It was a pity my family had had to find me.

I started to go to all and any sporting events, but as far as entertainments were concerned I was not deemed capable of sitting through an adult play – nor an opera, concert or ballet – so I was not taken to those things until I was nine or ten, although my sister Joan had already started going to them. Even so, that left revues, variety shows and pantomimes, all of which I adored. I remember two of the biggest theatres in London's West End – the Coliseum and the Hippodrome – putting on a lavish pantomime every Christmas in the late '30s, and I could always count on being taken to one of them by my parents. With luck, though not always, I would be taken to the other by an aunt or a visiting uncle – or to a pantomime at one of the intermediate theatres, like the Finsbury Park Empire or the Holborn Empire. Usually I enjoyed it regardless of what it was, but once at the Coliseum they had a curtain-raiser about ghosts, hideously green and green-lit – meant to be funny, no doubt, but I found it so terrifying I had to be taken out and brought back later for the pantomime.

The one among pantomimes that I liked the most was *Cinderella*. I liked it so much more than any of the others that I thought of it as the only really proper, full-blown pantomime, and if a year went by without my seeing it I felt deprived: I enjoyed seeing any of the others, so long as I saw *Cinderella* as well. This predilection continued beyond early childhood – I remember seeing a *Cinderella* in my teens, not for the first time one that contained the entire Crazy Gang; and during the scenes when the Brokers' Men try incompetently to take away all the furniture, while Baron Stonybroke and his ugly daughters try to stop them, and between them they break up the entire stage set, I felt as if I had arrived in paradise. That was also my first intimation that pure anarchy, the smashing up of everything, can bestow pure joy. Pantomimes in general made a deeply marked impression on me, and I still remember several of them individually, even details from them. For instance, there was always a specially written song that the leading comic or Principal Boy would teach to the audience and get them to sing, and I remember two or three of those whole, in spite of the fact that they are mindlessly bad songs, and that I heard them on only that one occasion.

I found variety shows absorbing in a similar way, and took everything in. These were to be seen on all sides then – every town of any size in England had at least one variety theatre, often two or three; and London had one in each significant suburb, from Golders Green to Wimbledon. Every show had at least two dance numbers, one in each half, in which the chorus girls were dressed in men's tailcoats and top hats, but all in pure white – I think it was in response to the then novel and sensational influence of Hollywood musicals, which were of course only in black and white – and it sent me into ecstasies, especially the colours, texture and shininess of the toppers. That anything could look like that was sheer delight to me. What the explanation of it was I have no idea – I have never been a fetishist of any kind. But whenever I was asked as a little boy what my favourite colour was I thought of those hats and said 'shiny white'. This seemed to others such a funny-peculiar answer that it became a family joke.

Once a week my parents went out by themselves, usually to a theatre. This was on Thursdays, because that was early closing day for the shops – the law required all shops to close for half a day during the week in order to compensate the assistants for having to work all day on Saturdays. I think I remember this change being introduced, but I may be wrong about that: as a child I sometimes confused my first awareness of something with its starting to happen. (Do I really remember Shredded Wheat coming in as a new thing, or is it merely that my family suddenly started having it for breakfast?) The theatre began at eight or eight-thirty, and most people ate beforehand. My parents used to eat in various places, sometimes at home before going out, but their favourite restaurant was Pinolis in Wardour Street, just about the cheapest restaurant in the West End that nevertheless kept up the traditional standards of a decent restaurant. It is now something else, but the name is still there on a gable high up above the pavement. It was the first proper restaurant I was ever to eat in, though it was not my parents who first took me there. When they were out with Joan and me we all used to eat more cheaply, usually in one of the Lyons Corner Houses, which I considered a great treat. How well we ate at any given time had to do with how well the horses were running. If my father was currently making money at the races it would be table-service and possibly a taxi, but if he was not it would be bus and a hot sausage roll eaten standing by a coffee stall on the pavement. I enjoyed this too, because it seemed to me a terribly grown-up thing to do: it was the way big men in caps and mufflers ate their meals. In those days there were coffee stalls in the streets all over London – it was the fast food of the time, the lead-item being the hot sausage roll, which cost a penny – and there were plenty of people who ate all their meals at them. When my parents went out without Joan and me they now regarded us, at least Joan, as able to behave responsibly, so they left us at home without a baby-sitter, and with enough money to get a meal from the fish and chip shop – which was more than okay by me. We promised to go to bed at a certain time, and I think we more or less did, Joan being always good about keeping promises.

My father and grandfather were both freemasons, my grandfather quite a senior one, and this involved them in going from time to time to formal dinners in the West End, sometimes with their wives. The usual venue was Frascati's. I enjoyed watching my father putting on his white tie and tails in front of the kitchen fire: they were well made and he, being tall and slim, wore them elegantly. It was the most extreme example of how we as a family, being in the clothing trade, were dressed at a higher level of quality than anything else about our standard of living. It also epitomised for me a certain attitude to going out: in those days everyone used to dress up a bit when they went out, whatever the occasion, and I came to look on that as part of the fun.

However, I did not always enjoy going out. I came to find horse-racing boring, and sometimes I had to be made to go to it against my will. The problem for me was the length of time between races, and then the shortness of the races themselves. When you watched a game there was something interesting going on all the time, but a horse-race lasted for only a minute or two and then it was all over – and another half-hour before the next one, with nothing at all happening in between. Dog-racing was not quite so bad, because the races were every quarter of an hour; but it was still pretty bad, because each race lasted only a matter of seconds. The racing itself, the sight of the animals running, was more exciting to me with greyhounds than with horses; but there would still be nothing for me to do between races. At any sort of races I was unable to get my father's attention: he was absorbed in the race card, and in discussing the form and the betting with various people who came up and talked to him (he and my grandfather always knew a lot of the people there) and keeping a close eye on the changing odds, and choosing the most advantageous moments to plunge in and lay his bets. I had to keep my mouth shut most of the time. The chief interest for me lay in the surrounding activity, the teeming humanity of it all, and that did indeed hold my interest quite a lot of the time, especially at horse-racing; but the afternoons were too long for me, and I would always get tired and bored before it was time to go home.

Like most newcomers to racing I was fascinated by the tic-tac men. Even more interesting were the tipsters; I loved listening to their spiel, because they had to sell each tip to their crowd without letting on what it was. Even as a child I would stand there looking at them and thinking: 'If you know which horse is going to win, why are you doing this? Why don't you make a mountain of money and go off and live in luxury somewhere?' The most spectacular of the tipsters was Prince Monolulu. He was there every time, a black Jamaican with a huge American-Indian headgear of brightly coloured feathers. He was a national institution, and the crowds loved him: his cry *I gotta horse!* was already a nationwide catch-word. My father disliked him and thought he was a dangerous piece of work, though he would never say why – looking back, I think he may have been an informer – but I saw him as a colourful rogue, hugely enjoyable to watch in performance. He was only the second black man I ever saw, and for many years the only one I was used to seeing. He often addressed the crowds at Speakers' Corner in Hyde Park on a Sunday, and was still doing this after the Second World War.

If only my father had left me at liberty to wander about among the crowds at the races I would have been happy, but he never did: although he paid me scarcely any attention, he insisted on my being with him at all times. On the few occasions when he left my side he would give me prolonged admonitions not to go anywhere. 'Now stay there. Right there. Don't move. Don't go *anywhere*. Don't go anywhere at all. I want to find you here on exactly this spot when I come back. If anybody talks to you, don't go with them. If they try to make you go with them, tell them you've got to be here because I'm coming back any minute, and I won't know where to find you if you're not here. If they say they're going to take you to me, don't believe them . . .' and so on and so forth. And then off he would go, and I would stand there kicking my heels on the spot, forbidden to wander off after my own interests.

The feeling that everything was going on too long was one I used to get also at football matches, though to a much lesser degree, and I remained still keen to go to them. For an hour or more I would be utterly lost in the game; but then, as it went on being more of the same, and especially if the result became a foregone conclusion, I would begin to feel that it was all just going on and on. The only sport I never felt this about was boxing: I found that absorbing from start to finish, and wanted more of it when it ended.

I caught the boxing bug early. I was still a tot when my father took me to a top-level programme at Harringay Arena. At the box office they tried to make him buy a separate ticket for me, but he said I would be sitting on his knee throughout and not occupying a seat. They were adamant. So he said: 'Okay, I'll leave him with friends nearby. I'll just have one ticket.' He then circled the building with me, looking for an open window at street level, and found one, the window of a large men's lavatory that was being crowdedly used before the boxing began. He took considered note of its position and then lifted me up and seated me carefully on the inside window sill. After the usual homily about how I mustn't move from that spot or talk to anyone, he disappeared, and three minutes later walked in through the door and lifted me down. The boxing, when it came, thrilled me as no other sport had ever done, and I still remember a good deal from that evening. The main bout was between the British heavyweight champion Ben Foord and the European champion Walter Neusel; and the rest of the bill featured another champion in Benny Lynch, and such leading figures as Harry Mizler and Dave Crowley. From then on boxing was my favourite spectator sport by a very long chalk, and with my father I went to programmes ranging from championship fights to local boys' clubs at Pitfield Street baths. He bought me a pair of gloves, and taught me a little elementary boxing, but I never pursued it – my mother was afraid I would break my nose. Boxing was far more popular than it is now, and every schoolboy knew the names of the leading boxers.

It was during my childhood that the promoter Jack Solomons began his career from a base in East London, and among other things founded the Devonshire Club, which proved a cradle of champions, and had a special atmosphere. My hero there was a boxer called Harry Lazar; I was sure he was going to be a champion, but he never was. There was a joker called Alf Paolozzi who used to clown around in the ring to raise laughs from the crowd, but I disliked that: it insulted his opponents and our intelligence. I believe that Randolph Turpin, one of the all-time greats, emerged from the Devonshire Club, as had Eric Boon shortly before – I felt privileged to see *him* just sitting in the audience. Because I was involved in fist fights every day, and enjoyed them, it thrilled me to watch professionals who were limitlessly better than I or any child could possibly be, and see their cunning and skill, and above all their speed. Among the lighter weights the fighting was so fast: I enjoyed that more than anything else, much more than the lumbering heavyweights, even though it was they who produced the knock-outs. I remember one heavyweight who, when punched on the jaw, simultaneously buckled at the knees as if his knees were wired directly to his chin.

There had always been an enthusiasm for boxing in my family, at least among the men, though even the women quite enjoyed it. When Eric Boon fought a championship fight with Arthur Danahar we made a family expedition to Tom and Ada Western's in Islington just so that the two families could sit together round the radio listening to it. There was a well-known story in my family about my grandfather going alone to a world championship fight, having paid more for his ticket than he had ever paid in his life, and arriving just as the bell went for the start of the bout. He managed to squeeze slowly past people during the opening sparring, murmuring his apologies. When at last he reached his seat, he ducked down to tuck his umbrella underneath it – at which moment there was a colossal roar from the crowd. He straightened up, to find that the fight was over, without his having seen any of it – it was the occasion in 1922 when Georges Carpentier knocked out Kid Lewis in the first round for the World Light-Heavyweight Championship.

Although I did not enjoy, necessarily, all sporting events, I did enjoy virtually all stage entertainments: they gave me a sense of internal wellbeing, a feeling of being happy inside myself. But I wanted it to be live, real, happening in front of my eyes, being created now: films were all very enjoyable, and I went to lots of them, but they had nothing on live performance, which was of an altogether different order of interestingness and depth. A live performance was a special occasion, unique. Above all else it was real, and I was there, involved in it, part of it.

My father too had this appetite for live happenings. In his case it was partly a reaction against the dullness of his work, and was insatiable. For him, this was where the point and satisfactions of his life lay – not least in the music and theatre that I was not yet old enough to go to. Almost every Thursday and Sunday, and perhaps late on a Saturday evening too, he would be off to something, whether with his wife, or father, or a friend, or by himself;

and the older I grew, the more often I would be taken along. He was a wonderful person to go with to anything except the races, because he was an enjoyer, and his enjoyment was infectious. He also knew how to draw me in to things: he would give them little build-ups, or, contrariwise, spring them as surprises. Once he told me we were going to ring the changes on Pitfield Street swimming baths in a few days' time and go instead to a bath in the West End. When the time came he told me to put on a suit, and I asked why I had to put a suit on to go to a swimming bath, and he said that this was an unusually posh swimming bath. When I was ready to leave with my swimming costume rolled in a towel he said No, no, this place provided us with those things, we didn't have to take our own. And so on and so forth. When finally we got to our destination it turned out to be the Palladium, and an all-star variety show – and of course he had calculated correctly that this would not be a disappointment for me: I was thrilled to bits, and enjoyed it all the more.

On outings like this he would perpetually feed my curiosity. If we went to a theatre he would talk to me about the theatre itself, and what it was known for, and what other shows he had seen there, and then tell me about the performers we had come to see. He would always point out people of interest, in any circumstances. 'Did you notice that man arguing with the programme girl as we were coming in? He's . . .' I have found as an adult that if I talk to people in this way they think I am trying to impress them, when I merely expect them to be interested. Fortunately, my father did think such things were interesting, and knew I would too.

In spite of his need for excitement at the end of a boring day there were many evenings when he stayed at home. Most often he would either listen to music or read. He was fairly well-read, especially in the popular classics, which he loved. It was chiefly through reading that he fed his interest in politics and current affairs – he never joined a political party, though he was a member of the Left Book Club. His political views were somewhere to the left of Labour and right of the Communists. He distrusted Labour for being too compromising, too willing to come to terms with the dreadful capitalism of that time – in this he was influenced by the recent behaviour of Ramsay Macdonald, the Labour leader and prime minister who had defected from his party in 1931. At the same time he distrusted the Communists even more, for their duplicity and their contempt for human rights. He was aghast when they made an alliance with Hitler, but declared that this was typical of them. I think he must always have voted Labour, but without enthusiasm.

In all his relationships he was sensitive and responsive while remaining firmly himself, and this gave him exceptional charm – in fact 'charming' was the word people most often used about him after having met him for the first time ('The most charming of all my parents,' said the headmistress of Joan's school). Everyone seemed to like him and to find him interesting. He had a highly dramatic way of telling stories, but apart from that his manner was equable. And yet somewhere deep down inside him there was a frustration, a sense of being unfulfilled. He had become a person of genuine culture, not out of any aspiration to do so but because he happened spontaneously to like music, opera, ballet, theatre and novels. He was as unselfconscious about the gaps as he was about his interests: I do not remember us ever going to an art gallery, or looking at the architecture of a building, and I am pretty sure he would have found any suggestion that he or we 'ought' to do such things absurd, if not unintelligible. You did what you enjoyed.

What he loved above all else was high-octane live performance, in sport and the arts alike: I believe it meant to him, among other things, that these people in front of him were being all out, living to the top of their bent, fulfilling themselves. He once commented to me, as if from a very great distance, how marvellous it must be to earn your living doing something you enjoyed. I do not think he ever doubted that the chief aim in life of any sensible person was to enjoy himself as much as he could without bringing harm to others, and he felt a keen empathy with individuals who lived like that, no matter what section of society they found themselves in, as if there were a freemasonry of enjoyers across the social classes. This belief that the civilised cultivation and fulfilment of the individual was the point of living may also have been one of the factors that set him aside from the two main left-wing parties, both of which had collectivist assumptions. There was no one in my family who had collectivist inclinations: quite the contrary.

The fact that I have drawn together various memories of sporting occasions and theatre outings may have given them an exaggerated emphasis, but it goes without saying that they were embedded in a daily or weekly life that was mostly routine. A certain community life did go on among the shopkeeping families at our end of Hoxton Street. They saw one another every day as a matter of course, and chatty conversations and gossip went on all the time, as did neighbourliness and helping one another. Occasionally on a Saturday night – after the biggest day's takings of the week, and with the prospect of an easy day next day – a group of them would sit up most of the night playing cards, and my father would usually be one of these, and often also my mother and my grandparents. A sense of family and neighbourhood were always there as a base from which he made his sorties into life.

I find it impossible to guess what he would have done if he had gone to Brighton College after all – and perhaps from there to a university. I never heard him say 'I wish I had been . . .' or 'I wish I could have . . .', and I do not think there was an imagined alternative life-path in the world of his fantasies, a shadow profession that he believed would have brought him fulfilment if only it could have been realised. His situation may have been worse than that: he may have found it impossible to envisage what fulfilment for himself could possibly be. But his going out was not just escape. He loved for their own sakes the things he did: the happiness they brought him was protean, exuberant and genuine – and, as an accidental side-effect, was fed on to his children as a wide-ranging delight in things that transfigured the background against which they grew up.

CHAPTER TWELVE

At the age of six or seven I moved up from the infant school in Gopsall Street to the junior school in Canal Road, which was closer to home but in a different direction. The change was dramatic. The new school consisted only of boys. All the teachers in Gopsall Street had been women, but in Canal Road all were men – except the one who taught the bottom class, a red-haired woman called Miss Fordham, and I jumped her class anyway. So it was all masculine now. It seemed to me suddenly grown-up. We called one another by our bare surnames, and that is how the teachers addressed us too, so I became a person called 'Magee'. Also, the fact that we were older – up to eleven – as well as being boys only, meant that we were a lot rougher and tougher among ourselves than we had been in the infant school. In some of the ten- or eleven-year-olds you could begin to see what they were going to become.

There were six classes, with number one at the top and six at the bottom, each containing forty-something boys. Twice a year we moved up a class. I went in at Class Five, under Mr Amphlett ('Squeaky'). The teachers stayed put at the same level and taught all subjects. Class Four was taught by Mr Lewis ('Flyballs'), Class Three by Mr Fink ('Finky'), Class Two by Mr Hickford ('Jumpy') and Class One by Mr Howell ('Ali' – this was 'Howelly' in a Hoxton accent). The headmaster was Mr Ogle, who had some sort of war wound that made him walk like Groucho Marx. At one time or another I was taught by all of them, but few teachers have ever taught me so much of value as Squeaky Amphlett. With his gold-rimmed glasses, Old Bill moustache, hairstyle like a carnation, and very cheap and faded pinstripe suit, he looked more like a boffin in late decline than a schoolteacher. Rote learning was his method, the whole class chanting in unison what was on the black-board, over and again, day in, day out. We enjoyed this, because it meant we spent most of the day shouting, all at once. When I left him after six months I had a firm grasp of the multiplication tables up to twelve times twelve, plus the Ten Commandments and the Sermon on the Mount – possessions of lifelong and in-estimable worth; and I can think of no other way in which I would have taken them in so thoroughly at that age. None of the other teachers used his method, but the education I received from them had the same character of being solid and foundational, useful for living. When I left that school at eleven I could read, write and reckon with the best, and was familiar with the most popu-larly known passages of the Bible. I have no recollection of anything else they taught me, or even what other subjects there were, if any: I suspect there were none – that this was it, the three Rs. Apart, that is, from singing.

When we had a singing lesson we would troop along to the assembly hall, where the piano was. This meant that we always sang standing up – but still in rows, as in class. There were circular wooden 'spots' in the parquet floor for us to stand on individu-ally, and our doing so spaced us out in the right way. (Our phys-ical exercise classes were also held in the assembly hall, and for years afterwards I thought that 'running on the spot' referred to these spots.) From the blue-covered song books I learnt beautiful songs such as Handel's 'Where'er You Walk' and Schubert's 'Who is Sylvia?'. We sang all the best-known old songs: 'D'ye ken John Peel?', 'There is a Tavern in the Town', 'Early One Morning', 'Sweet Lass of Richmond Hill', and so on. Although the thought

never occurred to me at the time, half the songs were American
– spirituals, work songs, sentimental ballads, such staples as 'The
Battle Hymn of the Republic', and jolly ditties like 'Polly Wolly
Doodle' and 'The Camptown Races'. This last, like a lot of them,
was unimaginably politically incorrect, with such lines as 'So I
jumped upon a nigger 'cos I thought he was a hoss'. It has always
seemed to me absurd to claim that such things poison the minds
of the young – I did not consciously reflect on what that line
meant until I was grown-up. Children can be amazingly imper-
vious to literal meanings in what they sing. Every morning, also
in the assembly hall, the whole school sang a hymn together, and
I sang these without having any idea what some of them meant.
When we had one beginning

> There is a green hill far away
> Without a city wall . . . .

it always struck me as a peculiar thing to say, because who would
expect a green hill to have a city wall anyway? We recited the
Lord's Prayer every day, but I never had the remotest idea what
'Hallowed be thy name' meant, or 'Thy Kingdom come'. These
were just things you said, or things you sang, because that is what
you did. I am not sure I even assumed that they were supposed
to mean anything. At the same time as this, outside the school,
there was a vogue for popular songs whose words did not mean
anything, and I sang those unquestioningly too, without
wondering why they did not mean anything.

As at Gopsall Street, the serious business of each day began
when a teacher rang a hand-bell in the playground and we lined
up in the open air in our separate classes. In this school, however,
we did not at that point troop off to the classrooms: we went to
the assembly hall, where Mr Lewis would be at the piano playing
a sprightly march tune as we entered: he had two tunes, only one

of which has stayed with me. We would stand in our classes facing a dais, on to which the headmaster stepped out before us. He would make his announcements for the day; tell us any news he had for us, and then give us a three-minute homily of an uplifting kind, perhaps tying it in with our current goings-on. The underlying theme, usually, was how important it was to behave decently to other people. Then we would all sing a hymn, and recite the Lord's Prayer, he would say a prayer, and we would march off to our classrooms.

On the way out we filed past two very old and blackened reproductions of portrait paintings that hung on a side wall, one being of Robert Burns and the other of Beethoven. I grew curious about them. I saw Beethoven's name as if it were 'beeth', which as a cockney kid I pronounced 'beef', followed by 'oven', the sort of thing you cook in. It was my first awareness of him, and 'Beef-Oven' is still my internal nickname for him. I asked my father who this Beef-Oven was, and I have a clear memory of us sitting in a bus together coming down Southgate Road and him saying: 'Most composers have lovely bits joined up with bits that are not so good, but Beethoven's music doesn't have any of those other bits; it's good all the time. It's all gold.'

Something I never realised in the junior school was that the people who taught us had not themselves had much education: they had left school in their middle teens and then taken a two-year teaching diploma. They were also quite poor. I recall Mr Lewis, who was comparatively young, collapsing during assembly, and the reason given afterwards being that he had had nothing to eat since the previous day. Mr Howell, the youngest and most popular of the masters, frequently spent the lunch break refereeing a football match in Clissold Park, and his lunch would consist of half a tuppenny pork pie clutched in a fist concealed in his jacket pocket: he would snatch it out for a quick bite whenever he thought none of the players were looking in his direction. One day I deliberately tweaked him by mentioning this, and he told me it was what he had for lunch anyway. So this was how the teachers lived. They always wore suits, because it was expected of them, but with most of them it was the same very cheap suit every day, bagging and shiny at the joints. None of them lived in Hoxton, and some commuted long distances – Mr Howell came from Catford, in deepest South London.

Their most difficult task must have been to keep order. Finky, red-faced and foul-mouthed, with a horrid moustache, permanently carried a stick in one hand so that he could on any instant whack any child within reach – and his whacks were fierce, meant to hurt. Whereas in Gopsall Street children had been smacked by hand, in Canal Road they were beaten with a cane. You stood out in front of the class and held your hand straight out sideways at shoulder height and looked determinedly the other way. It stung like billy-o. If the teacher gave you more than two he had to record it in the Punishment Book, which the miscreant himself would be sent to fetch from the headmaster's study – which meant that the boy had himself to tell the headmaster what he had done wrong. For serious offences you got three, four or six – never five, for some reason – and six was the maximum, though sometimes it came in the form of three on each hand. Twos and ones were happening all the time. I got two most days, sometimes twice – almost invariably for talking.

I moved up the school quickly, partly because I jumped Finky's class – a piece of good luck, for he was odious, the only unpopular master. Having skipped Miss Fordham too, and having been a year younger than my classmates to begin with, I arrived in the top class when I was eight. No one ever made any comment on this, neither the masters nor the other boys, and I took it for granted, thinking it a result of my mother's having sent me to school early. Half the boys in my class were not particularly taller or cleverer than me, so I did not seem to them different, nor to myself. When we all arrived for the first day of my third term, and a teacher in the playground told me not to line up for Finky's class with my former classmates, I misunderstood this as an instruction to stay where I was in Mr Lewis's class; so I lined up in Class Four when I was expected to line up in Class Two. I then went along to the wrong classroom, and spoiled the first drafts of two registers. Once I was in the top class there was nowhere else left to go, so after a term there I was made to repeat the course. But even though I was now going round for the second time I was suddenly no longer top of the class: there was a boy called Bourne, two years older than me, who was ahead of me at everything. When he left in the summer of 1939 the school would have had a problem what to do with me next, had not the Second World War broken out. At that point I was sent away from London in one direction while the school went off in another. We joined up later, but by then they thought that because of the gap it would be all right for me to repeat the course again.

Although the solid basis in reading, writing and arithmetic that I acquired at this school was of lifelong value to me, I did not find classes enjoyable, still less interesting. Most of the teaching consisted of endless repetition of the same basic points, and this I found unsalvageably boring: I took on board most of what the teachers said the first time they said it, and it did not occur to me that there might be many boys who were not doing the same. I had two main ways of escaping from this boredom: one was to talk about something interesting to one of the boys near me, the other was to drift off into a daydream, for which I was reprimanded frequently – it was called 'Not Paying Attention'. Nearly all the time spent in class was spent by me doing one or other of these things. The idea that anyone could actually like school would have been unintelligible to me.

What I did like, though, was life in the school playground, and in the surrounding streets on the way to and from school. There was something wonderful about the freedom of this life, with no parental control and no school control either. As the boys converged on school they would meet up in the streets and play, and fight, and sometimes become so involved with one another in what they were doing that a whole bunch of them would be late for school together.

In addition to the games I had played at Gopsall Street we used to play games of skill and chance that were also gambling games: for instance when we played marbles we won and lost the marbles themselves, and the same was true with tops and cigarette cards. Cigarettes were sold in stiff packets that nearly always contained picture cards. The tobacco companies issued these in sets of about thirty, with the individual pictures scattered at random among the packets; and the pictures would always be of something in the popular culture, such as film stars, football stars, boxers, or different makes of car. I remember one consisting of jokes that called themselves howlers. Children in particular used to collect them and try to make up sets, and they swapped them for this purpose. We also had special games we used to play with them, and treated them as currency in other games. In fact they were our chief currency generally. I was an enthusiastic collector myself, partly because both my parents were heavy smokers; and I particularly liked the game in which you tried to flick your card on to a surface in such a way that it overlapped an opponent's card, in which case you picked up both. Sometimes a group of us coming out of school would go into the crowded market and just ask for cigarette cards from strangers on all sides. 'Hey, Mister, got any cigarette pictures?' . . . 'Any cigarette pictures, Missis?' It was a quick way of getting them, because nearly all adults smoked, but most of us were very seriously forbidden by our parents to accost adult strangers, and it was difficult to do it for long in the market without being seen by somebody who knew one of us and put a stop to it.

As a variation on some of our more active games we would play them on roller-skates. Street hockey with a tennis ball became much faster and more interesting when it was on skates. Any game played on skates was liable to spread out over a wider area – a game of Release could ramify through several streets. Boys would turn wooden boxes into toy cars or dog carts by fitting roller-skate wheels underneath them. We became, nearly all of us, nippy and skilful on these skates: there was a copious second-hand trade in them in the market, and quite a lot of boys had acquired skates that were stolen – if you left a pair lying around anywhere you would certainly not see them again.

Lamp-posts and leaning-posts were used a lot in our games. The streets of Hoxton were gas-lit when I was a little boy (as were our classrooms at school) and the streets were still full of those famous old Fanny-by-Gaslight lamp-posts whose tops always made me think of policemen's helmets. Just below the lamp, a metal arm stuck out horizontally, for use by the lamp-lighter, and we hung ropes from these to make swings. A lamp-post could also serve as the base in Release. In addition to that, the posts were good for climbing up, and you could swing from the metal arm by your hands, or sit on it. Leaning-posts, a lot lower than lamp-posts and often stumpier, were scattered about everywhere, I think to tie horses to; and these were used for leap-frog. Some pavements were like steeplechase courses, with a leaning-post every few yards; and a line of boys would go leap-frogging one behind the other down the whole street. The shortest and widest of them were invaluable as wickets in such games as cricket and rounders.

There were public horse troughs at strategic points, usually cross-roads, and they were a natural focus for boys. But this could be dangerous play, because the carters got angry about us making the water filthy. In their fury they would hit us nearly as hard as if we had been grown-ups, so we risked injury by doing it. The police, too, treated mucking about in horse troughs with a kind of adult seriousness. However, where there was a horse trough there was usually also a drinking fountain, with chained metal cups, and we could drench one another satisfactorily with these.

Although most of our play was in the street, and often in gangs, I do not remember a child ever being run over by a vehicle. Most of the traffic was horse-drawn, and an approaching cart made a great deal of noise. In fact we played on the carts too. If one was passing with its tailboard down, and was moving slowly enough, we would run after it and jump up on to the back for a free ride. Usually the driver would feel the extra weight immediately, and turn round and see us, and swear at us to get off; and if we did not he would flick his whip at us, so we would scramble off after only a few yards. But if his load was heavy enough – or so high that he could not see the back of his own cart, and there were only one or two children – he sometimes did not notice, especially if he had been in the pub not long before; and then you might bum a ride half way across Hoxton. But you were always liable to be betrayed by envious children on the pavement yelling: '*Look be'ind yer!*' after the driver's retreating back when they saw you grinning at them smugly from his tailboard.

Girls' games were different from boys': basically, they were co-operative where we were competitive. They would throw balls to one another and catch them, perhaps bouncing them off walls in between. They liked hopscotch, and had elaborate variations on it. But favourite with them was skipping: they had group games that moved very fast, in which one girl would duck under the rope and take over from another in mid-skip, and two ropes would be going in opposite directions at the same time, all accompanied by rhythmic chants that they would shout in unison. These chants had a style all their own, with tremendously emphasised beat and bounce, and were often childishly improper: the chief topic I remember was Mrs Simpson's relationship with King Edward VIII. Because as a little boy I would not have dreamt of playing with girls I did not learn their chants; but four decades later, as the Member of Parliament for an East London constituency, I saw girls of the same age playing the same games and joyfully shouting chants of the same kind. One that then took my fancy went:

> Diana Dors
> Has no drawers.
> Will you
> Kindly
> Lend her
> Yours?

Another was:

> Ladies and gentlemen
> Take my advice:
> Pull down your pants and
> Slide on the ice.

These were precisely the kind of chants I had heard girls intoning when I was a child. Groups of girls used to sing songs together too; whereas there was nothing musical or verbal about the boys' play – except for certain formulae for 'dobbing up' teams or picking who was to be 'he' or 'it'. There were several of these, but the one most often used in the circles I moved in went (with the pointing finger jumping rhythmically from boy to boy on each beat):

> I know a
> Policeman,
> He knows
> Me,

> I
> Invited
> Him to
> Tea.
> 'Have a cup of tea, sir?'
> 'No, sir.'
> 'Why, sir?'
> ''Cos I've got a cold, sir.'
> 'Let me hear you cough, sir.'

(Pause. The boy being pointed at would give a dramatic cough. Then the chant and the pointing would move on:)

> 'Very bad indeed, sir.
> Ought to be in bed, sir.
> O
> U
> T
> Spells
> OUT!'

After a time I realised that by starting with the right boy I could make 'he' come out as anyone I wanted – myself, if that suited my game – and I worked out formulae for doing this. I expected others to do the same, and kept a keen watch, but never caught anyone at it – though for that matter I do not think I was ever caught out myself.

At the few games that were played by boys and girls alike the boys would be better if the game depended on running or strength, the girls if it depended on skilled fingers. Fivestones was a game I liked, and I was thought good at it by the boys; but when I saw girls of the same age playing it I realised that they were in a higher league than us, despite the fact that their hands were smaller.

All children love play, but I think my love for it was abnormally intense. I was like an addict with his drug: I craved it, I had to have it, and while I was at it my experiences were hyper-vivid and profoundly satisfying. All experience when I was a child had a bit of this character about it: whatever I did, whatever I saw, whatever happened to me, was as if cut into my awareness with an engraving tool. I found everything interesting, and therefore stimulating, and took it in with a permanently greedy curiosity, retaining then a memory of it that was often almost as clear and sharp as the original experience. If I saw, say, a film, I would be utterly lost in it while watching it, and able afterwards to recall accurately any scene or line of dialogue on demand. I sometimes nowadays find myself watching a film that I saw then and have not thought of since, and when I do I frequently know with complete certainty what the next shot or line of dialogue is going to be. I have tested this many times by uttering it aloud before it hits the screen, and the memories are nearly always accurate.

This near-total absorption and near-total recall were things that stayed with me until I was almost grown-up, but then faded as I emerged into adult life. They were bound up with a sense of the marvellousness and extraordinariness of everything, a feeling I find myself unable to convey in language. There are writers who have expressed it, most famously Wordsworth, but I think more so, in fact, Dylan Thomas (and perhaps also Laurie Lee, whose prose seems to me obviously under the influence of Dylan Thomas's poetry); and, possibly most of all, Thomas Traherne. I have, to my sorrow, no gift for their sort of poetry or prose, and am driven to recounting my experience in more everyday terms. To the eye and mind of someone in the condition I am speaking of everything seems wonderful, the world an amazing place disclosing miracles at every turn, and all of it imparting a kind of ecstatic pleasure. Every such person is a human being freshly arrived in his first world, Adam in his Garden of Eden. Everything

is pristine. But in the course of growing up we become habitu-
ated to the world, things lose some of their freshness as they grow
more familiar, and the edge of our wonder begins to wear off as
our surroundings become more securely known to us – though I
doubt whether it ever wholly disappears in someone who has felt
it at its most cuttingly sharp. The world blunts us. But in childhood this has not yet happened. And in my own childhood the
sense of the marvellousness of things which to some extent I felt
about everything was at its deepest and most intense when I was
playing. I was at one with myself then, fulfilled; I was *being*, full
out, engaged with heart and mind, full stretch, in a way I never
wholly was at any other time. And so I wanted much more to play
than I wanted to do anything else, and spent every free moment
I had playing. When I look back, it seems to me likely that –
among other things, of course – I was taking flight into something for reasons that had to do with being unwanted by my
mother: I needed almost desperately a way of expressing myself
and living out my emotions without being repulsed. But that is
pure speculation: certainly I had no awareness of such a thing at
the time. I also suspect that the unnatural sharpness with which
I experienced and retained everything was due, at least in part,
to a repressed anxiety from the same source. Certainly it was
around that time that a general anxiety came into my life. And
it did so on a very specific occasion.

I have related how I loved fighting, and used to get into fights
every day; and how, because I enjoyed it, I was good at it, and
would often attack boys older and bigger than myself with intense
fury, and usually beat them. Such courage as this took was based
on the fact that, although I naturally wanted to win, and did my
damnedest to win, I did not much mind losing; and when I did
lose I took a shoulder-shrugging attitude towards it – too bad, I
thought: better luck next time. In any case, win or lose, I had to
take a lot of hard punches, and collected plenty of bruises and

cuts; but I did not mind those either: I thought of them as a rugby-player might, as part of the game I enjoyed playing. This absence of any fear of losing, or of being hurt, even though I knew both might occur, contributed decisively to my success as a fighter. However, it all came to an end one day when I was eight, and picked a fight in the school playground with a boy called Harman. His clothes, I remember, were all of differing shades of brown. He had a big white face, and was strongly built. Something about the quietly determined way he reacted to my aggressiveness made me think that possibly I had miscalculated, and that Harman was going to be a more formidable opponent than I had bargained for – that he might beat me. I had made this sort of mistake a number of times before, and had accepted the consequences ruefully yet philosophically. But now, suddenly, I was seized with fear. And it was fear not of being beaten, not that only, but of being hurt. And I was not merely afraid, I was terrified. All I could think of was how to get out of the situation. In the opening lunges of what would have been our fight I pretended to stumble, and then pretended to have twisted my ankle. I stopped fighting immediately, having scarcely started, and declared that it was impossible for me to go on because I had twisted my foot. The panic that had come over me had come seemingly from nowhere. I had never experienced anything like it before and was bewildered, desperate.

Whenever a fight began in the playground a ring of boys closed round it to watch, and Harman and I had already acquired our ring. The bogusness of my behaviour was evident to everyone in it – I was pretending to be hurt in order to chicken out of the fight – and they minded this exceedingly. There was nothing in the world they loved more than watching a fight, and here I was trying to cheat them of it. They started jeering, and saying I wasn't hurt at all and was just a cowardy custard, and ought to bloody well have the guts to fight. Those who had noticed the beginnings of the disturbance, and had seen that it was I who started it in the first place, were especially derisive. *'You started it, and now you're scared. You're yellow! Go on! You wanted it! Now fight him!'* But I was much too frightened to fight, regardless of the consequences of not fighting, so I clung ridiculously to my pretence. I announced that I was going home, since I was unable to walk properly. At first the boys were unwilling to break their ring and let me go, and they obstructed me with their shoulders while they carried on jeering, and egged me on to fight. But I forced my way through them, limping like a ham actor, and headed for home – whereupon they all trailed along behind me, with Harman in the lead, roaring derision, imitating my limp, and chanting *'Cowardy cowardy custard!'* in unison, over and over again. In this way they followed me all the way home. When I got within sight of my front door I was swept by a new terror that someone from my family would see me being jeered at by so many of my schoolmates – and see me fleeing from them.

Even in retrospect I cannot relate the cause of this onset of terror to any particular event. If there was some episode or development in my life that brought it on, I was unaware of it at the time, and am unaware of it still. But after that débâcle with Harman my attitude to fighting was transformed. I would fight when attacked, but hated it, and was scared of being in any fight other than one I knew I could win without getting hurt. So I would still occasionally terrorise smaller or meeker boys – which was not quite as disgusting as it sounds, in that all boys of every age did that, and expected it as a matter of course – but otherwise tried to change every conflict into a slanging match. If someone threatened me physically I would do everything I could to turn it into a verbal dispute – the opposite of what the other boys did, which was to turn verbal disputes into fights. I became adept at using words to induce doubt and hesitation in the mind of a would-be aggressor – in fact my own aggression was now finding its outlet in words. With practice I developed a lash of a tongue that could be biting beyond my years. People said I did this because I had the gift of the gab, and knew I would win in a battle of words against another child, but the real reason was that I had an enormous urge to be aggressive, yet was terrified of being physically hurt.

This verbal assertiveness, and what might be called situation-management, had the unforeseen side-effect of making some of the boys start looking on me as a leader. My cowardice with Harman faded from their minds, and had in any case probably been known only to those who witnessed it – we talked surprisingly little among ourselves about anything other than our immediate concerns, and these were quickly forgotten, to be replaced by others. So my emergence as one of the leader-figures among my schoolmates had an immediate relationship with my hidden terrors, and was directly due to my loss of nerve. So long as I had been fearless I had felt no need of group protection, and was equally happy to be with a gang or to freeboot, but now that I was afraid I wanted the safety of being with others – and obviously the most advantageous relationship to have with others was to lead them. Verbally I was bold, always ready to provide a group with a formulation of a situation or an aim; and this was what a lot of the boys wanted – they wanted to follow someone who seemed to be self-confident and know what to do. And from them, too, I learnt how to keep them happy in that situation.

Our play ranged far afield. Beyond Canal Road, and the canal for which it was named, spread the De Beauvoir estate, running alongside Kingsland Road as far as Dalston. We and everyone else in the area pronounced it 'Bow-via', though I am told that the family who built it call themselves 'Beaver'. It was an airily open pattern of many streets and houses, built as a single development in the early nineteenth century for small but respectable middle-class people, before the descent of Hoxton into the abyss; and it always remained outside the abyss. Embedded in its pattern was a park square in and around which we often played. The estate as a whole was an unusually big area to be virtually without shops or pubs, and this made it an excellent playground.

Our other favoured direction for spreading beyond Hoxton was towards the City. We were especially given to invading Liverpool Street station, a vast hive of human activity that offered endless opportunity for mischief and play. Just to see so many big trains at once was glory in itself. The heavenly vault of the station would echo and re-echo with thunderclaps of chuffing, and parts of it would keep filling up satisfyingly with steam. We could spend half a day there with ease and fascination. On a Sunday we would often penetrate to the heart of the City. The streets were deserted, so we had them to ourselves, and could play our games in the roadway: an empty City was a wonderful playground. It also gave us a change from Hoxton, playing up against those mighty stone buildings. What impressed me was the total absence of human habitation, and the depth of the silence apart from our own noise. It was like playing in an abandoned world. There could be no starker contrast than that between Hoxton Street on a Saturday and the City the next day. And it was a contrast we often experienced, because the most favoured centre of our operations remained always, and especially on Saturdays, Hoxton Street market.

The crowdedness of the market enforced on us a certain looseness of operation: it was almost impossible for a gang of children to remain together there for long. We would invade it as a horde but end up operating in threes and twos – which might then, by chance, re-encounter and join up, but split again in different combinations. Our chief game was stealing from the stalls. This we did, not because we wanted the objects but because it was exciting. In fact most of us threw away what we stole, unless it was edible, because we did not dare to take it home, and we obviously could not take it back. So the stealing of it was the point, and for that reason we would steal absolutely anything. On one side of a stall a couple of us would distract the stall-keepers with an apparent attempt at theft that was really a feint, and when they made a grab for us another boy behind their backs would help himself off the opposite side of the stall and dissolve into the crowd. If the decoys were caught, which they often were, they were always caught empty-handed and protesting their innocence; and if they were accused of being in league with the thief they would deny all knowledge of him – and he, of course, was nowhere to be seen. The stall-keepers looked on us as an infestation of plague, and became as clever at foiling us as we were at out-witting them, so it was a fifty–fifty battle between experts, which was thrilling. We would also play hide-and-seek among the shop-pers, and they too got angry with us. We would break up the discarded wooden boxes of the traders into sticks, and fight with them, or set them alight; and we would rip up their cardboard boxes into stiff wooden squares which we could flick for long distances, sometimes dangerously when they winged at the height of adult faces.

Our favourite things to steal were sweets, and to a less extent fruit. This sometimes involved me in a conflict of interests, because the best sweet stall in the market was the one belonging to the Tillsons, who were close friends of my family, so it didn't seem right to steal from them. In any case whenever I played in the market I tried to join forces with Norman Tillson, and he could certainly not be expected to steal from his own stall. In fact if he was going to get up to any worthwhile mischief at all it was impor-tant for him to get well away from his shop and his parents, and from the neighbours who knew him, so that there would be no danger of being seen by them. You never got up to serious mischief near your own home. Norman had an extra problem in that he was ginger-haired, which made him stand out in any group of children: he was always the one people noticed and remembered. So once I had winkled him out we would head off for a different part of the market.

Norman and I were never at the same school, because for each of us there was always a school nearer home than the other's. So ours was an entirely out-of-school friendship. It was exceptionally harmonious – for instance we scarcely ever fought each other, which was unusual between boys: it was common for two boys who were the closest of friends to fight continually, sometimes quite savagely. We were different from one another in many ways, so perhaps we were complementary. He was remarkably good-natured without being a softie. By temperament he was equable, always sunny and smiling; few things seemed to arouse him to any great anger or excitement, and yet he was always game for anything; he took everything in his stride, got along with everybody, everyone seemed to like him. He managed to get himself into all kinds of scrapes, and yet somehow everything always came out right for him in the end. When my father gave me a book in the *Just William* series by Richmal Crompton, the character of William, and his appearance in the illustrations, reminded me instantly of Norman. There were many ways in which I was unlike him: I was highly strung, over-stimulated most of the time, talking non-stop, aggressive, nothing like as good-natured. I thought and moved more quickly than he did, but not to greater effect: he was unhurried but always effective, and his measured approach often reached its goal before my over-excited one, or reached the right goal when I was aiming at the wrong one. Physically we were in some ways opposites, too. He was of average height, freckle-faced, stockily built, round-headed and broad-chested; I was tall and skinny – taller than him, although six months younger – with a long white bony face, and dark wavy hair piled high on my head. (One of my nicknames was 'Curly', his 'Ginger'.) We both had plenty of strength and stamina, and never seemed to tire, but mine was nervous energy whereas his was physical resource. We were surprisingly closely matched in almost everything we did, and I think this had a lot to do with the success of our friendship: in any play or game that was competitive between us each would win sometimes and lose sometimes: there was nothing either could rely on winning. All in all, although we both had plenty of other friends – in our separate schools, and in our different parts of Hoxton Street – we were each other's closest friend. This friendship irradiated my childhood, and I look back on it with feelings of great warmth. Our adult lives separated us to a large extent by taking us into different worlds, but we have never lost touch.

The fact that we were at different schools had a number of practical consequences, for instance that we tended to meet chiefly at weekends, and then spend long periods together. It also meant that we did not know one another's friends well, if at all. There was one of my worlds that I particularly loved, which was almost part of my daily life, yet which I shared scarcely at all with Norman, and that was the canal. Canal Road, where my school was, ran alongside the Regent's Canal from Whitmore Road to Kingsland Road, and needless to say the water acted on the children of the school like a magnet, the more so because all the authorities in our lives – our parents, the school, the police – forbade us to play in or by it. The canal was not just a small stream, it was the width of an important river. It had a towpath along one side, and in Hoxton there were two bridges from which you could get down to it, one little more than a hundred yards from where I lived. We played by the canal for a part of most days. It was more fun even than the school playground, certainly more fun than a park, and almost as much fun as the market. We fished for tiddlers, hurled ducks and drakes across the water, played tag along the towpath. The bigger children swam, though I never did. It was only after I left London as an evacuee that I learnt to swim.

There was a perpetual traffic of barges along the canal – long, black, open wooden boats of immense heaviness, roped to gigantic dray horses that plodded with a like heaviness along the towpath – and we tried, nearly always unsuccessfully, to hitch rides on them. The horses were the great attraction: to us they appeared as big as elephants. To succeed, if only for a few seconds, in sitting on top of one was the ultimate achievement. But it almost never happened. However, there was a decent chance of being allowed to stand around with our hands in our pockets while one was being given its nosebag and the bargee crouched on his heels and smoked a cigarette. But mostly the bargemen looked upon children in the same way as the market stall-keepers did, and tried to chase us off. We refused to be chased very far, knowing that they were unable to abandon their horses or barges to run after us. We would retreat up on to the bridges and try to spit on their heads, or drop missiles into their barges. The bolder spirits would go down again to the towpath and try to snatch a swing of the rope between the horse and the barge, or pat the horse defiantly on the flank and run away, or jump into the barge itself and be chased around it and off again by the bargee. Boys whom the rest of us did not like threw stones at the horses, or jabbed at their sides with sticks. The bargees would shout at us in marvellously obscene language; and if the eye of any of them happened to fall on a policeman, we really did have to scatter and run.

What I liked to do best, if we were up on the road and saw a barge coming, was to run across and position myself where I would see it emerge from under the bridge. First of all you heard the horse passing through the tunnel under your feet – the sound shuffley and echoey – breathing loudly and sighing, with snorts here and there over the effortful *plod, plod, plod* of its footsteps; and then appeared its nostrils followed immediately by its face, eyes, whole head, then long body, with the taut rope stretching out behind it getting longer and longer as the animal's continent-sized bottom moved away up the towpath, alone in its private world of slowness and strain. Suspense mounted as the high-tension rope went on and on stretching out behind it, more and more appearing from under the bridge as if there would never be a barge on the end – until finally the tip of the barge would appear; and then, with almost impossible slowness, the whole endlessly long thing floated out into view as if it would never stop coming. By now the poor old horse would be almost disappearing at the other end of the rope, straining against it and evermore plod-plod-plodding – in addition to being already, most of them, ancient and exhausted – and the rope itself was so tense that even a child could see that it was dangerous; and now, by complete contrast, after all that effort and tension, the purpose of it all, came the effortless, tensionless, soundless barge, all ease and self-possession, unaware of what was being endured to draw it along. Where the man in this whole picture was would vary: usually he was trudging along beside the horse, often with one hand clutching its harness; but if he was tired he might have fallen back along the towpath; and he might sometimes be in the barge; it made little difference to me, because out of the horse–barge–man trio he was the least interesting one to look at. The whole thing was a sight I never grew tired of seeing.

The bridge we made use of most often to get down to the canal was in the next street to my home, at the point where Whitmore Road ran into the De Beauvoir estate and began calling itself De Beauvoir Road. The other bridge was at the bottom of Southgate Road. There, a big metal pipe looped up over the canal in a sharp curve, like a second bridge. Boys who were swimming would try to walk out to the centre of this and dive off, but because of its steep curvature they usually fell into the water before they got to the middle. Further along to the left of the pipe was the Gainsborough film studio, with its front on Poole Street and its back against the canal. It was gospel among us boys that all river and

waterside scenes in Gainsborough pictures were shot on this bit
of the canal, and that the whole of *Sanders of the River* had been
filmed here. It was known for a fact, we said, that local children
were paid small fortunes to appear in the films as extras. I waited
for the call to come to me, but it never did, nor did I know anyone
else to whom it did. But that did nothing to shake our faith.

It was in this studio during the years when I was playing
outside its back wall that Alfred Hitchcock made his best-known
films before leaving England for Hollywood, the last being *The
Lady Vanishes* in 1938. David Lean was also beginning his career
there as a film editor. But of course I knew nothing of such
people, except in so far as I saw some of their films and enjoyed
them. I got to know David Lean in the last three or four years
of his life, and took an especially keen-edged pleasure in quiz-
zing him about the Gainsborough studio in the 1930s, a whole
world that had existed at my elbow almost unknown to me at
the time.

This film studio, incidentally, is invariably described, even in
otherwise reliable reference books, as 'the Islington studio'; but
it is not in Islington, it is in Hoxton, in the next street to where
my grandmother was born – less than two hundred yards from
Gopsall Street School, and not five hundred yards from my family's
shop. The frontier between Hoxton and Islington was then, and
is now, the wall on the further side of the canal – Islington ends
beyond the opposite bank, and the canal itself is in Hoxton. The
studio was in the Borough of Shoreditch then and is in the
Borough of Hackney now, but it has never been in the Borough
of Islington. The obvious explanation for this misdescription, now
unshakeably established, is snobbery: Hoxton was so notorious
that the film company – for what may have appeared good business reasons – did not want to describe itself as being there; nor
did people with jobs there want to say that they worked in Hoxton.
The deception was made sustainable at a distance by the fact that

Hoxton is in the same postal district as Islington, so the studio's address was in N.1.

The canal was a world of its own, but I had no idea of it as existing anywhere other than in the places where I knew it. I never thought of it as coming from anywhere else, or as going anywhere else. It was a surprise to my grown-up self to discover that the canal at Little Venice was none other than this same canal, and that it was again the same canal alongside Queen Mary College in Mile End Road. To this day the Regent's Canal of my imagination is the canal as it existed in the Hoxton of the 1930s, and there alone, a sort of self-contained entity. Factories, timber-yards and workshops were backed up against the bank opposite the towpath for the whole of its length. The most widespread occupation in Hoxton was the manufacture of furniture, and most of the raw materials for this came by barge. There were timber-yards scattered all around, not only by the canal, and these the children used to play in, and steal wood from, and get thrown out of, in the same sort of way as they did the barges and the towpath. A group of us would drift into one of the wood-yards looking as innocent as we could manage, and ask for empty wooden boxes that we could take home for use as tables, or to put roller-skate wheels under and push the baby in; and most of the time we would be chased straight out again with a swear word for an answer. But if anyone were foolish enough to take us at our word we would be hiding in amongst his timber before he could say Jack Robinson; and then he would find it the devil's own job to locate us and throw us out – which of course was the game. There were some of these timber-yards that seemed to us as big as indoor forests, alive with smells, all the different aromas of recently cut woods, edgily fresh. But most of them were small – the furniture industry, here at least, was subcontracted and sub-subcontracted into an insect-world of minute operators. The number of separately demarcated jobs (always referred to as 'trades') was endless:

under people's names over pinched-in doorways you could see such descriptions as 'Wood Turner', 'Veneer Cutter', 'Upholsterer' and so on and so forth. It was nothing for an individual to sit all day every day at a lathe, year in and year out, turning out a particular kind of brush handle or chair leg, perhaps in a workshop with one or two companions. Most of the boys I was at school with would reply, when asked what they intended to do when they left: 'Learn a trade.'

The wood-yards, the source of this life-giving employment, needed to guard their treasures. Many families in Hoxton were too poor to buy coal, and were all the time scavenging for fuel for their open fires. The richest source of supply was of course the rubbish left at the end of the day in the gutters of the market, but the next best was the wood-yards. And scavengers could be choosy about quality: the beautiful and expensive heavy woods that would go on smouldering for hours were more likely to be stolen than the flimsy plywood that would go up in flames at a touch and burn out in minutes. Many were the loving products of the polisher's art that wasted away slowly in a poor man's grate. So such places as timber-yards and wood-yards were compelled to employ caretakers and night watchmen, with the result that this was one of the commonest local occupations. Several of my school companions had fathers who were night watchmen. I always regarded it as a dangerous and romantic job.

Naturally, the boys at school came from many different varieties of family. Some were always well clothed and fed, others sometimes, others never. Every now and then one of them would faint in class because he had had nothing to eat. Many were dressed in cast-offs, some in rags. Several possessed only one pair of boots or shoes, so when these were being repaired the mother sent a note to the teacher explaining that the boy was unable to come to school. I never saw a Hoxton child come barefoot to school, though in my aunt Peggy's childhood it had been an everyday sight. If there were some of my classmates who thought I was different, it would have been not because they thought I was clever but because they thought my family was rich. Two or three times I was in such exchanges as:

'You're rich.'

'No I'm not.'

'Yes you are.'

'What are you saying that for?'

'My Mum and Dad say you're rich.'

'How do they know?'

'They say you must be rich because you live in a shop.'

My sister says this happened to her often, but this may have something to do with differences between boys and girls. Most of the boys I knew would not have thought of such a thing unprompted. Left to ourselves, we accepted one another in a totally unthinking way. I had my special friends at school – Sausage Larner, Stanley Yeomans, Frank Moxey – but I had no idea what their fathers did, nor did it ever enter my head to wonder. I did not think of myself as better off than them, or indeed than anyone. If someone said I was rich I considered it ridiculous. Looking back, though, I realise that I was better-off than most of the other children, even though it had no part in my conception of myself. I also realise that, although this was not the way boys would have looked at things, it must have been the way many adults did. The grown-ups in my family thought of bookmakers and publicans as rich because they were the only inhabitants of their world who were better off than they were, and this is how the Hoxton poor must have seen the street traders and shopkeepers. In fact I now realise that they must have seen them as living off the fat of the land – and so they were, by comparison: they were well fed, and sent their children to school in clothes that had not been worn by someone else.

Although high-minded charities tended to steer clear of

Hoxton, seeing its people as criminal and undeserving cynics who would take you for a ride if you tried to help them, there was a significant amount of internally generated charity. 'It's the poor wot 'elps the poor', they used to say. Most local philanthropists were like my grandfather, only with more money, people who had grown up locally, or nearby, in poverty, and then prospered enough to be able to help others. The outstanding example – and they really did make a difference to the whole area – were two brothers called John and Lewis Burtt. Of a slightly older generation than my grandfather, they had been rescued from the streets as children and educated in one of the so-called Ragged Schools; then together they had built up a prosperous business as saddlers. At first they just opened their basement workshop to abandoned children such as they themselves had been, and gave them shelter, warmth, food, and a few second-hand clothes. But step by step, and over many years, their charitable operation grew until it occupied large premises, and had a staff of its own, in a square off Hoxton Street. It had a big dining-hall in which it fed I do not know how many children every day: no child in Hoxton needed to go a whole day without a meal, though many did. The Burtt brothers were experts at not being imposed on. How they managed this with regard to meals I do not know – it may have been connected with the system of home visits that they also operated, for they tried to investigate the family circumstances of every child they helped. If a child had grown out of its boots it could take them to Daddy Burtts and have them replaced with a pair that fitted – and might even, if lucky, be given a new pair – but it was always part of the deal that Burtts would take the old pair and have them repaired, if at all possible, to give to another child. They were not simply handing out new boots to whoever asked for them. The family had to make a contribution too, unless there were special circumstances. And new boots were never promised.

It was not only children they helped. During the First World

War they kept the nostrils of hundreds of families out of the water when their only breadwinner was abroad in the armed forces. Then during the succeeding Depression they provided expert help to hundreds to emigrate to a more decent life in places like Australia, New Zealand and Canada. By the time my memories begin, only one of the Burtt brothers was left, and he died in 1937; but by that time they were making an extraordinary difference to the life of the poorest people of Hoxton. And the institution they founded carried on after them. Its premises were gutted by bombing in 1941, but reopened after the war, and did not shut down finally until the 1980s. Its breezy slogan, 'Daddy Burtts for dinner!', deliberately aimed at children, was a local catchword. Many among my classmates were fed and shod there – I was continually hearing funny stories about the enjoyable chaos of their meals. I clamoured to go and eat there myself, but my parents would never hear of it – a family like mine would have considered itself (though not others) disgraced if it sent its children to be fed by a public soup kitchen. But some of my classmates seemed to assume we all ate there, and said to me things like: 'What, you mean you don't ever go to Daddy Burtts?', as if that meant I did not eat.

Social improvements at another level were being introduced throughout my childhood by new and crusading Labour Party majorities on both the Shoreditch Borough Council and the London County Council. Surprisingly, I knew about the separate existence of both of these councils, even as a child, because they impinged so much on our lives; and I think we probably had something about them explained to us at school. At election times, columns of us would march in step round the playground singing:

Vote, vote, vote for Mr [Whoever the Labour
candidate was]
Chuck old [Tory's name] down the stairs

'Cos old [Tory]'s got the flu
And he don't know what to do
So we won't vote for [Tory] any more
Oh lor'!

The only name I now remember chanting was 'Mr Jeger'. This was George Jeger, elected Mayor of Shoreditch in 1937; I was only seven then, so we boys must have been quite precocious propagandists – though I do not remember knowing anything about political parties at that time. I think as far as we children were concerned there was just a good guy and a bad guy; and we can have got that only from the grown-ups.

George Jeger went on to become a Labour MP, and when I grew up I came to know him. He was typical of the solid but anonymous and unromantic core of Old Labour activists. It was under them that the borough introduced electricity, and child welfare centres, and greatly increased the provision of such things as public baths, swimming baths, libraries, children's playgrounds, and the facilities in the parks. All these things had a direct effect on us children. I was taken on regular visits to one of the child welfare centres, and enjoyed it: I liked being weighed and measured, and having my chest bonked, and my insides listened to by the doctor – I found the stethoscope fascinating, and the doctor let me have a listen through it. The malt they gave my mother for me to eat at home was scrumptious. She and my sister used to go together to the public baths in Pitfield Street, simply to get a proper bath. 'They have hot water coming out of a tap!' Joan told me in tones of incredulous awe. 'And you can use as much of it as you like, nobody says anything!' But I never went. My father used to go separately to the Turkish baths, as many men did in those days. When I was a teenager he tried to persuade me to go with him, but because I knew it would mean taking all my clothes off in front of a lot of strangers I always said No. To this day I have never had a Turkish bath.

The London County Council carried out one of its biggest slum-clearance operations immediately behind our shop, on an eight-and-a-half-acre site that stopped with us, so we were on the new estate's boundary. Apparently there had been a veritable *kasbah* of ancient slums there in my earliest years, but I have no memory of them. What I do remember is a monumental block of flats going up over our back wall. First there was a forest of unbelievably high poles, intended for the scaffolding but as yet sticking up right into the heavens all by themselves. Then, stage by stage, the flats solidified out of the thin air round the poles. The whole estate was built of ochre-coloured brick, much better looking and constructed than the later, post-war council estates. Because of my own back wall I could not see the lower storeys, only the top two. Each of them consisted of a row of front doors opening off a long external balcony, all of them overlooking our back yard. In the top left-hand flat lived what became over the years a family of eleven, called Harmer: two parents and, eventually, nine children, whose annual arrival I came to expect. There were no lifts, so any time Mrs Harmer wanted to communicate with her children in the playground below she came out of her front door and yelled from the balcony; and because we were almost as near as they were we got the full blast of her call. We only ever heard her side of the story. (*'Mary, where's Johnny? . . . Is he? . . . Well go and fetch him. . . . I don't care about that, you can do that afterwards. . . . Do as I say . . . Don't answer back . . . Find Johnny this minute and tell him to . . .'*) This happened several times a day, and was part of our lives. When her firstborn, Bertie, became old enough, the task was delegated to him. Among other things he had to call all the children in for every meal, and this meant he had to call out each of their names in turn. He would come out on to the balcony, stand there like a bugle-blower, and hurl a fanfare of names into the face of the world: *'Rosy! Jimmy! Georgie! Elsie! Mary! Johnny! – Mummy want' yer!'* I would walk round past the front of these flats twice a day on my way to school, and all the children of my age who lived in them came to school with me. The whole estate is still there, and very much lived in.

One assumption that I absorbed in my childhood, I believe from my mother, was that a flat was not a proper home, but was (literally, you might say) a half-way house. Only if you occupied all the premises of a building was it your home: if you shared it with other families then it was not yours, and you were in a temporary situation. It was almost as if you were camping, passing through. You might have to live in a flat until you were able to afford a house, but that was all. Real homes were houses, like the tiny ones in Wilmer Gardens, or in Hyde Road (the extension of Hoxton Street beyond our end of it). We had a proper home, because the shop and all the rooms attaching to it belonged to my grandfather.

Those were years in which everything round us was changing fast, and my school, like everything else, changed while I was there. The biggest single change was the transition from gas lighting to electricity. But there were others too, including the school's name. This happened not once but twice, on the first occasion because the name of the street was changed.

London having grown up as a collection of villages, it contained dozens of streets called High Street until well into the 1930s. But there were also many other streets with the same name, especially such names as Park Road and Canal Road. This caused endless problems for the Post Office, and for visitors from abroad, even for Londoners themselves. So eventually the London County Council, under Herbert Morrison, issued instructions to the borough councils that most such names were to be changed into something more distinctive. My particular Canal Road became Orsman Road; and this meant that Canal Road School became Orsman Road School. I assumed that it was the same Orsman as that of the Orsman Christian Mission which occupied Costers' Hall, where my grandparents had met; but no one explained the name, and I did not think to ask. If Orsman was a person I have to this day no idea who he was. But then, after that change, someone had the thought of giving the schools themselves their own names – perhaps to make them independent of changes in street names.

One day at assembly the headmaster introduced the school to a man who was wearing a suit of noticeably superior quality to those of any of our teachers. He explained to us that we children of London were about to be given a greater pride in our locality by the renaming of our schools after famous local people. Hoxton, he told us, presented a problem, because no famous people came from there. A couple of famous people had worked there: St Leonard's Hospital had once been run by a Dr Parkinson, after whom a very famous disease had been named; and a deputy matron there called Edith Cavell had gone straight out to the Continent to be shot as a heroine in the Great War. But that was only two names, and those would be given to the two schools nearest the hospital. So what was to happen to us? Well: Orsman Road ran off Kingsland Road, and the opposite side of Kingsland Road – only the width of the roadway away – was Haggerston. And a famous man had been born in Haggerston. It wasn't Hoxton, admittedly, but it was jolly near. So we were going to be called after him. (I wondered if this would give me a pride in Haggerston, but it never did.) Our visitor told us that the man was a famous astronomer, and that he had discovered a famous comet that had been named after him. Everything seemed to be about people having things named after them. And now our school was going to be named after him too. We were going to be called the Edmund Halley School.

I have since been told that the preferred way to spell that particular Edmond is with an 'o', and that the first syllable of his surname rhymes with 'ball'; but the man who told us about him rhymed it with 'pal', and whenever we saw the name written it was with a 'u', so that is how it has been with me. The name was quickly accepted by the local community, which it might well not have been – there were a few people who went on referring to the school as Canal Road, but we who were there were soon describing ourselves as being 'up the Edmund Halley' (or rather, of course, 'Ali'). When the school was evacuated to Leicestershire at the outbreak of the Second World War, and continued its existence in Market Harborough, it retained its identity as the Edmund Halley. I look back on it with affection. But I wish the authorities had had either better information or more courage and called it the Marie Lloyd. She, reputedly the greatest of all music-hall artists, had been born in Hoxton, and incidentally was married in the church in which I was christened. In her Hoxton you got married either in a church or not at all, and in mine people would assume you were illegitimate if you had not been christened.

CHAPTER THIRTEEN

My inner life, of great intensity when I was a child, was not just a silent flow of observation and emotional response going along hand in glove with my outer situation: it was often in conflict with my outer situation. I remember many examples of this, and in each case the conflict was itself the experience that bit deeply enough to leave the memory. For instance once, in a corner of the kitchen, I was playing by myself and trying to make something fit, or work, or balance on top of something else, when it was beyond my ability to do so, and I kept failing; and my frustration mounted all the time until when, yet again, whatever it was failed, something inside me snapped and I rounded on the only other person in the room and shouted at them in rage: '*You done that!*' The other person, of course, had no idea what I was talking about. And I knew perfectly well that he or she had had nothing to do with what was going wrong for me, that I had yelled because my frustration was intolerable, and that I had simply had to let the blame and my anger explode on to something or somebody. But why had I done that? Why had I roared with such face-burning force – and felt with such incredible emotion – that something was somebody's fault when I knew it wasn't? I didn't understand it at all. The other person, whoever it was, took no notice and just went on with whatever it was they were doing; and I was left standing there in the corner burning in chagrined bafflement at my own behaviour.

This is typical of something that happened to me a great deal when I was a child. I was moved by overwhelmingly powerful emotions to do and say things that I knew to be unjustified, and I was perplexed at the time as to why I was doing them, yet I found the urge to do them irresistible. They took the form not of tantrums but of protest. For instance, I went through a short period of carefully, when I went to the lavatory, defecating on the concrete floor instead of in the lavatory bowl. I knew how out-rageous this was, and awaited a thunderstorm of shock and disgust from my mother, and a thrashing from my father; but to my great amazement none of this occurred. My mother reacted to it only once, and then quietly and in passing, without even looking me in the eye, to say that if my father knew what I was doing I would be for it, but she was cleaning up my messes before he saw them. (Perhaps I stopped making them because of the unsatisfactori-ness of this response.) All my life I have been subject to irrational emotions of sustained and enormous power that I have the greatest difficulty in controlling, and sometimes cannot control, but can deal with only by shunning situations in which they occur. I include in these the phobias that have plagued me in adult life – claustrophobia, terror of heights, terror of injections . . . The fact that I know them to be irrational is no help at all in control-ling them; on the contrary, it only serves to make them more alarming. My struggles against emotions I cannot master have been responsible for a great many things about the way I have developed.

They led me even as quite a small child to be exercised about the way I controlled, or failed to control, myself, because it was such an issue for me. I was rattled that I had no apprehension of how it worked. It was not just that when I was swept by inner forces into doing something I did not want to do I did not understand how it happened: when I did something that I *did* want to do I did not understand how that happened either. With something so tiny and trivial as bending my finger: how did I do it? I was mysti-fied. I would hold an index finger up in front of my face and say to myself: 'I'm going to count to three, and on "three" I'm going to bend my finger'; and of course on 'three' the finger bent. Then I would say: 'I won't do it on "three" now, I'll do it on "four",' and my finger bent on 'four'. And then I would do it on 'five'. How did I do it? I had not the foggiest notion. I tried catching the finger out by making a snap decision: 'One . . . [long pause] . . . two . . . [wait for it] . . . [no, not yet] . . . [still not yet] . . . *three!*' and my finger, impossible to fool if I actually had decided to bend it, bent on the split-instant of 'three'. There was no way of causing my finger *not* to bend if I made a genuine decision to bend it. And I could make it bend whenever I liked. I was completely at a loss as to what I was doing or how I was doing it. I would have expected there to be a feeling of connection somewhere, a mental equivalent of pulling a string attached to my finger so that when I pulled the string the finger moved; but there was no such feeling, no experienced connection of any kind. In fact there was no *expe-rience* of any kind between the decision and the bending finger, nothing at all, a void; and yet the latter infallibly accompanied the former. The most puzzling thing of all was that I was in complete control of it, and consciously so – without having any grasp of how it worked. How was this possible?

It was the classic problem of freedom of the will. Given that it has baffled some of the greatest philosophers of all time it is little wonder that it baffled me at the age of seven or eight. I had no idea then of its being a problem for anyone else, but there was quite a long period when I was in thrall to it, and thought about it for a part of every day, and kept doing these things with my fingers. I never solved it.

Some children are obviously withdrawn, and some obviously extrovert, but I seemed to be both. I was a sociable boy, playing happily with other children every day, making friends easily – and not only superficially, since I had an especially close friendship with Norman. I adored my father and my grandfather. So there was no absence of warm, strong relationships, or lack of ability on my part to form them. Yet at the same time I carried around inside me a gigantic world of intense emotions and thoughts which I made little or no attempt to communicate to others, which absorbed me quite a lot of the time, and which had no necessary connection with what was going on outside me. The two might sometimes overlap. I remember once kicking a ball with another boy up against two big closed wooden doors, like the doors to a wood-yard or some such place, in Phillipp Street, when I was struck by what seemed to me the impossible fact of the ball's moving. It was not the usual tennis ball but a big dark blue rubber ball; and I thought to myself that at every moment it had to be somewhere, some actual where, and what is more be wholly where it was – it couldn't be partly there and partly somewhere else. It couldn't have a blurred, ambiguous position or existence at any instant. But in that case I didn't see how it could get from one position to another, how it could leave one place and cease to be there, and be in a different place – how it could *move*. Obviously it did move, though. I was looking at it now, and there it was, moving. But that it should move seemed impossible, or so I now found myself thinking. I was perplexed. Something impossible was happening in front of my eyes. I went on racking my brains about this for a very long time, but was never able to think of an explanation.

More and more thoughts of this kind struck me as I grew older. The things that puzzled me most were, I was to discover decades later, among the problems that most exercised certain ancient and medieval philosophers: I grew up, I could say, a natural metaphysician – what are in fact metaphysical problems presented themselves to me spontaneously and frequently. I was highly exercised by them – not just mentally fascinated but emotionally involved: they used to worry me, and I would lie awake in bed at night wrestling with them. It never occurred to me to think of them as abstract. I saw them as being problems about immediate reality, concrete problems about the way things actually are. For instance, the problem of free will was a fundamental problem about me. How *am* I? How do I work? And the problem of movement was an equally fundamental problem about the physical objects around me, things I handled every day. How can they possibly be as they are? It made me see everything as puzzling, myself included. I felt an impelling need to think about these things, I *had* to think about them; and I was aware of at least a partial satisfaction when I did; but at the same time I found it frustrating, because I only ever had problems, more and more problems, never solutions.

Often when one of these thoughts hit me I would be transfixed by it. I would forget myself entirely, and be as if frozen in time, lost. My mother had an imitation that she used to do for other people, often in front of me, of me having a thought in the middle of putting my socks on. She mimicked me sitting balanced immobile on one haunch in an apparently impossible position, with one knee up and a foot in mid-air, both my hands holding a sock dangling in the air over the foot, staring unblinking out of the window, my mouth hanging open, my whole self absent, gone. This performance was always accompanied by derisive laughter on her part, but I never really saw what was supposed to be funny: it seemed to me natural that this was how you were if you had a thought. Actually, she did not realise that what I was doing was thinking, she thought I was daydreaming. This was what she said to others; and if she talked to me when I was in this state she addressed me as 'dreamer': 'Come on, dreamer, get your socks on.' I did daydream a lot, but that was something entirely different, and she seldom noticed when I was doing that.

The only other kind of experience that had the power to

transfix me in this way came from music. Apparently it did so from an early age: I am told that when I was out anywhere as a tiny tot and heard music – from a beggar in the market, say, or a band – I would sometimes stand stock still, rooted to the spot, gazing at the source of the music and completely lost in my own attention to it, and would then refuse to move, and have to be dragged away. I have a few scrappy, inchoate memories to this effect, and I remember that on those occasions the music seemed to me more startlingly meaningful than anyone talking. It seemed like an amazing breach of the natural order of things, as if an animal had suddenly spoken to me; and it was spellbinding in the same sort of way as that would have been. To this day I have never been able to treat music as background. It commands some of my attention whether I want it to or not, and in any situation in which music is audible I am unable to give my whole attention to anything else.

At home there was music every day, most of it from the radio; but quite often from the gramophone too; and in my earliest years occasionally from father's playing the piano. I always listened or half-listened to it, whatever else I might be doing. It was never just muzak to me, never just aural wallpaper: I always noted it in an active way, and remembered something of it. More often than when I was out in the street it would kidnap my consciousness altogether, and I would become lost to whatever I was doing, my whole awareness taken over by the music, so that it was as if I *was* the music. When the piece ended I would come back to myself as if shaken out of a dream. But, like a vivid dream, the music would still be with me, and I would have a fierce desire to hear it again. If it were very short and simple, like a popular song, I might have absorbed it at a hearing, in which case the easiest way to hear it again was to sing it, and I might go around singing it for days. But anything more complicated or longer would leave me in a tantalised state. If it were a piece of orchestral music I might not recall any of it at all, in specific terms, but be left with a frustrating memory of a sound-world that I had inhabited and that had taken hold of me while I was in it, and now made me long to return to it. At best, if such a piece were short and distinctively tuneful – like, say, a popular overture – I would half remember it and half not, half have hold of it but half not have grasped it, and this too would give me a sharp-edged longing to hear it again.

These desires could not be satisfied immediately if the music had been on the radio, but they could if it had been from one of my father's records. Then I would clamour for him to play it again, sometimes over and over until he went on strike and refused to play it any more. The two first records of his to which I responded in this way were the overture to *Die Fledermaus* and a hodge-podge from *Parsifal* played by the Philadelphia Orchestra under Stokowski. This conductor had taken some of the most imposing passages from Act III of that work and woven them together for orchestra alone, calling the result a 'symphonic synthesis' – a name which I made no attempt to understand or even, after the first attempt, read. I thought it beautiful beyond words, and indeed, so it was. I heard the *Fledermaus* overture as not only comparably beautiful and profound but also infinitely sad – it brought me to the edge of tears every time I heard it – with the result that the very first time I heard the two pieces they came across to me as being, to a degree that no musical adult would conceive possible, alike. In fact, when I heard one of them for the second time I mixed the two up, mistaking the chiming of the bell in one for the striking of the clock in the other. I am probably the only opera-lover in history who has ever confused *Parsifal* with *Die Fledermaus*.

Because I slept in the room where the gramophone was, and on most days my father was free to play it only after I had gone to bed, he would wait until I was asleep and then slip into the room without turning the light on and sit there listening to music in the dark. Usually I did not wake up, but quite often I did; and among my most deeply felt memories are of floating up into consciousness in a darkness that was all music. My head would fill with the music before I was fully awake, and then I would open my eyes to find myself surrounded by blackness except for a single pinpoint glow, golden-red, the point of a cigarette – in mid-air, so to speak – where I knew my father sat in his armchair. His phys-ical presence, although invisible, was tangible to me, and filled me with comfort and love. When he heard me stir he would whisper: 'Are you awake?', and turn the music up. And from then on he included me, telling me what he was playing, explaining any story attaching to it, and perhaps, when it ended, asking me if there was anything I wanted to hear.

One after another a series of brief, melodious popular classics dissolved into my bloodstream, works like the ballet music from *The Bartered Bride*, or Bizet's *Arlesienne* suite. My father had few recordings that occupied more than a single 78 rpm disc, because he could seldom afford to buy more than one at a time, so his collection consisted largely of overtures, arias and snippets – which of course made it all the more accessible and attractive to a child. He kept it in mind as a conscious ambition, which was fulfilled a few years later, to buy a whole symphony or concerto – the longest symphonies of Beethoven and Brahms occupied six discs, the big romantic concertos usually four or five. He had one work that was longer than either, but this had been given to him as a present, or so he said. Actually, I suspect he had bought it out of a big win at the races which he had then kept secret from my mother, giving her the present story as a cover. It was *Pagliacci*, Leon-cavallo's short opera, on ten or a dozen discs, in a plum-coloured album of its own. He loved this work, and played it so often he knew it by heart.

He had quite a few recordings of the popular music of the day, too, which were played at parties, and on occasions like Christmas – I do not think he ever sat down alone to listen to them in the way he did to classical music. For a long time these were the only records I was allowed to play when I was in the living-room by myself – he was prepared to take the risk of these getting scratched, but not the others. At first I liked the so-called novelty songs for which there was a vogue at the time. We had several of these, no doubt because they were fun for a family party to listen to at Christmas – 'The Whistler and His Dog', 'The Teddy Bears' Picnic', 'Minnie the Moocher'. There were also some Duke Ellington records, which sounded strangely empty to me, and a number of what are now called standards. It was these that I took to playing most, and I liked nearly all of them – some, in fact, I found haunting, like 'Smoke Gets in Your Eyes' and 'Stormy Weather' – though on the whole they spoke to me less than classical music, which I was able to hear only when my father handled the records. The nearest thing to an exception was a recording of three dances from Edward German's incidental music for Shakespeare's *Henry VIII*. This was an orchestral suite that occupied both sides of a disc, and was very simple music, just tunes with accompaniment. It had nothing like the musical quality of 'Smoke Gets in Your Eyes'; and yet I loved it more than anything else I was allowed to play. I think this must have been because it was orchestral: I found the sound of an orchestra magical; and at that age the fact that the music was so rudimentary probably made it all the more so. There was a long period when I would nip upstairs to put this record on not just every day but two or three times a day. The family got so fed up with it that I was given permission to play a limited number of the other orchestral records as well, though under threat of dire punishments if I should scratch or break any of them. Gradually, step by step, the whole of my father's collection was opened up to me over a period of years.

His greatest passion in music was Wagner, and he possessed

more records of Wagner's music than of any other composer's. In 1937 or '38 he discovered a shop in the West End where he could buy German records, and he excitedly bought several; not all of them by Wagner, but mostly. There were two main groups of these. One consisted of recordings made from the 1936 Bayreuth Festival production of *Lohengrin*, the other of snippets from *The Mastersingers* and *The Valkyrie* sung by a lyrical bass-baritone calls Hans Reinmar. I was still not allowed to touch these, but because Dad was so excited by them he played them constantly and I heard them many times. At first they sounded intriguingly strange, very foreign. It was the *Lohengrin* that got to me first. I began to find a side that father said was known as *Lohengrin's Farewell* peculiarly seductive, and wanted to hear it again and again. I developed an imitation of it, so that I could sing it myself. I sang this imitation-German so often that I can still recall parts of it: some bits are quite near the mark, but others bear so little resemblance to what I now know the German to be that I am at a loss to understand how I can have supposed that this was what was being sung. Anyway, it was what I sang. I started listening more to the other *Lohengrin* sides, and began to feel the same way about them, too, and to develop pseudo-German imitations of them: I found a duet-scene tricky, but managed it. The tenor was Franz Völker and the soprano Maria Müller, and I have felt a lifelong sense of indebtedness to them, especially him: he did not bark the music but sang it; and I thought it was the most beautiful music I had ever heard. It did not sound to me just like other music only better, it sounded *different* from other music and better. It came to me as something of a different order, something from another universe.

The Hans Reinmar recordings sounded much more strange to me, and strange for longer, especially the excerpts from *The Valkyrie*. The world of its chromatic harmony came across to me as weird; and the voice part was continually going to what sounded like a wrong note. It was a basic thing about tunes, I thought, that often during the course of listening to one you wanted it to move to a particular note and it immediately did, and this was satisfying. But with this music you expected the voice to move to a particular note and it didn't. Instead, it went somewhere else. I found this disconcerting. This music was much more 'difficult' than *Lohengrin*, I thought, even though it was by the same bloke. But after a while the wrong-note idiom began to develop a hypnotic appeal – I found myself going goosey all over when the tune moved not to the expected note but to what suddenly seemed a deliciously wrong one. And as the discords in the orchestra became familiar, more and more of them began to sound gorgeously scrunchy and unexpectedly warm. And then there crept in that compulsion to listen again, and experience those surprises, which surprisingly remained surprises, again, and then again. I was hooked. I thought the best of the Reinmar records was one that was called *Wotan's Farewell*. Even when I knew this by heart in my imitation-German, and loved it, it still sounded 'advanced', much more weird and complicated than any other music I knew. By that time its chromatic harmonies were more than eighty years old, yet they were a good deal more 'modern' than any others I had heard – far more so than popular music, and the hymns and marches that I heard outside the home, and more so than my father's other classical records, which consisted mostly of such romantics as Puccini, Verdi, Tchaikovsky, Dvorak, Mendelssohn, Grieg . . . It was part of the way I perceived Wagner when I first got to know him that his was the most 'advanced', 'difficult' and 'modern' of music. I remember listening with father to Elgar's *The Dream of Gerontius* on the radio and finding it musically unintelligible; and even more so Debussy's string quartet. Not only could I not hear any music in them, I could not understand how anybody else could. My sister Joan, who listened to the Debussy with us, said afterwards that it had sounded to her like somebody throwing lumps of dough against a wall. And I remember saying I agreed with her.

Nearly all father's records were either orchestral or operatic, so I heard scarcely any chamber music. Although he was a good pianist he had only one piano recording, which was of two pieces by Debussy, and in fact there was no chamber music at all, and no lieder. In his mind the chief reason for this was financial rather than artistic. When he went to lieder recitals and chamber music concerts he took it for granted that the tickets were cheaper than those for symphony concerts and operas, for the very good reason that they cost less to produce. So why, when he bought records, should he pay such a lot to hear one person on a piano when for exactly the same money he could get a whole symphony orchestra? He took a similar value-for-money attitude towards the length of recording sides, and would sometimes decide against buying a record on the ground that there was not enough music on the disc for the price.

Not everyone in the family responded to father's Wagnermania in the way I did. My sister developed a hostility to Wagner, chiefly, I think, because he played it so insistently; and my mother resented it as she resented all his passions. Only rarely did she want to go with him when he went to operas or concerts, though she did sometimes. During those childhood years of mine he was hearing in the flesh some of the most legendary Wagner singers there have ever been, and he talked to me about them in later years, but I had no awareness of this at the time.

For years he had had the old wind-up gramophone with which I was now familiar – I early on mastered the trick of rewinding it while a record was playing, thereby enabling myself to put the next one on with a minimum break – but he longed for one of those new radiograms that you plugged into the electric mains and did not have to wind up at all. The acquisition of any such item in our household invariably depended on his having a big win at the races, and for this one he actually changed his betting behaviour and started staking larger sums at longer odds. It was a high-risk strategy, but he was lucky, and it came off – he probably did more intensive homework than usual on his selection of horses. So we got our radiogram.

To me it looked magnificent. There it stood in the living-room, a polished wooden cabinet the size of (I thought) a small wardrobe, actually a typically 1930s piece of furniture. The sound reproduction was superior to the old gramophone, which now sounded tinny by comparison, and the radio was also better than the one we had downstairs in the kitchen. As always with a new thing, we made more use of it at first than later. Dad bought some needles made of fibre, and a special little grindstone for sharpening them: they did less damage to the records than the normal steel ones. Resharpening these fibre needles made me feel quite the little professional. In fact both Dad and I were childishly proud of our new radiogram. My mother, however, resented so much money being spent on something that meant so little to her. It had one or two trivial teething troubles – it may well have been bought on the cheap – and when one of these took the form of a faulty electrical connection that produced a red glow somewhere in the apparatus she pretended to believe that the whole thing was about to go up in flames and burn the house down, and threw a large basin of water over it. Even as a child I saw clearly what the psychology of this action was. My father's rage was well-nigh uncontrollable. One of the most blinding rows they ever had was over this. After the radiogram had dried out I thought it worked well, all things considered, but Dad believed for ever after that it worked less well than it would have done if mother had not doused it. Although he was not by nature a nagger this incident never ceased to rankle with him, and he never let it wholly die.

As far as the radio was concerned we still listened to more music in the kitchen than anywhere else, because that was where we were for most of the time. Radio had the sort of place in family life that television was later to assume. Everyone knew the most popular programmes, performers and catch phrases, and referred to them spontaneously in conversation. The hit programmes – those that were said to reduce public audiences of all other kinds on the evenings they were broadcast, because people stayed at home to listen to them – included *Band Wagon* and *Monday Night at Eight*; and there was *Music Hall* on Saturday evenings. These were continually written about in the newspapers, and their regular contributors became nationally known personalities. Because so many music-hall performers were also regular broadcasters I heard the acts of quite a number that I never saw. 'Can I stay up to listen to so-and-so?' was an everyday request from children; and there was a children's comic that recycled it all, called *Radio Fun*. Radio was the most widely shared element in the common culture. It was general practice for families to sit round a radio set and listen to programmes together. Nowadays the fact that they sat *looking* at the set seems ridiculous, but that is how it was. Variety shows, comedy series, dance music and sporting events were probably the most popular items. I absorbed it all so thoroughly that I remember much of it still, including particular songs – dozens and dozens of whole songs from that era have stayed with me. Each programme had its own theme tune or introductory song, and so did each star performer, and I remember those too. Many of the songs of the '30s are now standards, but at least as many were bad – feeble tunes, mindless words – yet I remember those just as well. The BBC was not allowed to advertise, but on Sunday mornings over a late breakfast we would listen to Radio Luxemburg, with its advertising jingles, and characters who were also a part of the nationwide popular culture – Master Okay, the Saucy Boy; the Ovaltinies; Salty Sam, the Sailor Man. I grew up with radio in the same way as children of a later generation grew up with television. But there was one big difference: radio always had a lot of classical music.

The popular songs really were popular: you would hear people singing and whistling them in the street; and children knew them as well as adults. I would perhaps see a boy address a line of song to the sky, and later ask my sister if she knew it, and she would half know it, and then I would hear it on the radio. That was how you got to know things. When I started to be aware of radio performances of these songs I was struck by the distorted (and I thought dislikeable) way the singers pronounced the words. And they sang down their noses, too. I did not like the sound they made at all, though I liked the songs very much. When I asked why they did this I was told it was because they were singing like Americans. When I asked why they were doing that, I was told it was because the songs were American. But I do not now believe that this was the true explanation: I think the explanation was that the American accent sounded classless to English ears, whereas there was no English accent in which those songs could then have been sung which would not have made them sound ridiculous to large sections of the population. *That* was the main reason why English performers were imitating the top American performers – who were better anyway, and whom we were also hearing daily on the radio, singers like Bing Crosby and Ella Fitzgerald. To a generation older than mine the songs that everybody knew (and which, for that reason, I also came to know) were chiefly from the music hall, and were British in origin, whereas to my generation new songs came from radio and cinema, and were mostly American. The '30s was the decade in which Britain came under the domination of American influences in popular song and talking film – and in both cases it was partly the classlessness of the American approach that invited this and enabled it to happen. We children of the '30s were the first in Britain to grow up with an everyday familiarity with things American – and therefore also, as in the case of British popular singers, imitation-American. This rise of popular culture presented Britain, whose class-consciousness was at its most acute about accents, with a problem it was never to resolve.

In the films, of course, the accents were genuine – at least in American films: in English ones, which were a tiny proportion of the whole, they were often ridiculous, not because they were pseudo-American but because they were pseudo. Both cockney accents and posh ones were only too often risibly 'off', and made audiences laugh. The most famous film star of all, probably the best-known individual in the world, was Charlie Chaplin, who was a cockney but who had scarcely ever been heard to speak.

Talkies were a still recent innovation, but even so they made an immense impact on the popular mind. The most famous people of any kind in the Britain of the 1930s were Hollywood film stars. Before television, leading politicians had nothing like the fame with the general public that they have now: even the prime minister was a remote figure to most people. The only moving image the population had of its rulers was what it saw on cinema newsreels. Meanwhile even children talked and played games about Gary Cooper, James Cagney, Spencer Tracey and the rest. Everybody, even the very poorest, saw films, even if they were in some cases only the old silent ones that were still being recycled in the mission halls for an admission charge of a penny. A normal cinema programme consisted of a main film, a B-feature, a news-reel, a cartoon, and one or two shorts – usually all of it American except for the newsreel and one of the shorts. In the bigger cinemas there might also be an organist, even a stage show. So the programmes were long; and this made them taxing for the attention-span of children. Many cinemas put on special programmes for children which consisted entirely of short films, all American this time, and mostly either one- or two-reelers (a reel lasted roughly ten minutes). There were always familiar ingredients in the mix – always a cowboy film, always a slapstick comedy, always a cartoon. And the programme always ended with an episode from a serial, which itself always ended with some sort of cliff-hanger, to make the children come back the following week to see how it turned out. These programmes took place on Saturday mornings, so they really were matinées in the proper meaning of the word. The children would queue to get in, and while they were waiting, vendors would come down the line selling peanuts roasted in their shells, which of course carpeted the cinema by the end of the show.

Throughout the films the kids would yell at the tops of their voices to the characters on the screen: *'Look be'ind yer!'* . . . *'Don't shoot!'* . . . *''it 'im!'* and so on. For me this was among the outstanding pleasures of cinemagoing. When Joan told me it was a waste of time I was nonplussed. The conversation went something like this:

'It's no good you shouting like that – they can't hear you.'

'What d'you mean?'

'They can't hear you.'

'Course they can.'

'No they can't.'

'Why not?'

'Coz they're not there.'

'Eh?'

'They're not there.'

'What d'you mean?'

'It's not actual people up there, you know, it's only pictures.'

'Garn!'

'S' right.'

'Course they're there. You can see 'em. There they are. So they've got to be able to hear you . . .' . . . and so on and so forth. It was only with the greatest difficulty that I grasped the fact that the cowboys and the rest of them were not actually there at all.

At first this was a disappointment of such epoch-making proportions that I thought I would never learn to accept it.

I had very marked likes and dislikes among the films, or perhaps
rather among the performers: I found the Three Stooges horrible,
but Charlie Chan was good, and Charlie Chase not bad, if a bit
wet. Mickey Mouse was weak, and Pluto boring, but Donald Duck
was funny. Walt Disney made two series of cartoons called Silly
Symphonies and Happy Harmonies, all of which I liked: the song
'Who's Afraid of the Big Bad Wolf?' came from one of them. Far
and away my favourites were the cowboy films. There were four
cowboys of iconic status: Tom Mix, Bill Boyd, Ken Maynard and
Tim McCoy. Which of them you saw depended on which cinema
you went to. At the Old Brit it was always Bill Boyd playing the
same character, Hopalong Cassidy, though why he needed two
names I never understood, and slightly disliked it. At the cinema
Norman Tillson went to, the Rex in Kingsland Road, it was always
Tom Mix being Tom Mix, which was the sort of thing I wanted.
At the cinema I ended up going to you saw Ken Maynard. I had
started out with the nearest of all the tuppenny rushes, the one
at the Hoxton cinema in Pitfield Street, where it actually did cost
tuppence; but I discovered (or rather Joan discovered) a superior
one farther away, the Victoria in Islington, at the end of New
North Road, only a block from Essex Road. It was a long walk to
get there, and it cost threepence, but the difference was worth it:
the films were better, and there were more of them. Sometimes
you even got a grown-up film in the programme, and always a
good one, none of that sloppy kissing. Joan stopped going after
quite a short time – I think she outgrew it – but I went every
Saturday morning until the outbreak of war. I would set out from
home alone – Norman refused to come with me after the first
time because he could not live without Tom Mix – but I made
my way there by a zig-zag route through the back streets that took
in a children's playground, where I always picked up companions.

It was only, and briefly, on Saturday mornings that I had that much money. After breakfast, Dad would give Joan and me our biggest pocket money of the week, taking it out of the shop till. She got sixpence, for being older, and I got fourpence. One Saturday, when I reached the Victoria, I found that the picture show had been cancelled. It was too late to get in to any of the other tuppenny rushes I knew – but now I had this fortune on me. I had never been in such a position before, with all that money to spend and nothing to spend it on. I became unhinged by it: I felt almost literally as if the money was on fire in my pocket and I *had* to get rid of it as quickly as possible, it did not matter what on. I scuttled back to Hoxton Street market and started frenetically looking round the stalls. Within minutes the money had gone – a penny here, a couple of ha'pennies there, and even, I think an unprecedented three-ha'pence somewhere. I felt exhausted by the sheer emotion of it all, drained. When I got back home, obviously not having been to the cinema but with all my money gone, I got a tremendous dressing-down from my father. He demanded to see the things I had bought; and when I showed them to him he angrily denounced them as pointless rubbish, which they were. I had not even wanted them when I bought them. The whole thing became a general family row, and there was talk of my not being given any more Saturday money. When one of the grown-ups remarked that the money had 'burnt a hole in my pocket' I was amazed that he or she should have understood so very precisely what had happened.

I was given money virtually every day, but normally it was a ha'penny at a time. With this I could buy an ounce of sweets. As I went through the shop each morning on my way to school, if my father was unoccupied I would ask him for money ('Dad, giss 'a penny'), and if he had a ha'penny in his trouser pocket he would usually give it to me, though not always. He never gave me more than a ha'penny, so if he did not have one on him I did not get anything. If I struck lucky I would be spending my ha'penny a couple of minutes later in the sweet shop on the corner of Whitmore Road and Phillipp Street. When I went out through the shop again on my way back to school after midday dinner I would try again. If I had missed out in the morning I would usually get something in the afternoon. Occasionally I would strike gold twice in one day. More often, though, Dad would say: 'I gave you something this morning,' or 'You eat too many sweets' . . . I was forbidden to ask Grandad for money, but did it nevertheless if Dad was not around. Grandad would give me a whole penny at a time, which was enough to buy a comic. There was little regularity in any of this. I could pretty well rely on a ha'penny a day, but quite often the total of what I received came to a penny, and occasionally even three ha'pence, though I never had that much all at once. So anything that cost more than a penny was out of my range. All this, of course, was except for Saturday morning. My father was constantly promising to reduce this chaotic system to order by instituting fixed and regular payments, but I was thankful he never got round to it. I knew what they would consist of: a ha'penny a day and fourpence on Saturdays.

My love for the things I spent my daily pocket-money on, sweets and comics, was that of addiction. I simply had to have them, could not imagine life without them, would have done almost anything to get them. It was an alive craving, a dependency, of which I was perpetually aware and which I needed to keep feeding all the time. It was not just that for me there was no bodily pleasure to equal that of eating sweets, and no mental satisfaction to match that of reading comics, it was that I was obsessed by the need for them if I did not get them. If I had not had a daily supply of pocket-money I would have stolen them.

My other regular object of expenditure, seeing films, came near to falling in the same category. Because the silent films in the mission halls cost only a penny, I and my friends went to them often. There we became familiar with the star performers of an earlier generation – Charlie Chaplin (dozens of Chaplin films), Wallace Beery, Rin Tin Tin, Popeye, Felix the Cat. We became familiar with standard melodrama – the moustached and sneery villain, the distraught heroine roped to the railway tracks, the approaching train, the hero galloping to the rescue, the completely impossible last-minute save. Our role was to provide the soundtrack. In this way I saw, at first, as many silent films as talkies. When my parents then started taking me with them to adult films the first were at the Stoll in Kingsway. This was a cinema that my mother particularly liked, and we all went there quite often – in fact, rather uncharacteristically, she took me there several times alone: it must be that she wanted to go, and could not just leave me behind. I thought the musicals in particular were wonderful: the songs in *Roberta* seized me so powerfully that I can still recall the emotion that flooded my insides as I sat there looking at the screen. We went as a family to cinemas in Dalston to see toughguy films, with actors like Paul Muni and Edward G. Robinson. On the whole, my parents were good judges of what to take me to, and I enjoyed nearly everything I saw. Films fed almost narcotically into my inner life. Throughout my early childhood my fantasies about my future derived more from the cinema than from any other source – I was going to grow up to be a cowboy, then a detective, then a gangster, then a cowboy again, then an airman, and so on – and all because of things I saw on the cinema screen. When my mother began to disapprove of the way I talked – unlike her, I had a cockney accent, just about the thickest imaginable – she put it down to the influence of the films I was seeing at the tuppenny rush, and talked of not letting me go any more. My reaction was near to panic. I knew perfectly well that films had nothing to do with the way I spoke – I just spoke the way everybody round us spoke – but I was unable to contemplate not being allowed to see films any more. Luckily, it never happened.

None of my fantasies, in fact none of my inner life at all, derived from reading books, because I did not read books, though I read comics from almost as early as I can recall. I started with *Chick's Own* and *Tiny Tots*, full of big coloured pictures, in whose captions all words of more than one syllable were hyphenated. Then I moved on to *Tip Top*, *Funny Wonder* and *Jingles*, which had a higher ratio of word to picture: these, which came out weekly, cost a penny. I was scarcely ever able to buy all three of them in the same week, but I always made sure I got *Tip Top*. My mother complained perpetually about the amount of money I spent on comics, and made moves to circumvent me, but I managed to foil her. I would put up with any amount of telling-off rather than not have them, so, as long as I actually got them, she could say what she liked. After I had read those that I bought myself I would swap them for others, one-for-one, with other boys. These would not be as good as my chosen ones, of course, but were better than nothing. When I had exhausted them I would swap them two-for-one at the shop kept by Davy Franks's parents. These were nearly all American comics which I would swap back again at the same shop two-for-one – so I became familiar with a host of characters like Li'l Abner, Dick Tracey and the Katzenjammer Kids.

I was just about beginning to feel that these had become overfamiliar when Norman told me of a comic that was new and different, called *Dandy*. I read it from its first number. So instant a success was it that it was closely followed by a similar one called *Beano*. In these we had such figures as Desperate Dan, Lord Snooty and his Pals, and Pansy the Strong Man's Daughter. My last and longest step, which I did not make until somewhere around my ninth birthday, was from these to comics in which the stories were told entirely in prose, with pictures that functioned only as illustrations and were actually superfluous. *The Wizard* was my favourite of these, but I also felt I needed to see *Hotspur* every week, and there were others too. My sister was reading *The Magnet* at this

* Pansy Potter

time, but I did not want to read about a school, I wanted to read about cowboys, Robin Hood, explorers, airmen, and lion-hearted English soldiers in battle with the Zulus.

Incomprehensibly to me, my family regarded it as a serious problem that I read nothing but comics, and became quite disturbed by it. They brought all sorts of pressure on me to read books, but I would not. Their snooty contempt for my comics did nothing to diminish my love for them. The intensity with which I read and absorbed them, and what they must have meant to me, were brought home to me decades later when I was writing a book in the reading room of the British Museum. Faced with writer's block I diverted myself by ordering up from the stacks the *Wizards* of 1939. Up they came, in crudely tied brown-paper parcels, covered with a dust so thick that it was obvious no one had asked for them before. As I read – I was in my forties now – the content came back to me in a degree of detail so astounding that I began to disbelieve that I could really be remembering it as completely as it felt like. So I put my memory to the test. When I came to a lengthy riddle in verse I immediately put my hand over it without reading it, looked up from the page, and recited it to myself. I write it out again now from memory:

What does man love more than life?
Hate more than death or mortal strife?
What do contented men desire?
What have the poor that the rich require?
What does the miser spend, the spendthrift save?
And what does each man carry to his grave?

I am pretty sure that that is accurate, perhaps give or take a word. And I had remembered the answer, too, which was 'Nothing'. As I read on I found myself remembering even unseen relationships – during another of the stories I thought suddenly:

'When I turn the page I'm going to find myself looking at a drawing of a cowboy having a glass of water shot out of his hand by a bullet' – and I had not even come yet to this incident in the story. I turned the page, and there it was. It was spooky. I had never before re-read a comic; and needless to say, I had never consciously learnt by heart any of the verses they contained. I had simply read the stuff once in my normal way, and now found I remembered it for life. It meant that when I read those comics for the first time I must have done so with a completeness of attention and digestion that was altogether unknown to me in adult life – yet with no awareness that I was doing so. I took in films in much the same way. In fact I took in a great deal of daily life in much the same way.

My forty-something-year-old self sitting in the British Museum perceived, as my childhood self had never done, what the comics' strategies were. Each issue consisted of half a dozen serials, and in each issue a new serial began. This was the selling point of the magazine for that week, and the subject of a brightly coloured picture that filled its front cover. One of these in a shop window in Pitfield Street, a lurid picture of a masked highwayman on a horse, had sold me *The Wizard* for the first time. The new serial was always the first story in the magazine, but the following week the continuation of it would be the second story, thus making way for the next new serial. The longer a serial had been running, the further back in the magazine it came, until it dropped off the end, so to speak: when its turn came to be the last story it would be wound up, either with the death of the hero or his elevation to a grand job, perhaps as the sort of man who often figured in stories as the hero's boss. So in every issue not only was there a new serial that began, there was also another that ended. Heroes were impossibly brave and strong, and omnicompetent: they could kill tigers and uproot trees with their bare hands, fight twenty people at once and make fools of them all, capture tanks unarmed, leap into their horse's saddle from the top of a castle tower, shoot aeroplanes out of the sky with a bow and arrow. But this meant that they needed a sidekick for less ambitious readers to identify with, and so they were always sustained by an inseparable and indispensable companion who was either a child or a slower-witted but admiring adult. Each episode would consist of these two getting into a dangerous situation that the sidekick could see no possible way out of, and then getting out of it.

In most of the episodes of most serials the characters and stories remained the same in all these respects, but they inhabited a carefully planned variety of settings: the Wild West, a boarding school, Sherwood Forest, the African desert, jungle, outer space – there was no end of them. And with these went a corresponding variety of vocabularies. In one you would find that 'in the very act of leaping on to the parapet Robin had plucked his rapier from its scabbard,' while in another 'Tex rested one hand on the pommel while the other pushed his Stetson up as he gazed out over the buttes,' and in a third 'the Red Macgregor looked up from his sizzling haggis and said threateningly: "I'll be giving a taste of my claymore to anyone who . . ."' and so it went on. ' "The carburettor's bust!" cried Sandy . . .' . . . 'The twelve-year-old baronet found himself expected to fag for the cock of the Remove' . . . and so on and so forth. I had, I realised, picked up an immense vocabulary from these comics without the slightest realisation that I was doing so: indeed, they must have been my most abundant source of new words. And not only words: I had acquired from them an elementary idea of all sorts of ways of life in other parts of the world, and other historical periods, admittedly in terms of stereotypes. My parents had been hopelessly wrong in objecting to my reading them, in fact could scarcely have been more mistaken, for not only had comics provided me with this inexhaustible supply of new glimpses into other worlds, and the vocabularies that went with them, they had also turned me into an intensely addicted reader at an early age. The sort of books my parents would have had me read instead would have given me nothing like as much, and might have turned me off reading altogether if they had been forced on me, and my comics withheld. I realised, with surprise, that the debt my mental development owed to comics was incalculable.

When reading them originally I had identified with the all-competent hero, and spent parts of every day lost in thoughts of myself doing extravagantly impossible things. One day at school – it was in Mr Howell's class, and I was nine at the time – we were told something about Napoleon, and the teacher said that Napoleon had wanted to rule everybody, to govern the world. And I found myself thinking: 'What a good idea!' I gave it a bit more thought, and then decided: 'That's what I'll do, I'll rule the world.' And from then on, that became what I was going to do. It was clear to me that Napoleon's mistake had been to imagine that he could beat the English, but I was not going to have that problem because I *was* English, so for me there was no such snag, and I could succeed where Napoleon failed. The English currently ruled a third of the world anyway, through the British Empire, and we were always being told what a good thing this was, and how beneficial it was for everybody else, and how much they enjoyed it and admired us for it. So all I had to do was take England over and then bring the advantages of British rule to everybody else. People were bound to like that.

I find it difficult now to convey the character and feel of these thoughts, because I was wholly unaware that they were fantasies. I supposed that they were facts, facts about the future. Without any question, they were what was going to happen when I grew up. There was no element of aspiration involved. I did not think of myself as hoping to do these things, or having to strive towards them, or anything of that sort: I did not even think of myself as wanting to do them, particularly. They were what was going to happen. And they were hyper-vivid for me, like dreams – more vivid, far, than existent reality. So I came to live in this 'reality' almost as much as I did in the world around me. There was a big difference between this and my response to comics. With those, I luridly imagined my present self doing the things the hero was doing, but precisely because it was my present self there was always a part of me that was earthed and knew that I was not doing those things, knew that I was a boy and that this was a game, like when you played cowboys, only you were doing it in your head – like when you said 'let's pretend', or 'just suppose'. But now, with this, there was no longer any element of contradiction between my present situation and my fantasy. I was naturally in my present situation because I was a child, but when I grew up I would rule the world, and both situations were equally real, one after the other. I was no longer earthed. My inner life had lost some crucial element of contact with reality. I was suffering from a full-scale delusion, a form of madness I suppose, and perhaps that is the only way it can be understood.

But the thing is, it was real to me. For hours I sat in the class-room absorbed in contemplation of what I would do when I ruled the world, and it was all as solid, real, familiar, factual and immed-iate to me as if I were thinking about the game of football I was going to play at lunchtime. I lived with it as part of my daily life, part of my everyday conception of myself. Like an infant crown prince, I knew that I was powerless in the present, but I also knew that supreme power was going to come to me inevitably, of its own accord, in the natural course of things. I would merely wait, and it would happen. And that was how things were . . .

I fed on these fantasies with, if anything, an even more famished avidity than that with which I read comics and listened to music, and would have reacted in a similar way if the fantasies had been denied me. I could not have borne it: I needed them in order to survive. Such dreams mistaken for reality were an essential part of me for some years, and grew more mature and sophisticated as I did myself without losing any of their intensity. For example, when I later emerged as an impassioned socialist in my early teens, socialism became the world-order that I would one day usher in, and whose advent was inevitable. As those teens approached I began, occasionally, and to specially favoured companions, to confide what I was going to do; but as a nine-year-old I kept it to myself. I realised that no one could be expected to see my future me in my present self, so I assumed that anyone to whom I let on would think it too absurd for words. So I said nothing. I felt no need to communicate any of it. People would see for themselves in the course of time. Meanwhile, I carried on a normal life in every other respect, as being the only thing I could do in the circumstances. To an attentive observer I would have presented the picture of a boy who for most of the time lived a life of rough-and-tumble with other boys, but who some of the time was lost in daydreams. And I assume this would have seemed commonplace. In fact, for all I know, it may be not unusual for little boys to have fantasies of unlimited power about their future selves – in which case experiences similar to mine will have been gone through by many of my readers.

In spite of what now seems to me the madness of my inner life I did not feel separated from other people but continued to relate to them in an active and normal way. It may be revealing, though, that I also had what was an almost overwhelmingly emotional fellow-feeling for animals. To some extent this had always been the case, but it became especially true now, and involved chiefly dogs and horses. Essentially, the feeling was one of identification: when I looked at a horse it was as if I *was* the horse; and if I saw it being ill-treated the inner painfulness of that to me was nigh unbearable. The intensity of these feelings made animals important to me in my everyday life, and I felt myself to be living in a world of horses and dogs as well as of people. We usually had a dog and a cat at home, and there were often other animals as well, ranging at different times from a tortoise to goldfish. My mother usually declared them a nuisance, and wanted to get rid of them, and the rest of us always had to fight to keep them. There was a dog, Bob, to whom I became especially attached. Once when I returned home after having been away somewhere my mother told me he had been run over and killed. I was grief-stricken. But that was as nothing compared with the feelings of betrayal I felt a little later when I discovered that there had been no such accident, and that my mother had taken the opportunity offered by my absence to have the dog put down.

CHAPTER FOURTEEN

Early on, when I began reading comics by myself, I was sitting on the bottom step in the kitchen looking at one when my mother noticed I was holding it at arm's length. She took me to have my eyes tested, and they told her I was long-sighted and would have to have glasses for reading. So from then on I wore glasses, not walking around but when I was reading comics, and in school. My mother complained perpetually about the expense of it, and seemed to blame me, but there was nothing I could do. The tests themselves were free, at least: they were carried out in Moorfields Eye Hospital, which stood on the edge of Hoxton, in City Road, and all the locals said it was acknowledged to be the best eye hospital in the world.

One day my mother gave me half a crown to collect my glasses from the optician in Kingsland Road. As I strolled there along Wilmer Gardens I kept spinning the big silver coin up in the air and catching it. I had to halt for a while at a point where some workmen were carrying planks out of a house, because they blocked the pavement, so for a moment I just stood there in the tiny crowd watching them as they brushed past us. Meanwhile I started flipping the coin again. One of the workmen wore overalls that were gaping open at the front and poking forward, and I caught a glinty flicker in his eye as it saw my coin in the air. At just the requisite moment as he was pushing past me he turned his body towards me so that the coin went down inside his overalls.

I froze in disbelief as my half dollar disappeared inside the bloke's clothes. Then I grabbed at his retreating back, but he shrugged me off. I ran round to his front and grabbed him again: 'Mister, my money's gone down your—'. 'Garn, get out of it. You kids are always—' and very roughly this time he threw me aside, and hustled off with his back to me. Although he knew he'd got my money he was not going to give it to me. There was nothing I could do.

Boiling with outrage, I ran home to tell my mother what had happened. To my bafflement there was an almighty explosion of anger against *me*. Everything I had done was wrong: I ought to have kept the money safely in my pocket with my fist clenched tightly round it, I ought not to have gone along Wilmer Gardens at all but taken another way to Kingsland Road, I ought not to have let go of the man but insisted on him giving me my money, I should have asked him his name, I ought to have called on his mates to help me . . . She went on and on as if she would never stop. I stood there with this volcano erupting over me. It ended with her saying that I would have to pay the money back. I was nonplussed. How was I, before whom money passed in ha'pennies and pennies, going to give her half a crown? She was adamant: all my pocket money would have to be handed over to her until she had all her half crown back. And that was indeed what happened. At first it seemed silly for me to go and ask my father for a ha'penny and then take it to my mother and give it to her, but it was the only thing I could do: I had no other source of money, except for my grandfather. I heard the grown-ups arguing about it, the men protesting the pointlessness of the exercise, my mother saying: 'He's got to learn.' It was my grandfather who, in effect, bust the sanctions by saying to me one day: 'Here's a penny for you and a penny for the debt.' So I took a penny to my mother and kept a penny. She was furious. But my father then started doing the same with his ha'pennies, and the situation ended in farce, my mother quietly enraged.

She was always grumbling about things I could not help. For instance, my being ill: although I have had exceptionally good physical health in adult life, as an infant I went through every childhood ailment imaginable; and my mother always talked as if it were my fault.

From my point of view one of the high points of my medical history was having my tonsils out: I woke up during the operation (I think they gave the merest whiff of anaesthetic to small children for an operation that was expected to last only a couple of minutes) and it was a nightmarish experience. I was in hospital a lot longer with scarlet fever, and that seemed like a whole chapter of my life. After the hospital came a convalescent home. That period left me with a grievance that I never got over. My parents and Joan came to the hospital to visit me, bringing with them a toy monkey that was almost as big as I was; but they were not allowed to see me because of the infectiousness of the disease. So they handed the monkey over to a nurse, who promised to deliver it to me. She never did. I did not know of its existence until I got home after my illness. Then my parents never stopped talking about it. It was the most expensive thing they had ever bought for me, and they could not get over the nurse's not having given it to me. They went on and on about it, every word exacerbating my sense of loss and injustice. Although I never saw the monkey I have as vivid a mental picture of it – with a yellow pipe in its mouth, I remember – as I have of anything. For years my parents went on mentioning it, and for years I went on feeling that the most marvellous toy I had ever possessed had been stolen from me – and by a nurse, could you believe it.

I felt this all the more because, among the toys I had actually possessed in my childhood, the one I had loved the most was a monkey, much smaller, called Joey. He was the size of a doll, and I took him everywhere with me, refusing ever to be parted from him. Usually I held him by the hand, which meant that he trailed along the ground, or in the gutter, beside me. Being a furry animal, he became indescribably dirty. Eventually the arm by which I dragged him came off, so I led him by the other. He lost his eyes, and perhaps an ear, and his nose, but I went on trailing this filthy one-armed wreck around as the object of my most intense love. My parents disposed of it when I was in hospital, and the magnificent new monkey they had brought for me there had been intended as its replacement.

The experience of having vivid mental pictures, quasi-memories, of things I had never seen, while knowing all the time that I had never seen them, was true especially of the period before my real memories began. However young I was, I always knew I had a past that stretched back beyond my real memory; in fact my illnesses were one of the bonds with that past – my mother would refer to my having been 'always ill' in ways I accepted but could not recall. She mentioned whooping cough in particular, and said things like: 'He's always had a weak chest'. As a tiny tot, it appears, I also had rickets and walked bow-legged, and this was caused by the fact that she had always been 'a bit anaemic'; so I had been born with a bone deficiency of some sort. None of this did I remember; but when I heard her talk about it, and say the same things over and over again – to other people, in my presence, in response to questions about me – it became vivid for me, and acquired a sort of second-hand reality: I knew that this person she was talking about was me, and was an extension of the me I remembered. The attitude she expressed towards this past me was chiefly one of exasperation for having been such a nuisance, and since this was continuous with her attitude towards my present self it helped smooth the story out into one person, all me.

Sometimes I pretended to remember things that I knew perfectly well I did not remember. For instance, my father once said to me: 'You know how, last year, you were smaller than you are now? And before that, you were smaller still – and the further back we go, the smaller you were? Well, once you were so small that I used to carry you around in my waistcoat pocket.' And I thought immediately of the kangaroos we had seen in the zoo, the tiny little baby kangaroo peeping out of its mother's pouch, and I identified with it intensely, and said to my father: 'Yes, I remember,' clearly seeing myself peeping out of his waistcoat pocket.

'No you don't,' he said in delight at my response, not at all the one he had expected.

'Yes, I do.'

'But you were much too small to remember. You were tiny, tiny, tiny.'

'I know. But I remember.'

And I knew I did not remember. But I thought my father would believe me if I said I did. He was so pleased by this that he made a long-running serial out of the things that happened when he was carrying me around in his waistcoat pocket, always asking me at the end of each episode if I remembered. When, as occasionally I did, I said No, he would provoke me into untruth. 'Oh, surely you remember that? You must remember that. You can't have forgotten *that*.' And I would grudgingly admit that I did, perhaps, after all, remember – though I knew I didn't.

Just as I was interested to hear about my own past, so I was also interested to hear about the pasts of other members of the family. What they had done before I was born had a Never-Never Land quality about it. I loved hearing about the time when my grandmother had been my father's mother: for instance, how she had found it impossible to get him out of bed in the mornings, and how she was continually shouting up the stairs, nagging him to get up, and how he used to lean out of bed and bang his shoes on the floor to make her think he *was* getting up, and then turn over and go to sleep. Many was the time, apparently, when the shop was going to have to be opened at nine and he was still in bed at ten to. I identified with him entirely, of course, and often asked for such stories to be retold.

There is a sense in which children take the world in which they emerge into consciousness as having been always there. For me our home, attached to the shop with my grandfather in it, was a fixture from beginningless time. I was well into adult life before I realised that my grandfather was not there during my first years, and had arrived on the daily scene only shortly before my memories begin. This must have been a big happening for me, for he always took notice of me, and was inclined to spoil me; and perhaps his arrival was what launched my continuous awareness of him as a fixture: certainly, in the life I remember, he was a daily presence. He was always in the shop, and every few hours he would poke his silver head into the kitchen and say to my mother: 'Can I come in for a quick wash? Just a sloosh [= sluice],' and then he would wash his hands and face at the sink.

His voice had a distinctive timbre that I still carry in my mind's ear, a Cockney throatiness of an earlier age that cradled within itself a hint of resilience, not just humour but a special brand of humour – solemn irony, straight-faced impudence, having you on – again very Cockney. There was something I liked about the way he used words. Quite a few of them, like 'sluice', I never heard anyone else use. Others he invented. He sometimes sang songs to imaginary words. He also invented nicknames. When Joan and I were small we both had our nicknames given to us by him. Joan had been unusually big at birth, and he had made some remark about her being a champion baby, but from the slogan 'She's a champ' her lasting name in the family became Champ. Mine was Chonk, though how he arrived at that, no one, not even he, could say. There were three people – he, my father and my sister – who called me Chonk quite often until about the time I entered my teens: it never occurred to me to mind, though it also never occurred to me to think of myself as Chonk.

Cockney rhyming slang came into my grandfather's speech in humorous and easy ways. All slang – people often forget this – is a kind of jokiness, uttered in invisible inverted commas; and so it was in my family. My father used rhyming slang much more than my grandfather, but also with more self-aware relish. When they fell into this vein together a suit was a whistle [and flute]. Somebody's wages were his greengages, and the rent would be either the Duke [of Kent] or the Burton [on Trent]. A car was a jam-jar, boots were daisies [daisy roots] and eyes were mince-pies. So, of a customer who had just left the shop, one of them might observe to the other: 'He tells his old lady he hasn't got enough money to pay the Burton, but he's just bought himself a new whistle, and now he's off to get a pair of daisies.' My father often addressed me as 'Me ole China' [plate = mate]. He had a conscious interest in rhyming slang, and possessed extensive knowledge of it, and for that reason I have known a good deal of it all my life; but it never came naturally to me to speak it in the way he and his father did. Somehow it seems to have died out between his generation and mine. None of my schoolfellows used it, though all of them, like me, were familiar with it from their elders. I suppose all slang is evanescent.

My grandfather's mock-seriousness extended to the use of biblical quotations. Once when he knew I was on my way to have a fight with another boy he admonished me: 'Remember, it is better to give than to receive.' If something happened to dash his hopes he might shake his head and say dismissively: 'It's a snare and a delusion.' Many of the things he said sounded, as that did, archaic to my ears: for instance when telling me to shut up he might say: 'Hold your noise!' When offering food he would sometimes say: 'Help yourself, and your friends will like you.' There was usually a stoic undertone to his humour, but it was genuinely impersonal, there was no self-pity to it – on the contrary, the implication was that we all had to accept the harshness of life and make the best of it, there being no use complaining: anyone who complained was slightly despicable. One of his stock answers to 'How are you?' was 'Mustn't grumble.' His facial expressions and bodily gestures, though slight, said much. Even the most fleeting gesture could be expressive: for instance if, while talking about someone, he gave a tiny, surreptitious tug at his earlobe, it meant that that person was trying to borrow money.

My father's expressiveness was more openly declared than my grandfather's, less oblique, less subtle; it was as if my grandfather had been schooled in being careful but my father had not. Dad had the same feel for language but with a larger and less archaic vocabulary. He had a wider range of interests, and read more: my grandfather devoured newspapers but seldom read a book, whereas my father was well read and always had a book on the go. His speech was as casually littered with popular quotations and allusions as that of someone with more formal education. But I never heard a biblical phrase from his lips. Shakespeare was his staple: he loved the plays, and seldom missed productions of them in London. I grew up familiar with dozens of memorable phrases that I discovered later were quotations from Shakespeare. If he had another favourite author it was Dickens. I have never been particularly drawn to Dickens, but since childhood I have known quite a lot about his books. However, there was nothing self-consciously literary about Dad's conversation, still less bookish. On the contrary, its normal range included the worldliest of worldly concerns, such as business, politics and horse-racing. But there was a liveliness to the way he spoke about them, and this expressed itself in a freshness about his use of words, drawn from his reading and his love of the theatre. His way of talking was naturally racy, and people enjoyed listening to it – I especially. It grew out of the fact that he was by temperament an enthusiast, with a great vitality of interest in whatever he turned his mind to.

My mother's use of language, by contrast, was sharp, waspish, and wholly unindebted to literary sources. She did in fact read a lot of books, but they were mostly travel books, and they left no mark on the way she spoke. Her observations tended to be personal, to the point, cutting, undercutting. Because I was subjected so often to the rough edge of her tongue there came a time when I started venting the same treatment on others. So I fear that the way I spoke was influenced by her – an in-your-face telling of uncomfortable truths, intended to keep other people at bay and deter them from getting at me, not realising that in doing so I was getting at them. I developed a line in mocking humour that was, again, essentially self-defensive. For my age, though, I made some good jokes. And one or two of my phrases stuck – I once nicknamed the family business 'Mags' Rags', and that name went on being used within the family ever after.

If I developed a tendency to make jokes at other people's expense it was because I was constantly being disparaged in front of other people by my mother. For instance, when she started forcing Joan and me to go to Sunday School, she said to several people in my presence that this was only to get us out of the way, not because she believed in anything to do with Sunday School. On the contrary, she assured them, she thought it was all a load of rubbish; but she was determined to have us out of the house, and could not think of any other way of getting rid of us on a Sunday afternoon. Looking back, it is obvious that she and my father, who always went for what they called 'a lie down' after the family's Sunday midday dinner, made love, and wanted their children out of the house; but that thought never entered my head at the time. I just supposed we were being thrown out because our presence was a pain in the neck.

The Sunday School we were sent to was at St Peter's Church in De Beauvoir Road. For some reason I liked this church – I do not remember liking any other. I neither knew nor cared what people were talking or singing about, especially having been assured repeatedly by my mother that it was a load of rubbish, but it was all very bright and cheerful. I think it may have been the equivalent of what people mean nowadays by 'happy clappy'. Certainly we used to clap in unison to my favourite hymn there, which contained a line that not only I but all the other children got wrong, and no one ever corrected. Week after week we sang what should have been 'My cup's full and running over' as 'My cup's full of running over'. So the opening verse went:

> Running over!
> Running over!
> My cup's full of running over!
> Since the Lord saved me
> I'm as happy as can be.
> My cup's full of running over

– with exuberant clapping throughout. I carry with me still a radiant, suffused memory of that church, bright with a mass of lights and the uplifting sound of all us children singing and clapping.

The only other members of my family who were part of the familiar set-up were my grandmother and her two daughters, Peggy and Hilda. But they all lived elsewhere, and I would go for days or weeks at a time without seeing one of them. What imposed itself on me about my grandmother was that she was hard and unbudgeable. There was no moving her, and no getting her to do anything she did not want to do. Children often learn how to get round their elders, and become fairly used to protesting or arguing when given orders; but there was no doing any of these things with my grandmother. However, though notoriously mean, she would always, at the end of each of my visits to her, say 'Wait a minute', go and fetch her purse, which was invariably in another room, unbutton it with great deliberation, take out a penny, hand me the penny, button up the purse, and then take the purse back to where it had come from, all with ceremony and emphasis, as if she were doing something really big. I think this was how she wanted me to perceive it, but it was also how she felt it. It was always at the last instant, too, as I was in the very process of leaving – as if she had been struggling with herself up to that moment about whether to do it or not. In these circumstances I thought it odd that she gave me a penny and not a ha'penny, which was what I was more used to receiving.

Hilda, her youngest child, still in her early twenties, lived with her. Small, bony, white-faced, highly strung, a nervous chain-smoker, Hilda came across to me as the ultimate maiden aunt, uptight and disapproving. She had big eyes and a hostile stare – she was always said within the family to resemble Bette Davis. She would fix one of my garments with a look of contempt, screw her features into an expression of disgust, and say: 'Ugh, I don't like that shirt (tie/jersey/pullover/coat) you're wearing. Haven't you got anything better than that?' For a child who did not choose his own clothes this was difficult to deal with; and she said it more often than not. She disapproved of most things, and most people, and expressed it with shattering directness. I disliked her, and kept out of her way as much as I could when I visited my grand-parents. In fact, the uncomfortable truth is – and I think it had an effect on my development – I grew up without feeling much affection for any of the female members of my family. In each case the reason came down to the fact that they were affection-less towards me, and made me feel unwanted, rejected. This may not have been how they did in fact feel: I suspect that my grand-mother and Hilda had mild feelings of approval towards me which they did not show. Joan wanted to love me, felt she ought to, tried to, and convinced herself that she did, while all the time resenting my existence. And my mother made no pretence of not resenting my existence. In adult life I have felt a powerful and permanent need for the acceptance and love of women while being unable to feel confident that I have it, or to give of myself in return; and I think the roots of this lie mostly in my childhood, especially in my relationship with my mother.

The only one of my female relations for whom I felt a warm affection was my aunt Peggy. I have referred to her so far in this book as Peggy because that is what I have been used to calling her since I was an adolescent, but when I was a child she was known within the family as Lily, and I called her 'Auntie Lily'. There was something directly affectionate about her nature, soft and outgoing, which there was not about any of the others. She liked me as a child, and acted on it spontaneously, and as a result I felt differently about her. But she was the one I saw least of: she was married, and lived farthest away, so I would see her only occasionally. In later life she told me she had married partly to get away from my grandmother, whom she could not bear. She also told me that the family financial disasters through which she had grown up made her determined to marry a man who had a safe job, not one who ran his own business. Her husband was a determined young fellow called Bill Pett, who worked in the Westminster Bank. Unlike the Magees, the Petts were socially ambitious and upwardly striving. Bill rose to higher levels in the bank than he had earlier dreamed of, and acquired a detached house and garden in a respectable suburb, and became financially well-off. Lily became Peggy. Her aspirations chimed with her husband's, and she made him a good wife. They were the sort of people the audiences for Alan Ayckbourne's plays become familiar with. Her anxiety not to be a drag on his career seduced her into being class-conscious, ashamed of coming from Hoxton, so she tried to gloss over her origins and lose her Cockney accent. The result, for many years at least, was grotesque. Her way of talking became absurdly affected, half Cockney and half pseudo-posh, accompanied by twitching distortions of the muscles round her mouth, jaw and throat, so that she embarrassed almost everyone she talked to. It made her, I fear, a figure of fun, much mimicked, and an object of disapproval for many. But she persisted with great determination (which turned out in the end to be her chief characteristic) and by her later years she was talking a rough approximation of standard English. But even at ninety she did not want people to know she came from Hoxton, and if I mentioned it in front of others she was ferociously embarrassed. Beneath it all, nevertheless, she had a good heart, and plenty of feeling for other people. It is sad that she should have bought the life she wanted at so high a price in inner conflict. But at the end of it all she felt she had been lucky. What had appeared to others to be so excruciatingly painful for her had in fact been the path she wanted to follow. She was the only member of the family (except possibly for my sister) who felt a conscious desire to escape from Hoxton, and she had escaped. In her own eyes her life had been a success story against enormous odds.

My sister and I used to hatch plots in the lavatory about running away, but our aim was not to escape from Hoxton but to escape from our mother. We agreed that we were not yet ready to cope for ourselves in the world outside, and therefore that our escape would have to be delayed until Joan was old enough to fend for us both. She reckoned this would be when she was fourteen. We were serious about it, and waited impatiently for time to pass, making all kinds of plans meanwhile about what we were going to do. But the question never arose. The Second World War broke out the day before Joan's thirteenth birthday, whereupon we were both sent away from home anyway, to keep us safe from the bombs that were expected to fall on London. When Joan's fourteenth birthday arrived she was living in Huntingdonshire and I in Leicestershire. Had we both been still at home I think we might well have tried to run away, though I doubt whether we would have got very far.

The atmosphere at home was not good for much of the time, so it came to me quite naturally to prefer being somewhere else, if only outside the house. My parents had rows which were of extreme verbal violence. They shouted at the tops of their voices, often both at once, she screaming obscenities at him and he telling her to go and get her mouth washed out with carbolic. The only times I heard her use four-letter words (never once did any other member of the family do so in my hearing) were when she lost her temper with him; and then, when her foulnesses became particularly vicious, he would tell her she belonged in the gutter. Usually it would begin over money, of which at times there was none. But however it began, it would escalate to take in the whole of their relationship, and the whole of their past, so that the same phrases came into different rows. In the early stages there would often be, from her, 'standing all day over a hot stove', 'working my fingers to the bone', 'waiting on everybody hand and foot', and 'I never stop looking after these kids'. From him would come 'You're better off than most people', 'You've always got plenty of good clothes', 'I take you out', and 'Most people never go anywhere'. In the later stages there was usually a lot of 'I wish I'd never had any kids', 'I ought never to have married you', 'I was much better off . . .' and so on and so forth. And then again more brutal abuse.

The shouting and screaming were terrifying to a child, and I dreaded these rows more than anything else in my life. As soon as one was over I began to live in fear of the next. They took place in the kitchen, where everyone was already on top of everybody else, and the noise bounced janglingly off the walls. Once, when I burst into tears, it had the effect of stopping them, so I tried it on as a deliberate tactic during other rows, but it did not work: they merely blamed one another for making me cry. Through all this the worst thing for us children was the knowledge that they hated one another. The everyday atmosphere at home was one of seething unspoken hostility.

Actually I do not believe there was anyone my mother liked. She would upbraid my sister for doing things for other people. 'You must never do anything for anyone else. No one else is ever going to do anything for you. They'll just think you're a fool if you do things for them. They'll take advantage of you.' This was said to Joan not once but many times. It was never said to me, perhaps because I was thought sufficiently selfish, or not yet old enough to need it; and I suspect also because I was not a girl. But I regarded it as a terrible thing to say, and just plain wrong. It also seemed to me impracticable: I did not see how you could live like that. My father was appalled when he heard this moral instruction being given to his daughter, and would interrupt angrily with phrases like: 'Kath, please don't say things like that to her,' to which my mother's reply was always: 'Why not? She'll have to learn it sooner or later.' Fortunately her words had little effect – which was no doubt the reason for their repeated use: 'I've told you before . . .' Even as a child I saw her as living in an amoral universe of her own, in which no one else could join her, or would want to.

There were at least three volcanic eruptions between her and my father which resulted in her going off and leaving us. She went each time to Bristol, and stayed with a married friend with whom she had once worked as a waitress. (Bristol seems to have had some powerful attraction for her – it was where she chose to spend the rest of her life after my father died. Perhaps it was the southern city that seemed to her most to resemble Newcastle. Just as I recall her taking us to Newcastle, so I can just remember a similar visit to Bristol, where the Avon suspension bridge made an impression on me second only to the prehistoric animals in the Natural History Museum, and I spent a freezing day on the beach in Weston-super-Mare that was my most hated experience ever of the seaside.) Each time she bolted to Bristol during the '30s Joan and I were not told she had run away and left us, we were told she had gone to visit friends in Bristol for an indefinite stay. But after a few days Joan always picked up what was really going on from the way the grown-ups were behaving and talking, and would pass it on to me. To us it was good news, and we hoped that she would indeed remain in Bristol indefinitely. But our father found it impossible to cope with us domestically and do his job, and our grandmother and Peggy, even sometimes Hilda, would appear on the scene and help out. To our disappointment, mother came back every time. I think it was because there was a limit to how long she could stay with friends, and because finding a place of her own, and a job she could live on, were harshly difficult for an unqualified young woman in those days. So, in the end, she would return against her will, grudgingly, expressing deepest reluctance; and for some time afterwards the domestic atmosphere would smoulder with sullen resentment. She wanted us to understand that she was doing us a favour that none of us deserved.

Every family has its way of getting along, no matter how unsuccessfully, and this was ours. It was bound to have an effect on me – it is probably one of the reasons why I have never been enamoured of family life, never cared for domesticity, and always taken it for granted that I pursue most of my interests, and much of my life, away from home. The fact that we were so disunited, and that my mother was so unlikeable, meant that the family as a whole had very few friendships with other families. Instead we each had our own ramifying personal friendships, and went our own way for much of the time, and lived in our own worlds, and did our own thing. I still have a tendency to carry on like this when I am involved in a relationship, and it sometimes causes problems: what might be called 'normal' family life does not come naturally to me.

The families to whom we related as a whole were mostly local shop- or pub-keeping families. We saw a lot of the Tillsons and the Ainsworths. When the Blitzes opposite moved out to Leighton Buzzard we went out there to visit them. We would all go together to visit my father's cousin Beattie, of whom he was especially fond: she was a good-looking and warmly attractive young woman who was dying of a tumour on the brain in a hospice in Hackney. I liked her, but was horrified by the hospice, and found the people there frightening. Otherwise, when we went out together as a family it was nearly always to do things by ourselves, not with others: say, to go to a theatre or cinema, or some sporting event.

The outings I enjoyed most were those I went on just with my father. One that sticks in my mind was a visit he made to a friend living in a retirement home for music-hall artistes. Another person there was a big red-faced conjurer in a brown suit who revealed to me some of the secrets of his trade. I was mesmerised to see how coins and playing cards were palmed. He would hold his empty hands out open and flat, palms upward, directly in front of my face; then turn them over, still empty; then back again, empty still. And all the time he was holding coins or playing cards in them. When his palms were upward, the object was flat against the back of his hand, held in place by a skilful nipping grip between the backs of two fingers, unnoticeable from the front. Then in the act of turning his hands over he would duck the two middle fingers under the object, concealing this movement with the bulk of the hand, so that when the backs of his hands were upward the object was flat against his palm, held in place by a similar grip. He could move a card or a coin back and forth so quickly that he could turn apparently empty hands over and back, again and again, without your seeing the object. And this was all done eighteen inches in front of my face, without sleeves, apparatus, or anything. There was no trick about it, exactly: it was pure skill, pure sleight of hand. As he said with a twinkle: 'The quickness of the hand deceives the eye.'

I found it unimaginably thrilling: first the impossible was done in front of my face, and then this incomprehensible thing was made comprehensible. It meant, of course, that he was able to make invisible playing cards appear out of anywhere – thin air, his mouth, my father's ear. He shuffled the pack as if playing a concertina. He showed me how to cut a card at the bottom, which he could see, and make it look as if it came from the middle. He returned it to the bottom, made it come to the top, and dealt it to an imaginary opponent. He let me shuffle the pack as many times as I liked, then shuffled several times himself, and dealt me a hand face down and told me what every card in it was before I picked it up . . . I doubt whether I have ever in my life been more fascinated by anything anyone has shown me. His parting words, uttered with a sudden and complete unjokiness, were: 'Never play cards for money with a stranger.' In that instant I realised that he was a wicked old sinner who had cheated a great many people. When I asked my father about this afterwards he told me that there were such people regularly working the passenger saloons of transatlantic liners, and he believed this man had been one of them at some point in his career.

The grown-ups in my world all had friends outside Hoxton, of course, but naturally as a child I did not; and not all that many people from outside came into my world. At school the teachers all lived in other parts of London, but I did not have what could be called a personal relationship with any of them. In the shop there were commercial travellers from elsewhere, and I would occasionally meet them in the City. There was a regular visitor called by others 'the insurance man', whom we visited once in Hendon. But only seldom did we as a family visit a family outside Hoxton. Almost every time we did I was impressed by how well-off they were. They had lavatories inside the house, which flushed without your having to stand there holding the chain. They had washbasins just for washing yourself in, in a different room from the kitchen sink. They had taps that hot water ran straight out of. Incredibly, many of them had fixed indoor baths with these hot-water taps attached to them. It was all amazing, and tremendous fun. A friend of Joan's called Gwen Taylor lived in a pub on the Haggerston side of Kingsland Road, and the rooms her family lived in, over the pub, were monumentally vast, gigantic – and the family had all these other things as well. There was a nice commercial traveller called Mr Harriman, and we visited him at his home once, and he had everything you could imagine. Strangely, perhaps, this never made me discontented. I took my home for granted as the basic norm, and thought what jolly good luck these other people had, and what fun it was to visit.

I suppose the figure from another world who impinged on my awareness more than any other was Mr Lowe, a local curate who was around for the last year or two of the '30s. His church, St Andrew's, was in the same street as my school, and was destroyed a couple of years later by the same bomb. When I first met him he was still in his early twenties, fresh down from Oxford, where he had read theology at St Edmund Hall. This was his first job. He had come to the East End with the intention of doing good, but once there he found himself hopelessly at sea. There was not much he could do that anyone actually wanted, and in any case he was an ineffectual personality: bespectacled and braying, he seemed just another of the silly-ass vicars familiar to us on stage and screen. People smiled at him, patronised him, and turned away. He found himself unexpectedly at a loss. He gravitated towards my family, and then became an almost daily caller. This was in spite of the fact that it was made clear to him that we were not churchgoers, not even Christians, and that both my parents were if anything antipathetic to religion. My father, who did not like him, found his visits too frequent, sometimes a nuisance, so he tried to pressure Mr Lowe into making them scarcer, but with no success. Mr Lowe went on coming. For a long time I assumed that this was because we treated him decently, and he had nothing else to do, and found my father interesting to talk to. However, when I met him again decades later, and discussed those earlier days with him, I discovered that it had been because he found my sister attractive. I do not think this occurred to anyone at the time, Joan being then a lumpy twelve-year-old. There was never anything in the slightest untoward about anything he did or said with regard to her, so no one thought it odd that he should so often invite her to his rooms. On our later meeting he told me how he had so enjoyed talking to her that he ceased to think of her as a child and thought of her as an equal; but how one day he had been passing her school when he saw her, together with another girl of the same age, emerge carrying cases of empty milk bottles to stack on the pavement; and because that sighting of her was unexpected he saw her through fresh eyes, and felt a shock of recognition that she was, after all, only a twelve-year-old child. He found this highly disconcerting. But some years later, when she was grown-up and living in a different part of London, he went in search of her again.

He had rooms in the vicarage beside the church, and I was occasionally invited there with Joan. What struck me most about him was the way he talked. It was like the Western Brothers – a pair of silly-ass toffs who were a famous act on the music halls, and a special favourite of mine – only he did not mean to be funny. Also, he gave nervous laughs after almost every sentence, and during these his tongue would come right out of his mouth. It was almost inconceivable to me that anyone should actually talk like this, and that of course made it interesting. In his living-room he had a mechanical frog whose red tongue came out down the front of his body to its full extent, and then went back in again; and when he showed it to me, and made it work for me, I thought it was exactly like him. Then he told me it had been given to him by some friends because they said it reminded them of him. He then laughed just like the frog, and said he was sure I found that very amusing.

This mention of the Western Brothers recalls an occasion at about this time on which I saw them and which was memorable for something else. They were taking part in a variety show at Shoreditch Town Hall, and as always they sat at a piano in white tie and tails singing satirical songs about current affairs. Because of my father's teaching I understood quite a lot of the jokes; for instance, there was one song with the refrain 'That'll be the day, chaps, that'll be the day' in which a typical verse went:

> When Chamberlain tells Hitler
> He can go to H- Halifax,
> That'll be the day, chaps,
> That'll be the day.

I was in the cheapest seats right at the back; and because this was not a theatre and the floor was not raked, I could not see over the heads of the people in front; so I left my seat and stood propping myself on a radiator against the back wall in the middle of the centre aisle, giving me a full and clear view. One of the performers was a woman ballad singer, and the very peak of her act was a long-sustained top note sung by her with arms flung wide. At just the moment when she was about to come off the note and bring her act to an end, the tension with which I was bracing myself against the radiator caused my feet to slip forward from under me on the polished parquet, and I went down with an ear-splitting and almighty *Crash!* The entire audience turned round to see what had happened, and watch me picking myself up off the floor, while the singer's climax and exit were ruined.

CHAPTER FIFTEEN

Being a shopkeeping family brings with it a certain way of life. The members who work in the shop are with one another all day every day in a working relationship, and also have a special relationship with whoever lives over and behind the shop. So they are all of them, both genders and all generations, on top of one another all the time. All are dependent for their living on a single source, the shop, which thus comes to tyrannise over them, so that as individuals they have to organise their lives around its requirements. Our shop had to be opened at nine and closed at eight (nine on Saturdays) and then opened again on Sunday mornings. And not only did there have to be always somebody in it during those hours, there had to be enough people to cope with whatever the level of trade was – and that, of course, fluctuated. The shop might be empty for a long time, and then fill up with customers. Small shopkeepers cannot afford to have too many of them walking out because they become impatient waiting to be served. During the run-up to Christmas my grandmother, my mother, and even my aunt Peggy would be roped in to look after people who came in to buy handkerchiefs, ties or socks, or to be reassured that their jackets fitted; or would help customers' children choose from among the Christmas toys and games that we gave away. Theoretically these went to people who spent more than a certain amount, but in practice they went also to many who spent less. My grandfather would give them to customers who ended up not buying anything at all, so long as they had children with them. This greatly disgusted my grandmother, who maintained, correctly, that many such people came in every year just to get free Christmas presents for their children. These toys and games were cheap, cardboardy stuff, but the children were excited by them. A sample of each would always appear in Joan's Christmas stocking and mine. The one I liked best, and got every year, was Blow Football, in which the players tried with fat little pea-shooters to blow a ping-pong ball through one another's goal.

Whenever there was an external demand on the whole family – a wedding, a funeral, anything like that – the first question was: 'What about the shop? Who's going to look after the shop?' As a child I did not understand why we could not simply shut the shop and go off together, but we never did. I looked on the refusal of the grown-ups to consider doing this as weedy and exasperating. I loved the shop in many ways, and found it a place of inexhaustible interest, but there was this one aspect of it that I came to resent from an early age, namely its inflexible command of our lives. I was constantly having what seemed to me adventuresome or interesting suggestions rejected with the same words: 'We can't do that because of the shop.'

Each day the serious business of the day would begin with the sound of the shutters going up. They were rollers made of heavy metal, as in Hoxton they had to be, and they made a distinctive sound, especially going up, with *snap!* at the top. (When they came down they made a *thunk!* at the bottom.) Because it was a double-fronted shop we had two of them, so the same sound happened twice. One of the shutters had a steel door in it which was our only front door, and which rolled up into the rest of the shutter. This made us in one important respect different from most other families in Hoxton. People who lived in ordinary houses did not lock their front doors. It was usual to have several families living in one house, and there would be children going in and out all the time, so locking the street door was not practical. It was also unnecessary, because the house would contain nothing worth stealing, only some old clothes and some even older furniture. Everyday life among most people saw them freely wandering in and out of one another's living spaces: if you wanted to talk to someone you knew well you simply walked into her house and knocked on the door of her room ('You there, Rose?'). But shopkeeping families could not live like that. We had something to steal. And for my family the only route between our living-quarters and those of other people lay through the shop, which had to be guarded, and which had no door to its double doorway unless the shutters were down.

Between us and the rest of the world, everything and everybody, including us, passed in and out through the shop all the time. So people could not just drop in, or at least had to be circumspect about doing so and come at a time when they knew they would be welcome. Most of those who visited the shop intending just to talk without buying anything were commercial travellers, who knew how to keep out of the way when customers were being served. If I was around they would often try to commend themselves by being nice to me, and many were the pennies I received from them – they did not want to be seen giving me as little as a ha'penny. Some of them always kidded around with me for a few minutes in an ice-breaking sort of way and then dismissed me with my penny, but there was one of a more gentlemanly demeanour, tall and slim, long-faced and (to my eye) distinguished-looking, called Mr Lyman, who used to talk to me seriously. I found him much the most enjoyable to meet, though he never gave me anything.

One or two of the men who came to see us regularly in this sort of way were not commercial travellers but had other functions. There was Mr Wells, who came to collect our insurance contributions. He always arrived on a bicycle, the only adult I knew personally who I ever saw riding one, and he always wore a raincoat that was streaked and darkened by the rain that fell perpetually on him while he was on his bike. When not on his bike he was never without a notebook and pencil in his hands. He was a good-natured nondescript of a typically English kind, a sort of character subsequently made familiar in the cinema through the Ealing comedies. I thought he was nice. But I never received anything from him either.

From almost my earliest awareness, what went on in the shop was, and had to be, an influence on my behaviour. 'Don't hang around in the shop' was the first injunction – pass quickly through it without getting in anyone's way. When the shop was crowded, that could be difficult, so when I wanted to go out my mother would open the kitchen door a crack and keep an eye on the situation until the coast was clear. Even if there was only a single customer in the shop I was not supposed to talk to my father or grandfather, but just hurry straight through – though of course I always did want to talk to them, so I would be happy to wait until there was no one about. Then I emerged, and chattered away with one of them until the next customer came in – at which I would be instantly ignored and expected to disappear of my own accord. The only times I was allowed to hang about alone in the shop, or play there, were when it was closed. It offered a so much larger area of floor space than anywhere in our living-quarters that I very much enjoyed playing there. It had big boxy open wooden shelves all the way up the walls, into which I could crawl, and in which large garments lay folded; and there was a pair of steps, and also a bruised old wooden ladder, to get up to the topmost shelves. There were two rows of suits and overcoats on rails; and, standing on the floor, two racks of clothes on hangers into which I could completely disappear – the clothes were all of a thicker, heavier cloth than men wear nowadays in an age of central heating. There were two counters, two chairs, a telephone and a till (mustn't touch either of those) and a pillar that was holding the ceiling up where once there had been a wall. Out of this my imagination made worlds.

When the shop was its ordinary daylight self it represented a grown-up world of which I was not yet fully a part in my own right. The things we sold, especially the suits, seemed to me unbelievably expensive – more expensive, as far as I could see, than anything sold in any other shop. (There were no furniture shops in Hoxton, even though the chief local occupation was making furniture.) That alone made it super-grown-up, and of course the suits themselves were what you wore if you were a grown-up man. In those days every respectable man, even among the poor, had a suit that he wore on Sundays. It might have been bought many years before from a second-hand stall (from somebody like my grandfather) and now be shabby and worn-out, but it was a suit nevertheless. In Hoxton most of the best suits had originated in our shop, even if they had since passed through many hands. The cheapest cost three pounds. For that you got two pairs of trousers – before the Second World War it was normal for men's suits to come with two pairs of trousers. There was a nationwide chain of stores that called itself The Fifty Shilling Tailors and sold suits even cheaper, but we thought ours were worth the difference in price.

For many people, buying new clothes was such an event that it was a ritual. They performed it, if they were going to perform it at all, on two occasions in the year: at Christmas (for the winter) and at Easter (for the summer). The forgotten pre-history of this had probably had something to do with churchgoing, but in the Hoxton I knew, scarcely anyone went to church. People had to save up to buy clothes, but if they lodged the instalments with us it ensured that the money would not be spent on other things, and we would give them a bit off the price – and, if we trusted them, let them take the clothes before they had fully paid for them. Many a final instalment was never handed over. It was a familiar part of our lives that people who had defaulted would cross the road to pass the shop if my father or grandfather was standing in the doorway.

This, incidentally, was a habit both of them were given to. Each, a good deal of the time when not occupied, would stand in the open doorway engrossed in watching the river of human life as it flowed past endlessly in both directions. None of the other shop-keepers did this, except occasionally: their transactions were much more numerous than ours, because they were mostly for smaller sums, and this kept them on the go inside their shops: they did not have the problem of long periods when nothing was happening. Years later, when I asked around for memories of our shop, this one came up more often than any other, a visual image of either my father or grandfather being 'always' standing in the doorway, the only shopkeeper in that stretch of the street to be doing so, perhaps casually exchanging greetings with the person doing the remembering. People also remembered how well they were dressed; but that was something they considered necessary because of their trade. My father's clothes were always an object of interest to me, because I thought that whatever he wore must be the thing to wear. I was particularly impressed by the fact that he had a zip-fastener in the front of his trousers where I and everybody else had fly-buttons. Zips did not come into widespread use for this purpose until quite some years after the Second World War.

The two men took a pride in selling only clothes that were well made and good value for money, and went to a lot of trouble to get them, and to nose out new sources of supply. At the top of their range were a few brands that were nationally known (and in some cases still are, such as Van Heusen shirts). Lower down the scale, most of the clothes were made by small suppliers in run-down parts of the City around Bishopsgate and Aldgate, some in Whitechapel and Commercial Road. My father and grandfather continually visited these suppliers (such trips were known as 'going to the City') and often had parcels to bring back, so as soon as I was old enough to provide a useful pair of hands I was taken along if I was free and required. I grew up thinking of the City as the place the Magee family went to get the clothes it sold. At first I considered going there a treat, because it meant being with my father on buses and even occasionally in a taxi, meeting people, all very exciting. Quite often one of the men my father talked to would give me a penny; and there were sometimes drinks too. But I must too often have been given parcels that were too heavy for me, because slowly I developed a resentment that became in time a hatred of carrying those parcels. It went so deep that its consequences remain with me to this day, an often unreasonable hatred of carrying things, and even more of being asked to carry things: if anyone asks me to carry anything a rush of resentment rises up inside me which I then have to dissemble. There was one occasion when a parcel needed to be fetched before a promised date, and none of the grown-ups could go, so a discussion developed about whether I was old enough to go alone. Opinions differed, but I was sent. I went in our usual way, by bus from Kingsland Road, for which I had been given the money. The parcel, which contained two or three suits, was too big for me to get my arms round, and the men who gave it to me said there was nothing for it but to carry it by the string. I set off with it towards the bus stop, but it was so heavy that the string cut into my fingers, and my hand began to bleed on to the parcel. I carried it in the other hand, and soon had two hands bleeding. The cutting nature of the pain set my teeth on edge. I could see myself just about getting the parcel to the bus stop, but no way could I carry it from the bus stop in Kingsland Road to our shop. I could think of only one solution, so I hailed a taxi and told the driver he would be paid by the shop to which I was delivering the parcel. I was surprised by the fact that he did not hesitate, by how easy it was – being quite a young child, and having almost no money, I expected him to cross-question me, and perhaps refuse, but he took me without the least sign of doubt. My father said afterwards that when he saw a taxi draw up outside the shop with me in it he felt a pang of alarm, because he feared that something bad had happened and I was being brought home in a cab. There was quite a to-do about my arrival, and the paying off of the driver, with a lot of loud joking. The family did not at all take the incident in its stride, but had an outbreak of amused outrage at my having had the temerity to command a taxi by myself. Nobody would listen to my protestation that it had been impossible for me to manage the parcel in any other way. My father said grimly that when he had been sent to the City to fetch parcels at my age he had had to go all the way on foot in both directions. Never again, he said, was I to take a taxi and assume he would pay.

However, I believe the reasonableness of my case did get through to him, perhaps helped by the darkness of his own memories, for he then took to saying things like: 'I'm going to the City tomorrow – would you like to come? You won't have to carry anything.' And those were the trips I now remember.

The men I visited with him in the factories and workshops were nearly all Jewish, a fact which by the age of eight or nine I was aware of without being told. To my child's eye and ear they seemed a particular sort of person, browner and noisier. They had bright dark eyes, like shiny buttons, and their hands were in perpetual motion as they talked. And they seemed to be talking all the time. Sometimes I could see they were trying too hard to sell something to my father, giving him what he would later call 'a lot of madam'. Some of them, though, were very funny, again in a particular way, which delighted me. Chuckling afterwards at something one of them had said, my father – who was relaxedly non-anti-semitic – would shake his head and murmur: 'Typical yid.' It would not have occurred to anyone in his world to think he was being anti-semitic in saying this, because it was the normal word used by everybody, including Jews themselves – I remember one asking him about someone else in the trade: 'Is he a Yid?' (The anti-semitic thing to say would have been 'Jewboy'.) Most of these Jewish businessmen struck me as sharper, quicker-witted than the adults I was used to meeting in Hoxton, and indeed so they must have been. My general feeling about them was that they were fun, enlivening: meeting them cheered me up. One or two tried to teach me phrases in Yiddish, which I have long forgotten. But there were Yiddish words anyway in the idiom spoken by my family and the people round us in Hoxton, words used among ourselves without any reference to Jews, most of them beginning with a 'sh' sound – stumm,[1] spiel,[2] shtick,[3] schnozzle,[4] schemozzle,[5] schmooze,[6] schlock,[7] schmeer,[8] schmalz,[9] schlep,[10] and more. A synagogue was always referred to as 'shul' without article ('He always goes to shul on Saturdays'). There were others too, such as kosher,[11] goy,[12] and of course the word yid[13] itself.

This reflects not only the fact that my family was in a trade in which most of the other people were Jewish but also the fact that inter-war Hoxton Street was itself half Jewish – a fact that I was not aware of when I was there. While I was writing the earlier chapters of this book I checked my memories against such sources as old copies of the Post Office Register, and was astonished to discover that throughout the whole length of Hoxton Street half the shopkeepers had what seem to be Jewish names. Some had changed their names – Mrs Benson on the corner, who I never

1. don't say a word 2. sales talk 3. a salesman's performance 4. big nose 5. *fracas* 6. soft soap 7. rubbish 8. grease 9. cheap sentiment 10. drag 11. squeaky clean 12. gentile seen through Jewish eyes 13. Jew.

thought of as Jewish, had changed her name from Bensusan. The Jewish population was a twentieth-century development, and mostly a post-First World War one. The Hoxton in which my grandparents had grown up had been ethnically all-British to an extent that had been noted at the time – by contrast with Clerkenwell on one side and Bethnal Green on the other. In my day it was still only the traders who were half of them Jewish – I do not think there were many Jews among the population of the surrounding streets, though of course there must have been some.

My family's particular trade, the rag trade, was so predominantly Jewish that it was we who were the exception. Even so, none of us thought of our suppliers as only one kind of individual. Several were distinctive characters to me, and there was one that I thought of as especially different from the others. The best maker of our made-to-measure clothes was a firm called Gottlieb and Rothschild, near Liverpool Street station. Bert Rothschild, a little, thin, angular, bony, birdlike man with flaming red hair, was an ace cutter, and made beautiful suits – he made most of my father's and grandfather's, and mine too (up to and including the time I spent at Oxford as an undergraduate – he died while I was there). He was a craftsman, wanting nothing more than to spend his time making the clothes he loved making. He was also shy, and hated dealing with customers. So everything to do with the business side of things, including selling, was handled by his partner Sam Gottlieb, a heavily dark, heavily built extrovert with the thickest lips I had ever seen and a bone-crushing handshake which I tried in vain to evade. Sam was often in our shop, where he taught me my first Yiddish words – to greet him and reply to his greetings – and always gave me a penny when he left. I enjoyed the pennies and the Yiddish, but I found him overpowering, and got a slightly sinking feeling when I saw him coming.

Made-to-measure clothes were far commoner throughout the

whole of society then than now, and many of the more prosperous members of the Hoxton community – shopkeepers, publicans, bookmakers, successful criminals – took it for granted that they had their suits made to measure. Others less well-off than they would still do it for a special occasion such as a wedding. In those days of cheap labour the price was little more than that of our best-quality off-the-peg suits, the ones we bought from Jack London, or a firm called S. Schneider and Son. All sections of society dressed more formally, and, unlike today, people dressed up, not down, for most leisure activities. Men who worked in overalls all week would put on a suit every Sunday. If people went out anywhere socially, if only to visit old and close friends, the men wore suits, and the women wore hats and gloves. It was customs like these that gave us the best of our trade.

Although we were nearly always referred to by other people as tailors we did not in fact make clothes: my father and grandfather, who wandered round the shop half the time with tape measures hanging round their necks, would take customers' measurements and telephone them to a supplier, then collect the suit when it was ready – collecting it made it cheaper than having it delivered. The customers chose their cloth from fat swatches that hung from brass hooks on both sides of the door, where they could be looked at in daylight: people were constantly taking them out into the street and standing on the pavement examining them. If the suit as delivered needed major alteration it would go back to the supplier, but minor alterations were done by us, some on the Singer machine in my parents' bedroom. If trousers needed to be shortened, my grandfather did it: two huge pairs of tailors' scissors were always lying around in the shop, and an impossibly heavy flatiron with which he would smooth out his finished work, using the top of one of the counters as an ironing-board. One of my earliest memories is of him sitting up on top of a counter, cross-legged like a tailor in a fairy story, sewing. He often used to do that: I think he sat there to stop the clothes he was working on from trailing on the floor.

Whenever my mind goes back to the world of our shop there are always cigarettes somewhere in the picture. Both men were continuous smokers, my father preferring Players and my grand-father Gold Flake. Grandad would often light a cigarette and then, when he wanted to free his hands to do something, balance it on its end on a counter, to be picked up later. But quite often he then forgot about it, so it became an increasingly tall column of ash which, if neglected, eventually toppled over – and if then left to burn itself out would burn the counter, which was a mass of cigarette burns. At least, the wooden one was: the other was glass topped, and showed burn-marks less easily. My father, a more avid smoker, was incapable of forgetting a cigarette, and often used one to light the next.

The atmosphere I grew up in was thick with cigarette smoke, and I took it for granted in the way most people then did. My mother was a heavy smoker too, so nicotine must have been coursing through my bloodstream when I was in the womb. So all-pervasive were smoking and its accoutrements that they were among the most familiar things in everyday life – cigarette boxes, cases, holders, lighters, ashtrays. Among its other functions, smoking was a social lubricant. As soon as two friends met, one would offer the other a cigarette, and the two would light up together with a certain amount of gesture before plunging into conversation. Strangers would ask one another for a light, or intro-duce themselves by offering a cigarette; beggars in the street begged for them, or picked fag-ends out of the gutter to smoke. There was something universal about smoking that it is difficult now to convey. It was commonplace that I as a small boy should be constantly sent out to buy cigarettes. Man-sized ones were sixpence for ten, elevenpence ha'penny for twenty. If you got them out of a machine, even the machine gave you a ha'penny change, which I was allowed to keep as my tip for going. There were also smaller and less strong cigarettes for women, advertised as more ladylike, though I suspect their real point was that they were cheaper. My mother smoked those.

If you went to an adult cinema the auditorium was thick with the smog of tobacco smoke, and so were the music halls and variety theatres. Some of the West End theatres forbade smoking, though most allowed it. My grandfather went once to a play at either the Apollo or the Lyric, two theatres that sit snugly side by side in Shaftesbury Avenue, each with a row of doors along its front. His was a no-smoking production, so in the interval he wandered out into the street to have a cigarette, and strolled up and down smoking. When he heard the bells ringing he went back in; the lights had just gone down, so he slipped into the nearest empty seat and watched the curtain go up – on a different play. He had walked back into the wrong theatre. But it took him a moment to realise this, and that moment was an alarmingly disorienting experience.

On social occasions there was even more smoking than usual. If a group of friends met to chat, or drink, or play cards, or listen to music, it would all take place in a room full of pea-soup smog. This was so normal that no one thought it odd, or even noticed particularly. On Sundays my father, mother, sister and I would sometimes visit my grandparents in Southgate Road, and by the evening every cubic inch of air in the living-room would be hazy, grey and acrid, as if one were out of doors in the thickest of fogs. The grown-ups would then sit down together in this, adding to it all the time, and play cards for several hours, with a great deal of coughing, and smarting eyes. When I was small I would be put to sleep on the sofa, and when it was time to go home my father would pick me up, still sleeping, and carry me into a taxi, and put me straight to bed at the other end. Sometimes I half woke up during this process – I have many memories of being bundled like a parcel along the front path in the dark.

Among the regular parties that took place at my grandparents' house was one on what we called Bonfire Night – Guy Fawkes Day it was, but we never called it that. For weeks before, I would save up to buy fireworks. A shop in Hoxton Street owned by a Mr Davis, who had brylcreemed dark hair and a saffron shop-coat, would give me a subscription card, and each time I took him a ha'penny he would stick a stamp on it. I tried to prevent this from impeding my normal intake of sweets by changing my pitch to my donors: 'Can I have a ha'penny for sweets and a ha'penny for fireworks?' With average luck I would get both. When Firework Day came (we talked of Firework Day and Bonfire Night) the great thrill in the morning was to go to Mr Davis's and choose my fireworks. I liked rockets best of all, but they were too expensive: one or two would take all my money. Next to them I liked things that made a big bang, but I was under a strict prohibition from my parents against buying them. Golden Rain I despised, it was like somebody peeing. So I settled for things like Jumping Jacks and Catherine Wheels. In the evening we would all go off to Southgate Road and light a bonfire in my grandparents' garden, and then stand round it letting off our fireworks, everyone having brought his own. There would be friends as well as family, so it would be quite a party. My excitement was always immense.

Like so many children, I adored setting fire to things; and to be allowed to do it as a legitimate activity was too good to be true. I found the bonfire itself mesmeric, and would stand close to it gazing deeply into its heart for long periods, hypnotised. The biggest thrill from the fireworks was provided by the rockets, which were my father's contribution, and which he would try to lead up to as some sort of climax to the party, sending them zooming up from milk bottles hidden in the flower beds. A wide-ranging and jolly background to all this was provided by fireworks and bonfires in neighbouring gardens, with all the laughter and shrieking surrounding them.

For me it was a strict rule that if I was going to be holding a firework when it went off I had to show it to my father before lighting the fuse. On one occasion I calculatedly did not do this, and of course I was going to say I forgot, because I wanted to let off a Big Banger and see what it would be like to be holding it when it exploded. I lit the fuse, held it stiffly out at arm's length, and prepared myself for the explosion. When it came it frightened me out of my wits, and felt as if it had blown my hand off. I yelled and cried, and there was an instant scurrying about, much alarm from the grown-ups. I was swept indoors, and my hand examined: it was charred-looking and viciously painful, at the same time stunned and stinging with pain, but turned out not to be injured. 'Don' arf give yer socks!' said my grandfather, as if confiding in me – the first time I heard this expression about socks for pain. From that day to this I have hated to be near loud bangs, even when I know they are coming.

At the end of Bonfire Night we would always walk home, so as to see the bonfires in surrounding streets, and attach ourselves for brief periods to those we liked the look of. Few people had access to a garden, so most of the parties took place in the middle of the road. Every street of any size had a bonfire party. It was the time for getting rid of anything unwanted that would burn. Things would have been saved up for weeks or months for this: rotting old doors and floorboards, broken fences and palings, derelict furniture with springs or stuffing hanging out, flea-ridden mattresses, boxes, unwearable and unsaleable clothes. At about the time our party ended, these street parties would be coming to a climax, so we would see them at their best. Neighbouring streets would be vying with one another to keep theirs going the longest; and as the partygoers became more and more excited round their bonfires – and drunker – they would get more and

more reckless about what they threw on the fire to keep it going,
until at the climax their still-in-use furniture would be going up
in flames, and the less drunk would be struggling with the more
drunk to prevent them throwing things on the fire. I would stand
there ravished with wonderment and delight, watching chairs and
beds being heaped on to already mountainous bonfires that were
as tall as I was – I once saw a piano sitting splendidly on top of
one, waiting for the flames to reach it. If a fire got out of control
the fire brigade, who had patrols in the streets all evening, would
come and put it out, and that in itself was a sight to see. Quite a
number of wives each year would secretly slip away from their
parties and call for the fire brigade in order to stop their drunken
husbands from incinerating more of their furniture.

Parties like those given by my family were almost embarrass-
ingly sedate by comparison, but still, I thought they were
wonderful, and in any case I knew they were going to be capped
by the street parties when we walked home – which would be the
real climax of our evening, anticipated excitedly by me from the
beginning. So long as we were still in my grandparents' garden
only modest amounts of beer and whisky would flow, if from unexplained sources; and there would always be a table just inside
the door to the garden with platters of sandwiches and pots of
tea on it from which people helped themselves. Half the sandwiches, the main course of our meal, would consist of cold roast
meat, the other half of a mixture of cucumber, sardine-and-
tomato, and cheese-and-pickle. This was the standard fare for card-
playing evenings too, and any other occasion when sandwiches
were called on in place of a meal because people were doing
something else. These sandwich meals were a common feature of
my childhood. They most often followed a day on which we had
a hot roast. On Boxing Day, for instance, before going off to the
pantomime in the evening, we always had cold roast turkey sandwiches, and then again when we came back from the theatre. On

special, one-off occasions we had prawns: with crispy fresh bread cut thinner than for anything else they were delicious, but you had to remember to cut the sandwiches into quarters before trying to pick them up or they fell into little bits all over the place.

On most Mondays we ate the left-overs from Sunday's roast in the form of cold meat and sautéed vegetables. If there was nothing left but vegetables we ate them as bubble and squeak, which meant sautéed cabbage and potatoes. With little or no cooking to do, my mother regularly made Monday her laundry day, as I believe families all over the country did for the same reason. The food everyone ate except the poor was much heavier then than now: puddings and pies galore, not only for main courses but also for afters; and heaps of vegetables, above all potatoes. At sit-down meals we never had fresh fruit; it had to be either stewed or tinned. And we always had to have a hot breakfast. The most basic thing most people spent their money on, before anything else, was food, because it was not only life's most fundamental necessity but also one of its most basic pleasures. When people lived in conditions that were otherwise primitive and harsh, food was the supreme consolation of everyday existence (alongside sex, which as a child I was unaware of in that capacity).

The great blow-out of the week was the Sunday midday dinner, but that was essentially a family occasion. If we wanted to entertain guests we would invite them to tea. This, in spite of its name, was a substantial meal, with two light courses surrounded by what could be limitless amounts of bread, butter, jam, sandwiches, cake and biscuits, and accompanied all the way through by cups of tea. The first course would be a hot snack, usually something on toast – eggs poached or scrambled, or perhaps sardines. Then there would be tinned fruit and cream, or a trifle. After that, guests would be encouraged to 'fill up on cake'. Other families who invited us laid on the same things; and when I found myself a couple of years later visiting various families in Sussex and then

Leicestershire the same things happened in those places too; I suspect this was the commonest form of inter-family entertaining during the years before the Second World War.

The greatest celebration of the year, incomparably, was Christmas. For my family, living as we did in a market street, the lead-up to it was long. Just as a certain flower blooms all at the same time, there would come a day when all the stalls broke into sprigs of holly and bright red berries; and between then and Christmas Day the market became ever more festive, selling more and more Christmassy goods. As the crowds grew thicker the stalls would stay open later, and would light themselves brightly in the dark evenings – hundreds and hundreds of lamps and lanterns, plus loops of coloured electric lights. Light, above all, is my memory, the market alive with it for the whole of its length. In cold weather each stall-keeper would have a brazier at one corner of his stall and stand beside it, and these too glowed rich-red all the way up the street. They were comforting for shoppers as well, especially those with little warmth or comfort at home. Children would cluster and huddle round them, making up cheekily to the stall-keepers so as not to be shooed away. I loved braziers with the same sort of feeling as I had for bonfires. The ones I liked best were the biggest and most open, which were those of the chestnut-sellers, some of which looked as if they were dustbin lids. I would stand beside them watching the vendor rake the chestnuts over the hot coals, nuzzling my face into the warmth and luxuriating in the smell. I got to taste them only two or three times a winter, but when I did I found them as rich as they were delicious.

Children were as sensitive to the advent of Christmas as was the market, and more excitedly. As soon as it appeared on the most distant of our horizons we would start referring to it in our games and chants. Some of these went back a long way, though that was a fact of which I had no notion, and in any case we appropriated them from any source that pleased us. Just about my favourite – because ha'pennies and the lack of them were my most continual and pressing concern – was used by the girls as one of their skipping chants:

> Christmas is coming
> The geese are getting fat
> Please put a penny in the
> OLD MAN'S HAT.
> If you haven't got a penny
> A ha'penny will do.
> If you haven't got a ha'penny
> GOD BLESS YOU.

We found we could do extra well for pennies and ha'pennies if we hung around near the doors of pubs. Often it was just as convenient to play there as anywhere else. Not only did the customers get drunk earlier in the day while we children were still around, but they would whiffle out of the pubs beaming with an indiscriminate benevolence not to be seen at other times. They were a soft touch ('Got a'penny, Mister?') and we did well out of them.

During the last few evenings before Christmas Day the pubs would be doing their noisiest trade of all year. If I was out late I would hear singing coming from each one, all the inhabitants of a pub singing in unison. The same small handful of songs were repeated over and again in the course of a single evening, the most popular being 'Nellie Dean' and 'Lily of Laguna'. They were sung in a particular style, exceedingly slow, blearily sentimental, almost lachrymose. Then, late in the evening, the drinkers would cheer themselves up before going home by having a knees-up. I never saw this, because I was not allowed into the pubs, but I have seen it since: they all linked arms in concentric circles and did a high-stepping prance like show horses, into and out of the centre.

What I did experience as a child was the unbelievable noise they made doing it: the stamping and thumping would shake not only the pub but the street, and on top of it all they would be singing 'Knees Up Mother Brown!' at the tops of their voices, over and over, bursting into cheers after each verse. The bars were so packed that it was difficult for anyone outside the pub to get in, so how those inside managed to dance I cannot tell. Every now and then a door would fly open and a few people would come catapulting out as if ejected under high pressure. In that moment there would be a sudden explosion of noise and light into the street, and the door would close again. Then when I got home to bed I would like awake in the darkness listening to drunks lighting their way home with song. The sound of a solitary drunk reeling along the street at night bawling a song was almost everyday, but during those few nights before Christmas there were choirs of them, one following another, some passing right under my window and others dim in the far distance, others at all distances between. Drunks never sang like other people: not only were they louder and more uninhibited, they were overpoweringly sentimental in a way that perturbed me. My father never got drunk, but that was because he had what I think would now be seen as an allergic reaction to drink: more than one glass of anything alcoholic made him sick. My grandfather got drunk quite often, I believe, but he was always decently behaved when he did, though it still caused rows with my grandmother, and sometimes the fallout from these would get as far as my ears.

All around us, the days before Christmas were hyper-active and overflowing with publicly expressed sentiment. This was true of our shop, which would be crammed with customers greeting one another cheerfully, and laughing, behaving quite unlike the way they did for the rest of the year. The shop sold several things that were standard Christmas presents – socks, ties, handkerchiefs, cuff-links – so we did a bumper trade in those. But it was also a time when our better-off customers bought new clothes, especially suits, so we had our highest sales in our most expensive goods. For two or three weeks before Christmas the shop would be crowded more or less perpetually with people, many of whom were buying made-to-measure clothes against a Christmas deadline. I was under especially strict instructions not to take up any room in the shop then, or get in anyone's way. My father and grandfather were on their feet and on the go without respite, and I saw them grow increasingly tired as the days went by. My grandfather became tetchy when he got tired, so I would have to start watching out for his temper. In a way, the arrival of Christmas Day itself, after all this, would come as a welcome end.

On Christmas Eve, Joan and I would hang up stockings at the end of the bed. I felt envious of friends who told me they hung up pillow-cases, not because you could get more in a pillow-case but because bigger things would go in. I asked around about this, and could find not a single example of anyone else hanging up a stocking, though there were lots who hung up pillow-cases. I passed this information on to my parents, but it made no difference: for them it had to go on being stockings. Although Joan and I were kept awake until a very late hour by our excitement, our parents would always wait until we were asleep before filling the stockings (actually I think they had stockings already filled, and simply exchanged them for our empty ones) so we would always experience the magic of waking up on Christmas morning and finding a stockingful of presents at the end of the bed. As a tiny boy I believed Father Christmas had brought them, but when disillusionment came early from Joan I was not greatly troubled: as far as I was concerned the presents were what mattered, and who had left them was of secondary importance.

Beside each of the bumpily bloated stockings were three or four parcels neatly piled, things too big to go into a stocking. These we made a dive for first. Any kind of board game, jigsaw puzzle, large toy animal or doll, humming top, anything like a cowboy set, any long object like a bow or a toy rifle, would be here. There was nothing very expensive; but in any case, looking back, I suspect that most of it was paid for by my grandfather, who would have thought of himself as buying the things on behalf of my father. Different families, regardless of wealth, have widely differing conventions about the level of expensiveness of the presents its members give to one another, and these can range from handkerchiefs and paperbacks to fur coats and vehicles. Each family seems to regard its own assumptions as normal. In my family the assumption was that if somebody wanted a thing he would buy it for himself unless put off by the price, and therefore if your aim was to give him something he really wanted, it would have to be a thing he thought of as too expensive to buy for himself. This meant, usually, that it was also too expensive for you to buy for yourself. So a present was both something special that the recipient really wanted and a sacrifice for the giver. In these circumstances, presents truly enhanced one's life, and were always afterwards treasured. A high proportion of the possessions that people most valued were presents; in ordinary conversation they would quite often say of a piece of costume jewellery, or an expensive garment, or a book: 'It was a present to me from so-and-so, by the way.' In this case my grandfather knew that my parents were not able to give Joan and me the presents they would have liked, so he provided some, and we accepted them as coming from our parents.

In the toe of the Christmas stocking there had to be a tangerine and three new-minted pennies. On top of those were a mass of small things, mostly things to play with: for me they would be such items as a whipping top, or a pea-shooter, a catapult, a mouth organ, a set of fivestones, a pack of cards, a bag of marbles, a box of spillikens. There would be a few quirky oddities too, as it might be a piece of comically shaped soap, or a funny hat, or one or two of the silly jokes and tricks that little boys delight in. These would all be separated from one another – and the stocking bulked out – with fruit, mostly apples and tangerines, and nuts filling up the smaller spaces, mostly hazels. Since I could be relied on either to break or lose almost any plaything within a year I was given many of the same things every Christmas; and very welcome they were too.

As for breaking things, I positively wanted to break anything that was mechanical, like, say, a toy fire-engine, and had an urge to do so that was beyond my power to control. The emotional satisfaction I got out of breaking such things was out of all comparison deeper and more serious than any pleasure I could get from playing with them, so from the moment they came into my hands my determination was to smash them; if possible without incurring the wrath of my parents, though that was a price I was willing to pay if necessary. I would try to make it look as if the smash-up had been accidental, but my deceptions were transparent. My parents did not understand me, though, and they remonstrated: how could I possibly not realise that if I broke my own toys I would not have them to play with? Could I not see that I was the loser? ('Oh no I'm not!' I would think with relish, rejoicing inwardly at a smash-up just accomplished.) They would shake their heads with incomprehension. But a disastrous consequence of this was that they stopped giving me toys of that sort. And when I asked for them, the reply was: 'No good giving you *that*, it'll be broken the first day. Waste of money.' So having discovered the exquisite pleasure of breaking things I had to forgo it.

The first victim of my deprivation, apart from myself, was my tortoise Joey. I started throwing him up high in the air in our back yard and letting him smash down on to the concrete. On a superficial view this was out of character, because I loved animals with a genuine and deep intensity, more than I loved any human beings except for my father and grandfather; my feelings of empathy with them were always sensitive, sometimes painful. But Joey had refused my love. Every time I lifted him to my face to stroke his nose and talk to him affectionately he jerked his head back into his shell and disappeared altogether. He rejected me flagrantly, over and over again, and I think I was making him pay. As soon as my parents realised what I was doing they stopped me, took him away from me, and disposed of him terminally. But I abused him horrendously before this happened, and my skin crawls now when I think of it.

There was one Christmas morning, when I was small, when Joan and I woke up and saw the presents there, piled, and the stockings filled, and leapt out of bed and started unpacking them and playing with them. They were an especially good lot, and I tried to play with them all at once. Overflowing with excitement and delight, I rushed into my parents' bedroom with stocking presents bulging out of all my pyjama pockets, a cowboy hat on my head, a board game in one hand and a huge metal humming-top in the other, wanting to show them off. I switched the light on so that my parents would be able to see properly, and pumped the top up to its maximum speed beside their bed so that they would be able to hear the hum at its loudest from close to. Seldom in my life have I been so violently blown up as by the roar of anger that came from the heap of bedclothes. *'What the hell are you doing? Do you know what time it is?'* ('Time? Time? What time?') My father's face when he sat up in bed was crimson with rage. *'It's three o'clock in the morning!'* he shouted in a voice that could have been heard out in the street. *'Go back to bed at once! Don't touch any of those presents till it gets light!'* I was shattered, hopelessly bewildered, disoriented. I thought this was the morning – if this wasn't, what was? I had no idea what three o'clock meant. He carried on shouting at me until I had switched off his light and gone back to bed in my own room, trembling with terrified incomprehension. *'Are you in bed yet? Well stay there till you're told you can get up!'* The shock to my system was so great that it remains one of the most powerful of all my childhood memories.

On a Christmas morning I would receive so many stocking presents that I was engrossed with them, trying out the new games with Joan, until it was time for the meal of the year. This we shared with my grandparents, either at our place or theirs; and there would always be one or two extra family or guests; so eight or ten of us would be sitting round the table. My grandmother was the worst cook known to mankind, so if the meal was to be at her place efforts were made to get it cooked by someone else, perhaps one of her daughters. The menu had to be always the same: giblet soup to begin with, then roast turkey accompanied by roast pota-toes and brussel sprouts, then Christmas pudding, then hot mince pies. Over the Christmas pudding, crackers would be pulled, and riddles read out, and we would sit round the table wearing paper hats until the end of the meal. We never sat down until after two o'clock, and it would be approaching five when we left the table. One year the grandparents arrived more than an hour after the food was ready – my guess is that my grandfather had got lost in a pub somewhere – and my mother put up a blistering row that ruined Christmas for everybody.

After dinner we would be jumbled up together higgledy-piggledy round the fire in a half-circle, some on cushions on the floor, some sitting on the arms of chairs. Presents would be handed round among those who had not seen one another earlier in the day. At this point Uncle Clem, who visited us from his barracks one Christmas, tried to give me an electric torch, which I refused to accept. I had been told over and over again by my parents that if any man tried to give me a present I was absolutely to refuse it, no matter who he was or what he might say; and in the presence of my parents I dared not disobey this instruction. When he appealed despairingly to my mother I naturally expected her to back me up, but she was angry with me, and ordered me to take the torch. I was bewildered. 'But you said . . .' at which she snapped immediately: 'This is different.' *What* was different she did not explain. Mystified, I took the torch.

For the men there were always cigars at Christmas; and port for everyone except the children. Boxes of dates and chocolates would make the rounds, and bowls of nuts and fruit. There were fruits we did not have at other times – figs, for instance, and (my very favourite) *glacés* fruits. It was a feast for the senses, and there was such warmth among us as we sat together round the fire that I could have imagined no greater happiness. Some of the things we ate at Christmas were so delicious that I did not understand why we ate them on only one day of the year – turkey, for instance, and tangerines. I knew they might be expensive, but thought we ought at least to have them on other special occasions, but we never did.

The only other family occasions that made anything like the impact on me that Christmas did were summer holidays. Birthdays were pretty good, but all they consisted in was getting presents: there was no party, or family gathering, although there might be a special cake. Even though we were totally non-religious as a family, when it came to eating we kept all the traditional feast-days: we had pancakes on Pancake Tuesday, and hot cross buns on Good Friday – which I would be sent out before breakfast to get, spicy hot, from Vooght's. Like everyone else, we always ate fish on Fridays. Such customs continued among the population at large for generations after their religious associations had been forgotten. We ate fish on other days too, of course, and were free to have pancakes any time we liked, but these mini-rituals were fun, and had significance for us because of the fact that we always did them. I was grown-up before I knew that Pancake Tuesday was Shrove Tuesday. And what Shrove Tuesday is I still do not know.

Every summer we went away for a fortnight's holiday at the

seaside. It was in connection with holidays that I first learnt the word 'fortnight', and it has retained holiday associations for me ever since. My father was silently proud of the fact that he gave his family two whole weeks' holiday each year: it must have been financially difficult for him. Most of my schoolmates never had a holiday, and those that did nearly all went for a week or less. There was something called the Children's Country Holiday Fund that sent some of them on day-outings to the inner Essex countryside, places like Theydon Bois. And there were some who went away every year with their families to work as hoppers in Kent. This got them out of London, and gave them a week or two in the country; but they had to work hard all the time picking hops, and by all accounts they camped in conditions that were even worse than those they normally lived in. By contrast I and my family stayed in a comfortable boarding house, and were free to enjoy ourselves. It was fantastic, I thought, and every year I started looking forward to it months beforehand, from the moment discussions began about where we were going to go, the assumption always being that it would have to be somewhere different from last year.

My father's favourite place anywhere outside London was Brighton, which he loved. He went there often to the races, or simply to have a day out, and he and my mother had spent a holiday there. But it has a pebble beach which is positively painful for children to play on. The classic seaside resort for East Londoners was Southend, and my parents had spent a holiday there too; but now that they had small children they considered it too rough and rowdy. The two earliest seaside holidays I remember were in Ramsgate and Margate, in successive years. We then tried Clacton-on-Sea, which we agreed was a disappointment; so the year after that we went back to whichever it was of Ramsgate and Margate that we preferred.

We travelled to these places not by train or bus but by

paddle-steamer down the River Thames, which was cheaper and much more fun. Boarding the ship at Tower Pier was an adventure in itself. During the trip I would be taken to watch one of the gigantic paddles at work. I found it flabbergasting, and it would continue as a huge ongoing memory from one year to the next. The whole thing was so much bigger than anyone would have imagined, so that from high up the water came cascading down through the slats in heaven-sized schlurps, like a god drinking soup. The sense of power, strain and heaving was colossal. And I loved having my skin made to creep by being told: 'It'll kill you if you fall in, so be careful.'

The bed-and-breakfast houses we stayed in were more comfortable than our own home, and I thought them luxurious. Their rooms were often bigger, and usually lighter, than I was used to, and they always had lots of armchairs and sofas. There was an indoor lavatory, sometimes even two, so you never had to go out in the rain. In the bedroom there was a wash-basin with endless hot water coming out of a tap; and somewhere in the house there would be a whole room with nothing in it but a bath – not a dark grey one made of zinc but a big pure white one, perfectly smooth. It was there all the time, and had hot water all the time. I was not much of an enthusiast for bathing, but this was impressive; and I would ask, to my parents' amusement, if I could have a bath, so that I could play with the taps.

The arrangement with the house was that we had two meals a day there: breakfast, which was like having a Sunday breakfast every day, and what they self-consciously called 'high tea', which turned out to be tea. If the weather was fine we would be out all day, mostly on the beach. If it rained we had plenty to amuse ourselves with indoors – games, cards, books, and in my case comics – and would use our rooms as a base from which to make excursions to places of indoor entertainment such as theatres, cinemas, amusement arcades and the rest – there was never any shortage of such things in a seaside resort during the holiday season.

To me as a child a fortnight was an endless time, and these holidays were like another whole life. Home was like a dream from which I had awoken: when I returned there it all seemed strange. What I loved above all were the days on the beach. I would paddle, make mud pies, get into games of beach cricket and rounders with other children, bury my sleeping father in the sand. With my bucket and spade I would construct elaborate sand castles, most of which were actually built by him, with more obstruction from me than help. We would try to position a castle so that the last, weakest lap of the incoming waves kept replenishing the water in the moat as fast as it sank into the sand. When we had finished with it, and were about to go home, there would be what was for me the culminating pleasure of destroying the castle.

There were entertainments on the beach which I relished with new excitement every day: donkey rides, Punch and Judy shows, band music from the promenade, the whole razzamatazz and hullabaloo of the pier. I always wanted to do more than my parents could afford – more donkey rides, more visits to the pier – but I was reasonably good about accepting reality, and hugely enjoyed what I did. The donkey rides combined two pleasures in one: there was the delightful, childlike animal itself, which you chose from several, each with its own name on its forehead, and you stroked it and talked to it; and then there was the thrill of actually sitting on its back and riding it along the beach – it was the only kind of horse I ever rode as a child, and while doing it I indulged all sorts of cowboy fantasies. As for the pier, even I was put out by how much it cost – you had to pay just to go on it, before you even did anything – so I saw my parents' point of view; and that made the visits we did make (probably two in a fortnight) even more exciting. At the end of the pier there was always a concert party, and it always put on special shows for children. What the word 'concert' meant to me until I was about nine was one of these shows. I still remember the songs, many with a distinctive character of determined jollity like 'Here we are, here we are, here we are again!' – but also the sublimely joyous 'Oh I do like to be beside the seaside!'

I suppose we formed a typical family group on the beach. My parents spent most of their time in deckchairs, either chatting or reading or snoozing or snacking, and smoking more or less non-stop, while my sister and I played somewhere around them, whether together or separately, in ever-increasing circles. Sometimes we had to be called back from doing something either dangerous to ourselves or annoying to others. We played a lot in the sea, and although I was the only member of the family who could not swim, the others were good about trying to keep me in the game, and I loved all the splashing. I made as many friends in the sea as I did on the beach, usually by getting into splashing-fights.

In the course of writing this book I have tried to stop myself from launching too often into passages with 'Words cannot express . . .' or 'I find it difficult to describe . . .', because they apply to so many of the things I am writing about, and are not helpful to the reader. It is obvious that we do not live in words, and that any attempt to transmute the tingle and smack of lived experience into language loses something essential to it. Even so, I have not so far felt the difficulty as much as I do now. The happiness of those holidays is something that, indeed, cannot be conveyed in words: the openness and freedom; the family together all the time, especially me with my father; the active dedication to having fun all day, every day, day after day, in circumstances intended to further that end; the cosy luxury of the boarding house; the vast sea and limitless blue sky, so unrelated to my normal environment; the beach, the pier, the other children; the sheer thrill and exhilaration of it all. And these were just those early holidays on the East Coast. The ones we went on to take later in the West Country were even better.

My father seems to have felt that we had come to the end of the simple bucket-and-spade holiday; and although I felt at the time that I would have been happy to go on with it for the rest of my life he was probably right. He wanted us to go somewhere different, somewhere less resorty, and do different things. So the next summer we went to Lyme Regis, in Dorset. Although famous as a beauty spot it was small, and not much frequented: there was little of the seaside resort about it in those days. We stayed with a fisherman whose wife took in bed-and-breakfast visitors. Early one morning he took us out in his boat and we, me included, fished for mackerel. The bay contained shoals of them, and they were childishly easy to catch – you did not even need bait, the mere glitter of your hook flashing through the water made them bite. From only a brief expedition we came back with a couple of dozen mackerel. I was thrilled: never before had I done anything like this. But everything about the holiday was different. Lyme was a beautiful place, and I had never before stayed in a beautiful place. Everyone kept saying how pretty it was, and even I could see that it was. It was also quiet and peaceful, and I, a townee to the marrow of my bones, had never been in a town where there were no crowds and no noise. Instead of the usual roustabout Edwardian pier there was the silent and massive stone Cobb that had been there since the Middle Ages. Usually it was deserted, and I loved walking out to the end of it and feeling myself to be in the middle of the sea. Everywhere in and around Lyme I felt in touch with basic, simple things in a way I had never done before, and it haunted me long afterwards.

My father was greatly taken with it, and with the whole idea of the West Country as a region to explore, so the next thing he decided was that he and my mother would have a holiday together in Devon without their children, so that they could move around freely just looking at things. The following summer Joan and I were lodged with a family called Taylor in the village of Uploders in Dorset (there was an Uploders and a Lower Loders) while our parents moved on to what were then no more than picturesque villages on and near the coast of North Devon, starting with Lynmouth, Lynton and Watersmeet. For me Uploders was a new life with a vengeance, the first time I had ever been in a village, or in the countryside at all, other than to pass through them in a vehicle.

Netta Taylor and her husband lived in a cottage with a small market garden, and he had a job two or three miles away in Bridport, I think at a brickworks. Every morning she would make up his lunch box in a biscuit tin, in which she put sandwiches and a flask of tea, and off he would go on his bike, while she stayed at home and worked in the garden. They had a son Roy, a year younger than me. He was a kind of boy I had never seen before. An only child, he had been engulfed with love since birth, in a small, quiet, safe environment, had met only a handful of people in his life, and was deeply shy. When the Magees descended he could not look at us but went bright red in the face and buried his head in his mother's skirts – and went on trying to keep it there when she moved, so that he was staggering around the room blindly and backwards in a doubled over position, his face hidden. To my incredulous eye it looked hilarious, like a comedian in a silent film, and I laughed as spontaneously as I would have done at Charlie Chaplin. Instantly my mother squashed me; but I went on eyeing this phenomenon with wonder and contempt. He had, I could not believe it, pom-poms hanging from his shirt collar. (He was dressed up to meet us, I now realise.) He presented himself to me as the last word in soft touches, the ultimate patsy. As I looked at him I found myself thinking that whatever he had that I wanted would be mine. My mother read these thoughts with experienced accuracy, and before she left she took me to one side and warned me in her coldest, toughest manner that if, when she and my father came back to collect me, they were told that I had hit Roy and taken his things there would be hell to pay. I needed always to remember, she said, that he was younger than me. I knew enough to take serious notice of a warning from this source, so I disregarded Roy from that moment on; and he made it easy for me by keeping well out of my way.

I went off every day and played with the roughest kids in the village, the children Roy was forbidden to play with – and very congenial they were. They would have made good Hoxtonians. From the market gardens and surrounding farms they stole anything they could get away with: their market gardens were my market stalls, and their farms my wood-yards: they were fellow spirits operating in a different environment. They taught me how to make my own bow and arrows, and also my own catapult, sturdier and more powerful than those that were sold in toy shops (which did indeed look like toys by comparison); and also what sticks of wood would hollow out to make the best pea-shooters. We enjoyed ourselves frightening the cows and sheep, and gazing with respectful awe at the bull. We loved watching grown-up men working, and knew which farmyards we could go to where they would talk to us, perhaps even toss a goody in our direction, and not just shoo us away. These children had been climbing trees all their lives, something I had never had a chance to do, and they could shimmy around high up in them like monkeys. They were used to ranging over far distances freely, with others or alone, across fields and hedges, gates and stiles, in places where there was nobody else around. I joined them in all this, and it was a great adventure for me. Everything, but everything, was so different from what I had known, even the houses and the roads; and the open countryside was incredible. The farthest afield we went was to Eggardon Hill, which they pronounced Egg'don and which looked to me like a mountainous green boiled egg that had thumped down into earth from outer space, pointy-rounded, so sharp-sided it tired you completely out to climb it, and almost as difficult to come down as get up (and then you still had to face the long walk home). I formed the assumption that the whole of England from London to the sea in all directions was like the country round Uploders. Londoners always divided Britain into 'London and the country' as if that was all there was, and this was the country. If you didn't live in London, or at the seaside, you lived here. I knew there were one or two untypical towns in the country, like Newcastle and Bristol, but basically non-London was this, I thought.

That summer must have been a hot one, because an all-pervading memory is of a heavy, almost intoxicating drowsiness hanging over everything, thick with the buzzing of insects. The smells were heavy too, unfamiliar, more powerful than open-air smells in London – when I was back home afterwards the strongest single impression I retained of life in the countryside was the engaging smelliness of it all. And it had all been new to me down to the smallest details: just being in fields, lying in long grass, catching wasps and butterflies – or, back in the cottage, living on a stone floor, pumping water in the kitchen, looking through a window at a garden. I had never seen anyone have a lunch box, or leave for work on a bike. Mr Taylor once took me somewhere on the crossbar of his bike, and I had never sat on one before. He got angry with me for my fidgetiness. 'You'll have us under a car if you don't sit still.' I was a highly strung child, never still for ten seconds, and actually, I think, pretty jerky, but I had no idea that I was moving around all the time. I believed that I *was* sitting still, and that Mr Taylor was just making a fuss. I had exactly the same trouble with barbers.

The village street ran downhill, and along one side of it trickled a firm little stream of clear spring water. At a couple of places this splashed out above ground from a pipe, and at these points the villagers, many of whom had neither pump nor tap in their homes, filled buckets. Buckets and pails were a great feature of life. I kept seeing milk being carried around in pails. It was like no other milk I had tasted: as thick as cream all the way through, and not white but yellow. There were places where rows of huge urns of it were regularly left all by themselves at the roadside for collection. This puzzled me: how could everybody so take it for granted that these would not be stolen? It seemed to me almost an offence against nature that they were not, so I fantasised about putting this right by hijacking the milk urns.

While I was in Uploders a gymkhana (delicious word, I thought) was held. All the winners in the riding events seemed to come from two families, one called Bishop and the other, if I remember rightly, Clark. Everything ended up as the Bishops versus the Clarks, in events involving riders who ranged in age from my grand-parents to me. It gave me pleasure to see children of my own age riding real horses. I liked their clothes, too, especially the jodh-purs and hard black hats. I wished I could have been up there on horseback too. As it was, my active pleasures were confined to the funfair; but that was pretty good as well. The village children were straggling around it in twos and threes, trying out the various sideshows. I prospered at the coconut shy, being an accurate and forceful thrower, and walked around clutching coconuts. Joan had gone off somewhere to run in a race. Not wanting to leave her purse with her clothes on the grass she had given it to me to look after. Suddenly the man running the fête summoned all of us boys around him and informed us with mock militariness that the official teatime in the marquee had come to an end, so there was no more tea for grown-ups, but he wanted all the food and drink finished up, so it was ours now, free, and we must absolutely make sure not a crumb of it would remain. That was an order. The boys gave a '*whoop!*' and waved their fists in the air, and hared off to beat one another to the tent, their bodies doubling into a sprint.

I remained standing near the man, taking it utterly for granted that what he had said did not include me, assuming that if I moved he would instantly send me sprawling with a swipe round the head, and bawl: 'I don't mean *you!*' Roy Taylor, who had positioned himself beside me, saw that I hung back, so he hung back as well – at which the man, who knew him, beamed down at him and said gruffly: 'Go on, go on!' So Roy hurtled off after the others.

The man then walked away to attend to the next thing, and I was left standing there alone. I did not dare go to the tent. I could not understand why. There was no one to stop me. The only people there would be other boys whom I knew already and was friends with. But I had not the courage to go. I was baffled by it myself, and dismayed with myself. My most poignant feeling was an uncomprehending astonishment at the instantness and lack of fear, or even hesitation, with which all the boys had assumed that it would be okay for them to rush off and demolish the tea. Even a little squirt like Roy Taylor had the guts to go – by himself, too, not with the others. And I had not. I was perplexed and depressed, and simply did not know what to do with myself. Clutching my coconuts, I wandered off disconsolately alone into the crowd. My feet, all by themselves, made their way to the coconut shy. I had long ago spent all my money, but now I remembered that I had my sister's purse in my pocket. I took it out and looked inside, and was amazed to see how much it contained – all her money for the whole of our holiday. At once, frenetically, I began spending it on the coconut shy. I did not hit a single coconut, and I spent all the money. After that it was like waiting for execution. Horrified by what I had done, and appalled at the prospect of having to tell it to Joan, I sat on the grass and waited – waited what seemed like for ever, with my knees up and my chin in my hands. When she came, and I broke the news, she was shattered. She could not believe, still less could she understand, what

I had done. But I had done it, and that was that. I told her, to provide myself with a pathetic shred of justification, that it was with her money that I had won the coconuts I was holding, and tried to give them to her, but she angrily refused to touch them.

The culmination of the holiday was our return home. For some reason our parents did not collect us, as we had been told they would; I expect they had a blazing row and went straight back to London, probably separately. In any case, Joan and I had to go back to London alone, and were allowed to make the long rail journey unsupervised. This was thrilling for both of us, she being ten and I seven. (One of several things that attach a date to that year is that we had been into Bridport with the Taylors to see a new film called *With a Banjo on my Knee*. It was, incidentally, the first film in which I saw Barbara Stanwyck: I remember liking the way she sang, though I have no recollection of ever hearing her sing again. That film was made in 1936, so our time in Uploders must have been the summer of 1937.) On the unforgettable return journey we had to change trains at Yeovil, and that made the adventure all the more hazardous and exciting. The Taylors had given Joan as big an armful of flowers as she could carry, to give to our parents, and this made it almost impossible for us to cope with our luggage. The guard on the first train, the local one, had been tipped off to help us, and did, so we had managed so far. And of course we managed again. Rail journeys in those days took much longer than they do now, and this one seemed to take all day. Our compartments were stiflingly hot, and by the time we arrived in London the flowers were hopelessly wilted, not worth the trouble of carrying. But the journey itself was one of the most tremendous experiences we had ever had.

Our parents had hoped that if only they could get away from their children they might be able to draw closer together. But it did not happen, and I believe it now became clearer to them that their marriage was never going to work. Certainly they never again attempted to go off anywhere alone together. But their experiences in Devon had a side-effect which, though trivial by comparison with their marriage's survival, was considerable in its effect on the life of the family: they persuaded my father that the only way to travel around somewhere like the West Country, looking at interesting places, was by car. So he decided he needed a car.

Not many families in the Britain of those days had cars. In places like Hoxton there were scarcely any at all. Among the trading community a slow changeover from horse-drawn vehicles to vans was beginning to occur in the middle and late '30s, so a few tired-looking second-hand vans could be seen parked further up Hoxton Street during hours when the stalls were not there; but the change was still in its infancy. The only person I knew with a car, apart from some of the commercial travellers who came to our shop (and not all of them), was Norman's father, Albert Tillson, in the sweet shop two doors away. He ran a little wholesale business on the side, selling cigarettes to traders who operated on so small a scale that proper wholesalers could not be bothered to deal with them – such people as made things available to neighbours from supplies kept in their living-room. It was from these beginnings that many shops in poor areas developed, and the shops themselves were often conversions of what had formerly been living-rooms fronting the street. Most of Albert's customers of this kind were in Leyton, so he bought a little Morris Seven to buzz around them quickly. Norman often accompanied him on these trips, and I went several times. They were my first visits to Leyton, and my first acquaintance with those later-familiar streets.

Whether Albert Tillson's having a car had any influence on my father I do not know. It may have done, once he had formed the desire for one, because there it was, staring him in the face every day from its parking place only a few yards from our front door. At all events, he set his heart on one. This immediately caused ructions between him and my mother. She was implacably opposed to spending so much money on something we had done perfectly without up to now, when what we really needed was 'a decent home'. Anyway, what would we do with a car if we had it – where would we go? Surely he was not thinking of buying one just to use once a year on our holidays? She was in permanent revolt against our living conditions, insisting that these could be immeasurably improved if only we took seriously the need to do so – which my father, she said, having lived in them all his life, did not. Given the fact that, when the *Luftwaffe* bombed us out four years later, we moved into a roomy modern flat, she may have had a point – though it was probably only the improvement in living standards brought about by the war that enabled us to afford the flat. I suspect the truth is that my father, not having much money, wanted to spend what he did have on the enjoyment of living – sport, music, theatre, books, opera, ballet, day-trips, holidays – and was not prepared to forgo these in order to have a higher material standard. Of course he would have liked both. The huge boost to the economy, and to the living standards of most of the population, that came with the war – when my father found himself doing two jobs, and then my mother went out to work – enabled us to have both. But before the war he had to choose, and this being so he was in no doubt where his choice lay.

Since even from his point of view there was no purpose in having a car if he could not drive it, he started taking driving lessons. I became emotionally involved in the will-he-won't-he drama of whether he was going to pass the test, and when he returned home from taking it I went out towards Hyde Road to meet him. I retain a sharply etched picture of him as he walked towards me in his gingery-brown raglan overcoat, his face unrevealing. 'Did you pass, Dad?' I shouted to him as I approached from a distance. He smiled and looked down, and nodded without saying anything. He was so pleased he could scarcely speak.

There followed the most earnest high-betting commitment he ever embarked on. In order to buy a car he needed to win more money than he had ever possessed at one time. What risks were taken to do this, and what sacrifices made, I do not know, but he won his car – a fawn-coloured two-door Austin Ten, second-hand, registration number AUV 917. When I asked him how much it cost he was uncharacteristically coy, and would not give me an answer at first. I persisted, and he said: 'Well, I'll give you a clue. There's a two in the number. And a five.' 'Fifty-two pounds,' I shouted. He looked at me with surprise, and murmured quietly and shyly: 'Yes.' This was not his normal way of behaving. Years later, after his death, when I was grown up, I made some reference in conversation with my mother to his having paid fifty-two pounds for the car, and she said: 'Fifty-two pounds? Good God no! He didn't pay anything like as much as that. It was twenty-five.' My belief is that he lied to her – or, more likely, to avoid literally telling a lie, played this coy game with her in a way that caused her to draw the wrong conclusion.

The first time we as a family drove out in the car was on a day-trip to Oxford, one Sunday. Of Oxford I remember nothing at all. What I remember is being sick in the car. As was always to be the case, my parents were in the two front seats and I was with Joan in the back. There was a long period on the journey during which I felt sick but was afraid to say so, because I assumed I would be shouted at and told I had no right to feel sick, and had to jolly well not feel sick. Then suddenly I vomited. There was a tremendous fuss about this, and I really was shouted at well and truly. My father told me that in future, if I felt sick, I had only to tell him, and he would stop the car and let me out to be sick at the roadside. I was astounded to be told that it would be all right to be sick, and even all right to say I was going to be sick. This was an attitude I had not encountered before. But I was pleased to go along with it, and it worked. For the rest of my childhood

I was car-sick on every journey as a matter of course, and it caused almost no bother, not even to me: I did not think about it until I actually started to feel sick, and then I would tell my father, and he would stop the car, I would get out and put two fingers down my throat to make myself sick, after which I felt fine again and forgot all about it. It became a routine.

We often drove out on Sundays to places of interest near London; and always on bank holidays, on whichever day there was no football match. I was greatly impressed by the fact that coming back invariably felt shorter than going out. It was on these return journeys that I became aware that I had something close to total recall. Going out I would gaze with absorbed fascination at everything we passed – every single shop, house, pub, hoarding, and so on – and coming back I would not only recognise them individually but remember the order they came in, for instance the order of the shops in a long high street. It makes me wonder whether I was brushed with a touch of autism. Be that as it may, I took in almost everything, and remembered not only it but where it was in relation to other things. And it was involuntary. It made car journeys marvellously interesting for me. Another new world, the world of the road, entered into my world; and it was different every time.

Motoring through all the neighbouring areas to destinations that were sometimes not far away – Epping Forest, for instance – made me begin to see Hoxton in some sort of context. We always set out from Hoxton, and returned to Hoxton, and each time I would be seeing it in relation to somewhere else, not only as to where it was but also as to its character. It had always been my world, but the realisation began to dawn on me that Hoxton was not everywhere. Day-trips did more to teach me this than summer holidays, because those were in such total contrast with my normality that I might as well have been on the other side of the moon. Day-tripping insinuated something quite different, namely the continuity of Hoxton with other places, the way it was set in the warp and woof of everywhere else. I became used to the idea that people lived elsewhere, and in different *sorts* of places; and although the fact that they did not live in Hoxton was obviously a misfortune that you would never actually wish on anybody I became familiar with it as a fact.

Out on the open road we were in a world that was motoring and nothing else. There were two motorists' organisations with mass membership, the Automobile Association and the Royal Automobile Club. My father chose the AA (which automatically led me to think it must be better). It employed roving mechanics who patrolled the roads on motorbikes, with sidecars containing their kit: if you wanted their help you flagged one down and he fixed you up there and then. They wore military-style uniforms, complete with peaked cap and black leather gloves, and if on the front of your car you carried an AA badge they saluted you as they passed. My father turned out to be an excellent driver, but he never learnt how a car worked, so we used these mechanics a lot. The car was perpetually serviced on the road, and I always felt that this added to the interest of the journey.

There was amazingly little traffic by the standards of today, and motoring was a leisurely activity, quiet and restful: there was plenty of opportunity to look around. Many were the places of interest we visited in the Home Counties, and soon we had driven through most of what might be called London's countryside. Once visited, each place became a possession, a place I had now been to and knew, so that henceforth any reference to it brought the actual place itself before my mind. On the busier roads innumerable houses had boards outside advertising bed and breakfast: the lowest rate was two shillings, and the sort of places we stayed in cost two and sixpence, though we avoided spending the night away from home if at all possible. We never used the car for any destination in London: for those we still went by bus or tube.

People used their cars very differently then from now. For instance, it was common, if not normal, for private motorists to lay their cars up for the winter, and then take them out again in the spring. We did this too. But there was no doubt about it, the great event of the motoring year was our summer holiday, and it had been for this above all that my father had bought the car in the first place.

He thought, correctly, that having a car would enable us to fuse a bucket-and-spade holiday with a holiday spent visiting beauty spots, especially as we would be spreading it over a fortnight, not just a week. He chose Torquay as our base, and asked the AA to recommend the most scenic route to it that would pass through Uploders and Lyme Regis. And in the summer of 1938 we motored down through unspoiled countryside, visiting old friends on the way and chuntering around what even to me at the age of eight now seemed like old haunts. Torquay, when we got there, was big and grand: it was more spectacular visually than the other resorts I had seen, and I was impressed by its uncluttered openness, the fact that there were so many parks and public gardens in which things were laid on for us to do. I liked its luxury hotels, and all the palm trees. And we were lucky with our boarding house, which was unusually bright and comfortable – and where for the first time I saw a dinner gong. The man let me do the necessary banging on this each six o'clock, and it was the most enjoyable moment of the day. There was a family from the North staying in the same house, and I had never before heard North Country accents in the flesh, so to speak, though I had heard them from music-hall performers. I have always remembered the moment when – after we had woken up one morning to find flood water pouring down the street, and had all gone out to the front steps to look at it – a young woman standing there said to me: 'Ee, it's *ter*rible!' Here was a marvellous new world in sound.

We alternated days on the beach with days out and about in

the car, sometimes driving along the coast to deserted coves with golden beaches, sometimes to other resorts, and sometimes inland. We decided that Paignton's beach was better than Torquay's, so the following year we made Paignton our base, and had an even more enjoyable holiday of a similar kind, visiting a whole new lot of places, including those we wished we had seen the previous year. I do not remember what we did in which year, but the two holidays together have provided me with lasting memories: the thick redness of the Devon earth; those deserted coves; the unforgettable sight of a regatta; country villages asleep during the day, untouched by modernity; thatched cottages; cream teas; place names like Newton Poppleford (which I have used ever since to stand for any tiny out-of-the-way place); the bleakness of Dartmoor even in summer. I was thrilled to see Dartmoor prison, which I had read so much about in my comics. We visited Buckfast Abbey, where I saw monks for the first time, building their own church. I was riveted by the sight of a horse being shod by a blacksmith in Cockington forge: the sparks shot out like bullets every time the hammer hit the hoof, and the red-hot metal gasped and sizzled when it plunged into water. We went to a fête (and I have an idea to the races too) at Newton Abbot. We watched a cricket match at which one of the captains had a marvellously *haw-haw* face and voice, and talked like the Western Brothers. His only concern was not to be run out by his partner – '*Wait! Wait! Only one run!*' He obviously had no idea he was ludicrous, and was a great pleasure to watch. In a big tent out in a field one evening we went to a circus; and when the clown asked for one of the children to come up and help him I went, only to make a complete fool of myself: I couldn't blow up the balloon, couldn't stay on the revolving table, couldn't do anything right. The audience laughed indulgently all the time, but it was like family laughter, and I assumed they were laughing at the clown, which after all is what clowns are for. My father told me afterwards that he had overheard two people wondering aloud on the way out whether I was part of the act. (Possibly he did, but I doubt it.) The things about the whole experience that made the most lasting impression on me were the giant multi-coloured pom-poms on the clown's shoes, and the fact that they were not shoes but slippers.

CHAPTER SIXTEEN

The first public event I remember is the Silver Jubilee of King George V in May 1935. This is because of the street parties. Bunting was hung out over the road between the houses in all the little residential streets round us, and for a day or two a Christmas-like atmosphere reigned, including our having a holiday from school. The children had their own separate street parties. Long tables were set out down the middle of the road, and we all sat down to a splendid tea, at which each of us was given a mug with pictures of the king and queen on it. You drank your tea out of this brand new mug, and then took it home – it was yours. Everyone said what a wonderful thing it was that the king had been there so long. Then eight months later he died. The phrase 'the nation was plunged into mourning' had more truth in it then than now: people cared, and talked about it, so much so that even at the age of five I experienced it as an important event.

My father showed me the huge pictures of the king's funeral in the newspapers, pictures in which nearly everything was black. This led him to point out other pictures in the same papers, and tell me about those too. A war was going on in a place called Abyssinia. I had heard about this, because it had caused the word 'Abyssinia' to become slang among us boys for 'I'll be seeing you' (we pronounced the two almost the same anyway). My father explained to me in almost fairy-story terms that there was a country called Italy that was ruled over by a Bad Man called Mussolini, who had attacked Abyssinia, which was full of people who were so poor that they had no chance of winning. He based the story on the pictures, and played up the Bad Man killing the Little People aspect of it; and what with that and the fact that it was my father telling me, I was engrossed. Not only was this a good story, it was real, actually happening. Would the Bad Man get his deserts? If so, who was going to give him what for, if the Abyssinians couldn't? My obvious interest led my father to do something for which I remain permanently grateful: he developed a habit of telling me the big news story of the day by explaining the pictures in the newspapers, always keeping the story simple, and always letting me know what he hoped would happen, thus filling the situation with suspense. Because of this I actually *remember*, directly, events like the Abdication and the Spanish Civil War, and figures like Franco, and the Hitler of the 1930s – these were all alive for me when they were current news. And in many cases the view I got of them was not far from the one I would take today. My father was, I think, a natural liberal who thought of himself as a socialist; and in foreign affairs he was first and foremost anti-Fascist. This caused him to cast Mussolini, Franco and Hitler as super-villains, which seems to me not a wrong assessment. It made them interesting, too. About Stalin and Russia he was ambivalent: on the one hand Russia was trying to be something called socialist, which he thought was Good, but on the other hand Stalin was a dictator, and that was Very Bad. In other words Russia was trying to be Good but had fallen into the power of a Bad Man, so things there were actually Bad even though they were supposed to be Good. With luck, though, and because they were trying so hard, things there might become Good when the Bad Man was no longer around. Therefore we must not be *anti* Russia, we should stand up for it if other people ran it down, because they were showing they didn't realise it was *meant* to be Good and was *going* to be

Good. Largely because what my father said was gospel so far as I was concerned, some recognisable version of this view of the Soviet Union, and of Communism generally, remained mine until my late teens.

In the days before television, when radio was still in its infancy, people's awareness of a world outside their own was fed mostly by newspapers. I was aware of the beginning of television in November 1936, but I remember it as a newspaper event. For a long time there were exceedingly few people with television sets, and transmission was suspended during the war anyway, so it was years before I saw a television set other than those on display in shop windows. Our daily paper was the *News Chronicle,* a liberal one that dealt with serious issues seriously yet in a popular style. It was excellent, actually, and since its demise no other paper has played that role. On Sundays we had the *Sunday Times* and *Reynolds News,* a well-meaning socialist paper owned by the Co-op. On weekday afternoons successive editions of London's three evening papers (the cry '*Star, News and Standard!*' was heard many times a day from boys passing in the street outside) came flowing into the shop, with the racing results. *The Star* was, I believe, a sister paper of the *News Chronicle,* and was the best one for the racing results, so my father preferred it; but we saw plenty of all three. So there were always lots of newspapers around. This abundance of papers was very much part of the family's way of life – everyone seemed to spend a lot of time reading newspapers and talking about what was in them. My mother complained constantly about the way they cluttered the place up. When I think of my father and grandfather in the shop, there are four activities I remember them in more often than any others, apart from talking to me: serving customers, standing in the doorway, smoking and reading newspapers.

The death of George V brought to the throne the at-first popular Edward, Prince of Wales. Suddenly, the populace at large was engulfed in the story of his love affair with a married woman, who had only just got a divorce, and was not even English anyway but American. I heard it said that there were many people who insisted that a woman like that could never be Queen of England, but all the people I actually heard express a view were on Edward's side: the people of Hoxton, at least, wanted him to have his way. And so did us children. Why should he not marry the woman he wanted to, and go on being king, was what we wanted to know. It was the first time for generations that the 'scandalous' sex-life of a sovereign had become public. People of all ages found it irresistible to talk about, and it entered even into schoolboy jokes and schoolgirl skipping chants. My father said the powers that be were using Mrs Simpson as an excuse to get rid of Edward because he was sympathetic to the unemployed, and he ought not to give way to them. When he did we were devastated. My father had all along said that they would never let him get away with it; but the children had not expected him to lose, because, after all, he was the king. We were even glummer when, in his place, we got someone nobody had heard of, called King George VI. However, for his coronation there turned out to be street parties the same as there had been for his father's jubilee less than two years before, and that was jolly good – bunting everywhere, a holiday from school, a sit-down tea in the middle of the road, and a mug with a picture of the king and queen on to take home and keep. It was an identical replay, no doubt based on the same set of instructions. Both my street parties were in Phillipp Street, with children from my school; and I believe both were paid for by the London County Council, because both mugs had the LCC crest on them on the opposite side from the pictures of the royals.

Before and during the Second World War people in general were patriotic in a way that they never again went back to being, and this included having a John Bull-ish attitude to the royal family. It was taken for granted that England was superior to other nations, and that the English were superior to other people – and that the British Empire was the leading force for good in the world, because it provided decent government to people who were not yet developed enough to govern themselves, training them for eventual self-government, when they would become democracies like us. Only people of ill will could possibly object to any of this – but, as the third verse of the national anthem said, 'Confound their politics, frustrate their knavish tricks'. The second verse of *Rule Britannia* had it about right: 'The nations not so blest as thee must in their turn to tyrants fall, while thou shalt flourish great and free, the dread and envy of them all.' In the minds of most English people, that is how things were. And the personal embodiment of it all was the king. Many people hung portraits of the king and queen in their homes – you could walk into a slum and see a picture of the king on the wall, sometimes a page torn from a newspaper. All this was connected with people's sense of their own unique importance as English people. They might be poor, but, for all that, they were superior to everybody else. In this way the king functioned as a buttress to the self-esteem of the ordinary English. It was because he was our king that he governed a third of the world, so his glory was ours. Every year the nation celebrated Empire Day. At school the headmaster asked the boys to arrive on that day wearing anything uniform-like that we could lay our hands on, to show that we were an imperial people – a Cub's cap would do, he said. I belonged to something called the Lifeboys, which was a cadet organisation of the Boy's Brigade, just as the Cubs were a cadet organisation of the Boy Scouts; and as a Lifeboy I had a sort of sailor's hat: so I wore that, and walked about all day wearing it. Other boys did the same. It appears grotesque now, but it was normal behaviour at the time.

Along with these imperialist assumptions went a whole lot of other attitudes. Foreigners, because they were different from us,

were funny, as well as unfortunate, and were not to be trusted –
in comics the villain was often a foreigner, the hero never.
Everyone who was not white was inferior to everyone who was;
and the definition of 'not white' was extreme: it included Latins,
who were dagoes – so, as someone famously put it, 'Wogs begin
at Calais'. Because of all this, Londoners took it for granted that
London was the capital of the civilised world. My father told me
that Piccadilly Circus had been called 'the hub of the universe',
and that if you stood in it for long enough, watching the people
go by, you would sooner or later see everybody. I grew up taking
it as a fact that London was the most important place in the world,
and the only serious place to live in.

My feelings about London consisted not only of wrong ideas
but also a deep emotional attachment to the real place. I started
acquiring a sense of its past surprisingly early, partly through
school, partly through the Geffrye Museum in Kingsland Road.
This long, beautiful row of almshouses, dating from the early eighteenth century, displayed a series of ordinary English rooms as
they had been from Elizabethan times to the present day. The
social level chosen had to be one that would go with small rooms,
and so was that of small-time London merchants, people who
made a modest living in trade in the City up the road. Because
it was City-oriented, yet in a positive way ungrand, it showed me
the past of a London I recognised, and I could see its continuity
with the present. I found it compellingly interesting. I identified
with it personally, and thought of it as showing me my own history.
And because the museum was free I dropped in many times, often
with Norman, sometimes alone. I got to know it by heart, so to
speak. I felt a special affinity with Restoration London. The look
of it all – the clothes, the furniture, the pictures of other buildings – had deep-rooted appeal for me, as if they constituted an
alternative life to my own; and what little history of it I picked up
was pleasingly dramatic: the Great Plague, the Great Fire.

> In sixteen hundred and sixty-five
> There was hardly a soul who was left alive.
>
> In sixteen hundred and sixty-six
> The whole of London burnt like sticks.

This was something I was learning at school. Oddly, as it now seems, the only history we learnt at the Edmund Halley was London's history – somebody there probably had a theory that this was the only history that would interest us. But I suspect that this was a peculiarity of my school – at Norman's they were more international in their outlook, and it was from him that I first discovered that

> In fourteen hundred and ninety-two
> Columbus crossed the ocean blue
> And there he found America too.

The London of my childhood was about to suffer inflictions as great as the Great Plague and the Great Fire. The blitz began when I was ten, and in it 30,000 Londoners were killed and a third of the buildings in the City destroyed. Something like a third of Hoxton was destroyed too, including many whole streets; and we as a family were bombed out of our home. All this lay only just out of sight in the near future. But at the time, in the '30s, the worst London disaster I was aware of was nothing more than the Crystal Palace fire. The chief building of the Great Exhibition of 1851, which, after the Exhibition, had been moved to South London to be preserved, burnt to the ground in 1936 in a spectacular conflagration. Even as far away as us in Hoxton, families went out into the streets to look at the redness in the sky. Doing that is all I remember of it now – that and people talking about it for days afterwards.

The earliest awareness I had of the existence of forces that were going to bring down in wholesale destruction the London I knew must have been also my earliest awareness of the Blackshirts. That is what the members of the British Union of Fascists, the political party founded by Sir Oswald Mosley, were called by everyone, including themselves. It was also what they called their first newspaper, *Blackshirt*. They had a tremendous impact even on us children in the area I lived in. Unlike Mussolini and Hitler, who came from unprivileged backgrounds, Mosley was a rich aristocrat, a sixth baronet, educated at Winchester and Sandhurst and the inheritor of a fortune while still a young man. He was a demagogue of rare charisma. I heard him speak many times when I was a child, and again after the war when I was grown up – and then met him. On one occasion I spent a whole day with him at his home in France, a day during which we talked at length about, among other things, his activities in Shoreditch during the 1930s.

As a young man, Mosley was the wonder-boy of British politics: a tall, imposing, sinisterly handsome figure of dangerous charm, highly attractive to women, an outstanding public speaker. After fighting, with genuine bravery, in the First World War he was elected to the House of Commons as its youngest member at the age of twenty-three, and served there first as a Conservative, then Independent, then Labour MP. In 1929, still only thirty-three, he was appointed Chancellor of the Duchy of Lancaster in the Labour Government formed in that year – after having been seriously considered for the job of Foreign Secretary. At that stage it appeared self-evident that he was a probable future party leader and prime minister.

But something happened. There was some deep instability in his character, as might have been suggested already by his too-frequent changes of political allegiance, and his privately notorious, apparently compulsive womanising. My guess is that what triggered the political change was his experience, in the 1929–31

Government, of being right about central economic policy when all his colleagues were wrong. The Government had found itself trapped in a world economic crisis. In these conditions it seemed obvious to everyone else in the Government that what had to be done, however unpalatable, was to drastically reduce public spending. Mosley, however, was a Keynesian before Keynes, and believed – rightly, as it turned out – that the proper policy was to implement a massive programme of public works, thereby creating employment on a large scale and pumping purchasing-power into the economy, while at the same time improving the social super-structure. It was what Roosevelt did with such success in the United States, as the New Deal. But in the British Government Mosley's was a lone voice, and he lost the battle.

Britain plunged deeper into recession as a result. I believe that this created in Mosley an overwhelming conviction that if only he had the power to implement his policies without the constraints of other politicians or parties it would be the best thing for the country. So he embarked on a political course aimed at estab-lishing himself as a dictator. His model was Mussolini, who, after a prominent career as a socialist, had created an independent Fascist movement and come to power in a government in which he was Prime Minister, Foreign Secretary and Minister of the Interior. Even the trappings of the British Union of Fascists were in imitation of the Italian movement – the black shirts and uniforms, the Roman salute, the use of the word 'Fascist' itself, which Mussolini had introduced. Mosley went for meetings with Mussolini in Rome, and the Italian dictator gave his movement regular and secret financial support. While these things were going on, Hitler, another admirer of Mussolini at that time, another would-be dictator who consciously learnt from him, came to power in Germany. It was subsequently alleged that Hitler gave Mosley secret support too, but I do not believe this to be true in the same significant sense. They met in Berlin twice; and on the second occasion Mosley got married secretly in Goebbels' house to Diana Mitford, his second wife. The two were entertained to dinner privately after the ceremony by Hitler; and what has come out since indicates that Hitler was not impressed by Mosley, did not believe that he was going to come to power in England, but believed that any future government in London that might be sympathetic (not to say subservient) to the Nazis would be led by politicians of an altogether different stamp, namely appeasers in the Conservative Party. He regarded money spent on Mosley as money thrown away.

However, Mosley was impressed by Hitler. German influences on him and his movement began to appear alongside the Italian ones, for instance heavy, belted raincoats and red armbands with a flash-and-circle emblem. Far and away the most substantial thing that Mosley took up from Hitler was the use of anti-semitism as a political instrument. He had come to believe that the only way to impassion a whole people was by arousing them against a perceived enemy, and he saw Hitler as having successfully done this in Germany by the use of anti-semitism. He imagined he could do it in Britain. But whereas Hitler had an emotionally felt hatred of Jews, and what is more an emotionally felt desire to wipe them out, with Mosley it was a cynical calculation. In himself, I believe, he was no more anti-semitic than the general social circles in which he moved. But he was more than willing to exploit anti-semitism if he thought it would carry him to power on its back – and it seemed to him that Hitler had shown how this could be done. It was a miscalculation. Or perhaps Hitler was right about him, and he was not a person who would have achieved power anyway. The full explanation, whatever it is, is bound to be complicated, but the fact is that Fascism in Britain was an almost total failure.

Mosley was determined, like Hitler and Mussolini before him, to come to power constitutionally, but his movement never succeeded in getting one single Member of Parliament elected, or even a local councillor. It never succeeded even in becoming a nationwide movement. It stirred up a great deal of activity in some areas, but little or none in others – in the whole of Scotland it only ever had one parliamentary candidate, if I remember rightly. At first, Mosley had despised the idea of getting involved in local politics – he was aiming for supreme power on a grand scale – but the thinness and patchiness of public response to him pushed him eventually into concentrating his efforts on those areas where he seemed to be having some success. This was already a response to failure, and after a couple more years his move-ment began to peter out altogether. It was on its last legs before the Second World War began. But that was not how it seemed if you happened to be living in one of the areas in which the Fascists concentrated their greatest efforts during that crucial couple of years. And it so happens that I was, albeit as a child, in one of the three boroughs where they were more active than anywhere else in Britain.

The situation is described in the book *The Fascists in Britain* by Colin Cross (selected quotations beginning on page 149):

It was in the East End of London, principally in Bethnal Green, Shoreditch and Stepney, that British Union from 1936 onwards at last found a mass following. This was the Old East End, shortly to receive a mortal blow in the air raids of 1940 and 1941 and to be essentially destroyed in the massive post-war building schemes . . . British Union never actually captured the East End. There the forces of anti-Fascism always remained stronger than those of Fascism. But what Mosley did do was to capture, especially among the young, enough support to become a serious contender for local power. His success was the more impressive against the background of the fact that a quarter of the population was

Jewish and implacably opposed to him. And he achieved it in a relatively short time . . . That the East End would prove the most fruitful area for its activities does not appear to have been foreseen by British Union . . . The East End successes changed the bias of the whole Movement . . . The effort British Union put into the East End was on a scale unprecedented in British politics. With open-air meetings every night, rallies every weekend, it was like a perpetual general election . . . Even the children joined in, Mosley forming Blackshirt cadets for youths aged between fifteen and eighteen and a Fascist Youth for children from eleven upwards. Gangs of Jewish and anti-Jewish children fought each other in school playgrounds, Joyce [William Joyce, later known as Lord Haw-Haw] commenting with satisfaction in *Action* how 'Jews and Blackshirts' had replaced 'Cowboys and Indians' as the favourite game.

This is how things were in Hoxton when I was seven and eight. Small as I was, awareness of the Blackshirts was part of my daily life. Their main meeting place in our area was just behind the shop, in Phillipp Street, which I had to pass along at least four times a day to and from school. They were not allowed to hold their meetings in the market, because that would cause an obstruc-tion, but they made use of the 'circus parade' method of adver-tising a meeting and raising an audience for it by marching through the whole length of the crowded market, starting at the other end, past our shop, and round the corner into Phillipp Street, where the meeting would then begin. Trailing along behind the marchers would straggle a long crowd gathered up through the market, mostly men and boys, very few women, virtu-ally no girls; and this would then constitute the audience. Innumerable times during those years I stood on the pavement and watched them march past in column of three, all dressed in black from head to foot. I found the blackness alienating, not attractive: it made these men look like the villains in cowboy films, who always wore black and rode black horses, whereas the hero always wore light-coloured clothes and rode a white horse. But they were satisfyingly formidable villains. Most of them held themselves proudly erect and marched snappily, their arms swinging shoulder high, keeping themselves in step by chanting loudly to a punchy, left–right–left marching rhythm: '*The Yids!* [beat] *The Yids!* [beat] *We gotta get ridda the Yids!* [beat]', over and over again, non-stop. I always wanted to follow them round to Phillipp Street and see the meeting, because there were always fights, but for the same reason my parents forbade me to go. I often went all the same, usually by not starting from home: if I knew a Blackshirt meeting was coming up I would go out somewhere else, and then from there to Phillipp Street. It gave me never-ending pleasure to see grown-up men fighting: it was like watching cowboy films come to life.

Of what was actually said at these meetings I understood hardly anything at all, but that did little to diminish my pleasure. It was like watching opera in an unknown language. Whatever it was they were putting over was basic, emotional, sentimental, melodramatic, and obviously important. A man in a black shirt (actually it was not a shirt but a tunic) stood on a little folding platform made on the same principle as the stepladder in our shop, and talked down to the crowd in a manner that was shouty and hectoring but at the same time pleading. The crowd was lively, and people in it would shout questions or objections back at the speaker, to which he would then respond – often he visibly rose to the questions, and appeared at his best in answering them. At some of the meetings an electric rumour would suddenly go round the crowd. 'He's coming! Mosley is coming! He's coming to speak at this meeting!' And then Mosley himself would sweep into the street with his entourage. A great cheer would go up, and as he walked straight into the middle of the crowd people jostled round him, wanting to shake his hand or just touch him, while the speaker up on the platform shouted words of welcome to the leader and announced that the platform would immediately be given over to him. Up he climbed, as if emerging from among the people themselves, and addressed them. He made a common practice of these surprise visits; it kept his people on their toes at all the meetings simultaneously, though he personally was able to speak at only a few of them; and he adored the gladiatorial acclaim that unscheduled arrivals provoked.

Even to my childishly ignorant eye and ear he was a different proposition from the other speakers. He looked vastly more impressive, and was in complete command of the crowd – no implied pleading from him. Also, I understood more of what he said. Most of it was still above my head, but there was something that got through. The essence of it, really, was: 'England for the English!' I grasped about two of his points. One was that floods of people who were not English were pouring into our country and taking away the jobs of English people, so that what we had to do now was kick them out and let the unemployed have their jobs back. The other was that, after we had done this, Britain would be *Great* Britain again. The first of these points was clear to me, but I found the second perplexing: since we were already the greatest nation on earth I did not see how we could become greater. But obviously he thought we could.

His crowd-control was masterly. Seeing it again years later, and discussing his methods with him, I came to understand his technique. There was quite a lot to it, but two things were particularly important. One is to start very quietly, so that the audience has to create a hush to hear what you are saying. This itself draws them all tightly together; and the thing then is to carry them all forward together, slowly and gradually, almost imperceptibly stepping up the volume, the tempo and the hard-hittingness, until by the time you reach the climax of your point or argument you are shouting as loud as you can, and using the maximum of gesture to incite an explosion of applause. This explosion must be allowed to rumble on for its full length – you must not interrupt it by starting to speak again. When it has died away altogether, even then you do not immediately resume speaking, as the crowd expects you to, but allow a few surprisingly long moments of complete and unexpected silence. This screws up the tension and expectancy of the crowd. Then you start again, but very quietly, as at the beginning, and repeat the cycle. This whole technique was, incidentally, Hitler's. In Mosley's later years it became formulaic to a point at which his gestures could appear unconnected with what he was saying, but I do not think this was so when he was in his prime: he seemed then to have the audience in the palm of his hand, and to be controlling them in the sort of way a conductor controls an orchestra.

The second striking aspect of his conscious technique had to do with his use of gesture. This was different from Hitler's, and better. None of his gestures were small – for instance he never, as almost all speakers do, wagged his finger at an audience. At a point where Hitler would wag a finger, Mosley would step forward on one foot and lunge towards his audience with his whole body, in a lithe, athletic-looking movement, one arm outstretched to its full length – and his head stretched forward along the line of the arm – the whole gesture culminating in a finger as firm and penetrating as a spear-point. Actually it was a fencing movement – he had been a champion fencer since his schooldays, and had fenced for Britain in the Empire Games of 1935. My description of it makes it sound stagy and over-exaggerated, but at an open-air meeting – or, I take it, in a large auditorium or arena – it did not seem so: it was done with elegance and compactness, and came across as appropriate and effective, though certainly melodramatic. The effectiveness was connected with the fact that the audience was responding to him as if he were an actor, in such a way that his body language was expressing something for them as well as to them.

Under the influence of my father as I was, I regarded Mosley as without question the supreme local baddie, the star villain of where we lived, in the same sort of way as Hitler, Franco and Mussolini were star villains elsewhere. The choice of all-black uniforms for his movement was a serious error (as, I am told, Mussolini's colleagues came to think, in retrospect) and also, in Mosley's case, so was the villain's moustache. But he was a star in spite of it all, a class act, and I found him enthralling to watch. There were other Blackshirt speakers who said crude, horrible things about Jews, and hurled four-letter words about them from the platform, but Mosley never did. I know now that he was saying anti-semitic things, but it was not in that crass way; and this being so they passed me by. Because of his fine-tuned control of the crowd it was always better behaved for him than for other speakers, at least at small local meetings such as those in Phillipp Street, which were the only ones I ever attended. When he was not there, and one of his bully-boys was up on the platform dishing out abuse, the crowd, as usual, behaved like the speaker, and was crude and abusive back. It was in that atmosphere that violent heckling used to break out, and then turn into fist fighting. And I enjoyed watching this even more than I enjoyed watching Mosley.

As an interested observer, I soon came to understand the practised way in which persistent hecklers were dealt with at these meetings. There was always a loose circle of minders hanging around on the edges of the crowd, not in uniform, and therefore looking like members of the audience; and if the speaker wanted a heckler removed he would flicker a glance in the direction of one of these, and three of four of them would close in on the heckler, pushing their way through the crowd towards him. One would always approach him from in front and one from behind. The one behind, unseen, grabbed the man's arms suddenly and pinned them to his side while at the same moment the one in front, who appeared to be coming up to him to remonstrate with him, kneed him in the testicles. As the heckler doubled over violently the one in front uppercut him in the face; and since the heckler was jerking into the blow it almost always did him serious damage. The two minders so far involved would then drag the man, doubled up and sometimes bleeding copiously from the face, out of the crowd to the empty belt on its edges, where they would either just dump him or hit him a few more times, or hand him over to other minders who were standing about. If it should happen at the point where the two minders attacked the heckler that someone standing nearby in the crowd, perhaps a companion, moved to the man's aid, he would find the third and fourth minders there waiting for him and immediately giving him the same treatment. It was smoothly worked out, and no doubt had been rehearsed in private. It seldom failed. The best thing, though, was when several members of the crowd turned against the minders simultaneously: then, for a few moments, there would be a fight on equal terms between two groups, or perhaps with even more goodies than baddies. There would then be a marvellous situation in which the speaker was trying to carry on with his speech while a fist fight involving eight or ten people was going on in the middle of his audience. But then the other minders on the periphery would move in, the fight would escalate, the meeting would break up, and most of the crowd would dissolve into the surrounding streets. At some point someone on the goodies' side might try to call in the police, but they seldom arrived before the street had cleared of its own accord.

It was not until many years later that I discovered that a large number of the back-up minders were not Blackshirts at all but local Hoxton roughs who had been used to working at the racetracks and were now being hired at seven shillings and sixpence a time. One of the people who has explained this to me is someone called Frank Hawkes, who was in the same class as me at school, a couple of years older. In the '30s his father, Nobby Hawkes, was a painter and decorator hired by the hour, which meant that he might work through a weekend at repainting some business premises and then have no work at all for a week or a fortnight. Theirs was a typical Hoxton situation. It was Nobby's wife and mother who kept the family going, especially his mother, Frank's grandmother, in whose house they all lived, and who actually brought Frank up. (This family pattern was a common one in Hoxton, and people often said that it was the women who kept everything together.) When Nobby had no work as a painter, which was most of the time, he did anything for a few bob at the racetracks – the dogs as well as the horses – and that was where he spent most of his days, usually as a bookie's minder. This too was casual labour, piece-work, and the jobs were handed out at two of the local pubs. (Three or four years later I got to know one of those and its publican well – my family slept in its beer cellar during air raids.) In almost every way Nobby Hawkes was a typical small-time Hoxton rough, staying out of prison by the skin of his teeth, more by good luck than judgement. He had been one of the foot soldiers in the Battle of Brighton in 1936, and had been arrested there by the police, but released without charge. Since then, with most of his erstwhile leaders and bosses in prison, times had been hard, and he was having to scratch around for a living. When at home he went down to the pub each evening in the hope that jobs would be handed out for the next day. 'This new bookie Mr Gold is going to want four people tomorrow at Newmarket. Ten bob for the day, and you'll be taken there and back. Who wants to go?' For Nobby and his pals the concentration of Fascist activity in the area came as a godsend. 'The Blackshirts want a dozen people in Dalston, Sunday morning. Seven-and-six. Who's on?' And that was how it worked. From the Fascists' point of view they got a dozen extra minders at a big meeting for a total cost of less than a fiver. And for the minders it was money for jam – a job they could walk to, where they might have to do nothing other than just stand around for a couple of hours. Seven-and-six for a Sunday morning! None of them had the slightest interest in politics; and if they voted at all, which I would guess most of them did not, they probably voted Labour.

The street politics of the Blackshirts in those years affected the whole life of the community down to the school playground. During the borough elections of 1937 most of the children in my school were singing, 'Vote, vote, vote for Mr Jeger', but there were some who sang 'Vote, vote, vote for Mr Mosley' (who was not a candidate). I remember playing Blackshirts in the school playground. And I have a specific memory of seeing a line of boys marching in single file, swinging their arms shoulder high and chanting: '*The Yids! The Yids! We gotta get ridda the Yids!*' and one of them, seeing a boy approaching their path, shouting: '*There's Buckley! He's a Yid! Let's get Buckley!*' and the line breaking up and the boys piling on to Buckley, who went down under a rain of blows squeaking plaintively: 'I'm not a Yid!'

All this colourful, high-profile, dramatic activity at so many different levels of life gave the impression that there was a great deal more support for the Fascists than there actually was. In the borough elections they did not even come second. Both of the Labour candidates in Shoreditch, where each party was required to put up two candidates, polled more than 11,000 votes, while each of the Fascist candidates, who came third, got about 2,500. And that year, 1937, represented the high-water mark of their success. In the elections for the London County Council six months later the Fascists came second in Shoreditch, but it was a very bad second; and after that it was downhill all the way.

By the end of the year the British Union of Fascists was splitting up into separate organisations. Among the figures leading the split was William Joyce, who had been one of the BUF's two candidates in Shoreditch. In this capacity he had come into our shop, ostensibly to buy something but actually to canvas. Needless to say, we did not have what he wanted. Describing this incident to me during the war – when Joyce was nationally famous as 'Lord Haw-Haw', Hitler's chief broadcaster to Britain from Berlin (for which he was subsequently hanged) – my father said that two things about him had been very surprising: one was how intelligent and well educated he was for a Blackshirt (I have since learnt that he had a first-class honours degree from London University), and the other was the size and fierceness of a razor scar on his face, extreme even by Hoxton standards. It is almost certain that I heard him speak in the flesh, probably more than once, but I cannot find any specific memory of it, or of him, whereas I have vivid memories of Mosley.

The extreme right became as fragmented just before the war as the extreme left always is, and in similar ways, with former friends and colleagues splintering into ever-smaller sects and passionately hating one another. I remember standing as one of a small group of people by the lavatories in the middle of Hoxton Street listening to a forlorn young man in a shabby overcoat who radiated the impression of being permanently all by himself, and would not have been imaginable in a Blackshirt context. He was talking about how all the country's ills were being caused by aliens who came in and took everything we had away from us. He used the word 'alien' in almost every sentence, and I became curious to know who these aliens were. When I got home I asked: 'Dad, what's an alien?' My father said he needed to know the context, and I found myself telling him about the young man, and answering questions about what he had said. Then my father said: 'Well, actually, the word "alien" means something different and strange; and if it's used about people it means people who come from a strange country. It's obvious your bloke was talking about Jews, foreign Jews. Did he use the word Jews at all?'

'No. I don't think so.'

'Well, anyway, it's obvious from what you tell me that that's what he was talking about. He must have been some sort of Fascist, I suppose.'

I came to realise that my father, and also many of the families around us, regarded Fascists not as just another kind of person but as unacceptable, beyond the pale. My father explained to me that in Germany, where Fascists were in power, they were doing terrible things to Jews, who for that reason were running away from Germany and coming to England – which is what the Fascists in England were now complaining about. If Fascists were in power here, he said, they would do terrible things to Jews here as well. Whenever he spoke about the Blackshirts his face and voice became grim. By contrast, our Jewish neighbours and near-neighbours had an attitude that was closer to hysteria. They knew so much more than we did about what was going on in Germany; and they knew only too well that there was an element of anti-semitism in British social life. For them the Blackshirts represented a very real danger that the same thing could happen in Britain as was happening in Germany. Because of this, two or three local families emigrated to the United States. The rest stayed, but felt threatened, and expressed open fear and hatred of the Fascists. One or two of them, when they knew that the Blackshirts were about to march past our shops, pulled down the shutters and bolted the door until they were well and truly past. Some of their young men used to go to the Blackshirt meetings to get involved in fights. I had a vague idea that they had a street organisation of their own to fight the Blackshirts, but I never knew any more than that about it.

None of the non-Jewish families we knew were in favour of the Blackshirts, but there were several who thought they were un-important. I remember Albert Tillson saying that they were just rubbish, and were never going to get anywhere, so there was no need to worry about them or take any notice of them. To me they did not seem unimportant, though. For a while they came close to dominating our streets; and on one occasion they threatened my father. He was alone in a street in a Jewish area, on his way to or from one of our suppliers, and he encountered a group of (he said five) Fascist thugs who started calling him a Jewboy. Like me, he had a big nose with a bulbous end; and in the fashion of the '30s he often wore his thick dark hair slicked down with Brylcreem; and he was always well dressed; so in that area the thugs evidently took him to be a Jewish businessman. They barred his way and became more threatening, working themselves up, until one of them made a lunge at him, and he had ignominiously to run away. It was only by climbing some scaffolding that he managed to shake them off, and then only because they could not be bothered to chase up after him. He arrived home white-faced and shaken, and poured it all out to us. I believe that this incident permanently influenced his attitudes. It certainly affected mine. I began to understand that these Fascists were seriously disgusting people, and not just interesting baddies who were putting on a show that was fun to watch. Growing slightly older, as I now was, helped the process. The feeling around us hardened that the Blackshirts were bringing something hideous into our lives.

During those couple of years before the outbreak of war I had as yet little idea of there being a national government that was running the country. I had a firm grasp of there being a borough council in Shoreditch, where I lived, and of there being above that a London County Council that ran London as a whole – we heard a lot about it at school – but at any level higher than that I became vague. The stories my father told me from the newspapers were, I think without exception, about foreign affairs. The Spanish Civil War was a tremendous drama, long-running and powerful. For a long time it was accompanied in my mind by the Japanese invasion of China. Then came Munich, something in which the whole population, including children, felt themselves to be involved, as they had been in the Abdication. The Nazi–Soviet pact had my father gasping – nothing so strained his wish to take a tolerant view of Communism, and actually his tolerance went into abeyance until Hitler invaded Russia in 1941. He made these pre-war events vividly alive for me in a way that has accompanied me through life, and was to provide a motive for later study. It was comparatively easy for me to grasp the idea of one man running a country, and I knew from him that Hitler ran Germany, Chiang Kai-Shek ran China, Mussolini ran Italy, Stalin ran Russia; and when the Spanish Civil War came to an end early in 1939 I knew this meant that Franco was taking over Spain. But there was nobody in Britain who corresponded to these people. We did not seem to have anyone running us. It was not that I felt we ought to – my father's teaching gave me the firm view that dictators were Not A Good Thing – but he had given me no idea at all how Britain was governed. There was Mr Chamberlain, of course, but he was ridiculous, a figure of fun whom children used to imitate in the playground, with his umbrella and snotty-nosed expression, looking at other people down his moustache. It was obvious that he could not be running anything, he was just up there doing the talking. But who actually was running things? I hadn't the remotest idea. My father told me nothing that I can remember about Parliament, or the parliamentary parties, or the civil service, or the Cabinet. I suppose it is just possible that he did tell me and I found it all so boring or unintelligible that I have no recollection of it, but I do not think this is so. Certainly he tried explaining a lot of things to me that, after his explanation, I still did not understand. But his political interests seemed to be entirely in foreign affairs at that time. At Munich he thought there was going to be a war, and wanted one. When it did not come he explained to me that this did not mean there was going to be no war, it meant that the war was going to break out later than he had expected. He regarded this not just as inevitable but, with deep regret, desirable. His view, in a nutshell, was that Hitler had to be stopped, and the sooner the better, and that the only way of stopping him was going to be by force.

Partly because this was his attitude, and partly because I was reaching an age when I could understand a few things in the news by myself – occasionally and briefly I was beginning to look at a newspaper alone – Munich was the beginning of my awareness that my own life was affected by what went on in the world outside England. Was there going to be a war? Everybody was talking about it. I saw the newspaper placards, heard Hitler's voice on the radio – I had never heard a man sound like that, raving and screaming, obviously a lunatic. At first, when war seemed to have been averted, a general sigh of relief went up – though not from my father, who said it was all shameful and monstrous – but very soon everyone went back to talking about war again. In fact the commonest of all topics of conversation among the grown-ups became: Do you think there's going to be a war or don't you? Customers debated it in the shop. Opinion was divided. The Jewish suppliers I went to with my father always asked him what he thought about it.

Talk began of preparations for war. People said there was going to be rationing. This sent earth tremors through Hoxton. How could a market survive if there was rationing? The shopkeeping families were even more alarmed than the stall-holders about the effect it would have on them, and everyone talked about it. At school we were told that if a war broke out the entire school would be sent away to the country somewhere, teachers and all, so as not to be bombed. It was either when I was still in Hoxton or during the first few weeks of the war that we were issued with gas masks at school. These were a problem for me. The size of my head had created difficulties with school caps, and now it did the same with gas masks: the one provided for children was too small to fit me. I could not get it on, and when it was forced on it was agonisingly painful, and clamped my jaw shut, so that I could not speak. It was obvious to everyone that I would not be able to wear it. However, the next size up was too big: it gaped at the sides, and would let the gas in. The teachers were stumped; but regulations said I had to have a gas mask, so they gave me one I could put on. The teacher who gave it to me said: 'You'll just have to hope the Germans don't use gas.' They never did, which really was lucky for me, because at no time during the war did I have a mask that would have kept it out.

Mine was a generation of children that was psychologically prepared for war before it came. We understood that if it did come it would change our lives. And I, having had my father expounding foreign affairs to me from the newspapers for a matter of years, possessed a childlike understanding that its coming would be determined by what happened in places like Germany, Czechoslovakia and Poland. The idea that what was going on in such places was nothing to do with me or with real life – the idea common in prosperous communities in time of peace – was one I did not encounter until I was well into adult life; and when I did I found it, for a long time, not easy to understand.

CHAPTER SEVENTEEN

Four roads met at the corner just past our shop – Hoxton Street, Pitfield Street, Hyde Road and Whitmore Road – and the space at the crossroads was wide and open: it is now a roundabout. Whitmore Road falls away from there towards the canal, so in that direction there is a downward slope. Among my most haunting recollections are those of constantly seeing horses struggling to get up that slope. Local cart horses tended to be overloaded as a matter of course – and underfed too, often – so there was nothing unusual about seeing a horse pulling a load that was too heavy for it. Along the lower, flat part of Whitmore Road things were not too bad for the horse, but when it came to the upward slope it would start to be dragged back by the weight. Its hooves would strike frantically outwards for a firmer grip on the cobbles, and there would be huge metallic clangs, and sparks flying upwards from between its shoes and the cobblestones. If the cart began to slide backwards the carter would yell swear words at the horse and slash at it with his whip, repeatedly, often standing up in the process. Worst of all was if the cobbles were slimy with rain, and the horse's hooves just kept slithering back over them, bringing it to its knees, while the driver went on whipping it viciously, and striving to force it onwards and upwards. I have seen horse and cart get almost to the top and then slide all the way down backwards with the horse on its knees, or even on its side. This, in the pouring rain, was an unforgettable image of failure, collapse, hopelessness. The drivers would then give up and, reviling the horse with extra curses, turn round and take another route.

The problems this caused were much discussed locally, and eventually the borough council changed the sloping surface to one on which horses could get more of a grip. To my great pleasure, workmen came and tore up all the cobblestones at the crossroads and replaced them with square-cut blocks of a hard, black, rubbery composition that gripped better than cobblestones when dry, and better still when wet. My father and grandfather asked the council if the stones that led out of the crossroads along the narrow part of Hoxton Street could be changed at the same time in the interests of noise-abatement, but this was refused. The road outside the shop went on consisting of cobblestones until long after the Second World War.

Whenever workmen needed to take up this surface, as they did constantly to get at pipes and cables, it meant taking up the cobbles, and I loved watching them do that. They worked in threes, usually. They would first of all wander about in the roadway separately, calling out to one another, looking for a weak join between two stones as being the place to drive in an iron spike. This was accompanied by much discussion, sometimes argument. Then one of them would crouch on his heels and hold out, fully at both arms' length, a giant pair of metal tongs whose other end held the spike over the spot. His two comrades, with sledgehammers, would stand at right angles to him, opposite one another, and smash down their great hammers alternately on the spike. Their movements were fluidly continuous, in marvellous counterpoint with one another, each swinging the sledgehammer in a huge circle and hitting the spike at just the moment when the other's was at the farthest point away on its circle: then up came the other hammer, arcing high over the man's head, and down *bang!* on the nail. The men formed a right-angle triangle and, with tremendous drive, created two flying and interlocking cycles of *bang!* swing, circle, *bang!* swing. The combination of rhythm, geometry and movement thrilled me.

The navvies, as they were called (I knew a song that started: 'I'm a navvy, I'm a navvy, working on the line / Peas pudding and gravy every dinner time'), looked huge to my eyes, muscular and tough. It never occurred to me to think of my father as less than manly, but these were extra manly. They were poorly, dirtily, raggedly dressed, and that added to the impression of toughness they gave me. I found them impressive, and there was a time when I wanted to grow up to be one of them.

Also physically immense were the men who delivered the coal. This, like almost everything else, arrived in the street by horse and cart, and stopped outside each shop or house in turn. The cart was piled high with hundredweight sacks of coal and, sitting on top of those, the two men who were delivering them. These wore a garment that they made from the sacks, a hood protecting their hair from coal dust, plus a long broad tail spreading down like an apron covering their backs. One of the men would come into the shop to ask how much coal we wanted, then slide away the coal-hole cover in the pavement outside, go to the cart and heave a hundredweight sack of coal on to his back, take it to the hole, and bow his head right down to his knees so that the coal showered out of the sack over his head and into the hole, down into our coal cellar. Not only the clothes but the faces and hands of these men were black with coal dust. When they came into the shop they were delicately careful not to brush against anything or anybody. They too seemed to epitomise masculinity. I envied them for being as dirty as it seemed possible to get.

In pretty well every street in Hoxton each house had a coal-hole cover in the pavement outside, a hangover from a long forgotten age when they had all been middle-class one-family homes with servant-basements and coal cellars. In my time most of the cellars were inhabited by people, though some were still coal cellars; and as the '30s went on, and living standards improved, the cellar population declined, and more and more of people's homes reverted to being coal cellars.

Milk was another thing that came by horse and cart, and was delivered from door to door, in this case every day. There was one milkman who would always give children a ride – we called him Milky – but the fact that he got down and disappeared every few yards made being with him boring; so each of his child-passengers would slip away after only a few minutes, and he had a ceaseless turnover of travelling companions. He emitted a yodel to announce his arrival, '*Milk-a-lay-eée-dee!*', going up into falsetto on the *eée.* We children giggled at this because we said he was saying 'Milk a lady!' – with us it was anything for a joke about tits. His cart was small compared with the mountainous coal-carts, and the horse not much more than a pony, so he was a downbeat acquaintance altogether, but, still, the softest touch there was for a free ride. Then, one day, the horse and cart were no longer there. Instead, Milky was driving what he told us had to be called a float. It was like an unenclosed van, full of milk crates, and he sat at a steering wheel and drove it like a car; but it made almost no sound, just a low, electric hum, as if driven by batteries; and it moved more smoothly than a car, almost creepily. There were no more rides.

So many people worked in the streets that even away from the market there was perpetual street life. Many of those involved had special cries. The rag-and-bone men would trudge past in the roadway, shoving handcarts and shouting: '*Any old rags! Any old rags!*' and then with a long, moaning sound, '*Bones! Bones!*' The man who sold pigs' trotters shouted, over and over, '*'apenny knuckles!*', and men with trays hung from their necks by leather straps '*Ice-cream! Ice-cream! Anyone for ice-cream?*' With the news boys it was either '*Star, News and Standard!*' or, if they had only the *Star* and needed something longer than that to shout: '*Star! A-dorp-di-der!*' Costermongers who had lost their pitches or never had one would wheel a barrow round the streets, staying perpetually on the move, shouting '*Apples a pound, pears!*' or whatever it was. There were carts pushed by scrap metal dealers, old clothes men, and people buying and selling broken furniture. The muffin man did not shout, but rang a bell like the one teachers used in our school playground: he walked along the pavement balancing a big square tray of muffins on his head with one hand while ringing his bell with the other. There were many other sorts of pavement sellers too, usually trying to sell you things from trays hung round their necks like the ice-cream men. Even for events that happened only once a year, like the Oxford and Cambridge Boatrace, vendors would appear on the streets for days or weeks before-hand, in this case selling favours. Few people take that much notice of the Boatrace now, but in those days it was an occasion for the whole population, known to all as Boatrace Day. Everyone took sides, and wore favours, which for most people consisted of tiny plastic dolls dressed in light blue or dark blue feathers. I supported Cambridge, because I preferred the colour. Also, I had been born on Boatrace Day, and Cambridge had won. The word 'boatrace', incidentally, was cockney rhyming slang for 'face'.

In addition to people selling things on the open pavement there were door-to-door salesmen – bundles of firewood for a penny were the most popular item – and also people who called on every house offering to do jobs in the home. I remember a knife-sharpener who came regularly and honed the shop's scissors as well; and there was a straw-weaver offering to mend chairs and carpets. There were always any number of people asking to clean the windows. Postmen, insurance men, tally men and foot-ball pools collectors also called from house to house. On the street corners, bookies' runners alternated shifts with policemen. At

331

dusk I often saw the lamp-lighters making their way from corner to corner, from lamp-post to lamp-post, carrying the long poles with which they turned on the gaslights. Only rarely was I out in the morning early enough to see the same men turning the lights off with the arrival of daylight – when I did it looked ghostly and weird, the switching off of lights in the light, leaving light.

If a group of men working in the street stayed in one place for long enough they expected to be serviced, at least with tea. All the workers' cafés employed boys, young teenagers straight out of school, to carry tea round to men at work. One of these boys would carry in parallel, either at his sides or on his shoulders, two wooden poles from each of which half a dozen cans of tea hung on metal hooks. When they were empty they jumped about and jangled. The tea was already milked and sugared, very sweet. Its cost, I believe, was a penny a can, and a boy had strictly to take as many pennies back as he took cans out – though a bunch of workers would often treat him to a can, which they would ask him to stay and drink with them. Tea boys were among the commonest sights in the streets; they seemed to be everywhere. Navvies in particular drank tea endlessly, theirs being such sweaty work. When a boy arrived at a group of them there would be joshing and ribaldry all round as they broke off and drank the tea, and the young boy would try to show them that he understood what they were talking about, and they would try either to catch him out or shock him.

Social change tends often to be at its slowest among the poor, so visiting a poor area can be like a journey back in time. When I think now of all this street life that I took for granted in the '30s – really, I grew up on the streets – I realise that it was a world that Dickens would have been at home in. Not only was most of the physical plant of Hoxton, the actual streets and houses, as he knew it (and he did know it), but in it I was also seeing the end of a way of life much of which was familiar to him, indeed some of which was unaltered since his day. It was all then very much closer to the London of Dickens than to London as it has become since the 1960s.

Although the social revolution that was to be precipitated in Britain by the Second World War was the supreme destroyer of that world and that way of life, significant changes were taking place already in the '30s; and because they were changes, I noticed them. It was a startling change when the lighting of the streets and schools switched over from gas to electricity: the world looked different. Such sudden changes seemed to be milestones, like the change from cobbles to rubber, or from a wind-up gramophone to a radiogram. In Southgate Road the trams disappeared, and newfangled trolley buses took their place. There came a day when my father and I went to Kingsland Road for our haircuts and found the barber no longer using his old hand-clippers but applying *buzz-buzz* electric clippers to our heads. The ice-cream men suddenly stopped trudging around on foot with their trays and appeared one day on tricycles shouting '*Stop me and buy one!*' Alongside this sort of change was another kind that went on steadily all the time, and which even as a child I associated, no doubt vaguely, with progress: the smokers around me stopped using matches and started using cigarette lighters; the stuffed old horsehair furniture in people's homes was replaced by furniture with springs, and linoleum by rugs, even carpets; horses and carts were gradually giving way to cars and vans, boots to shoes, milk and beer in jugs to milk and beer in bottles, bread that you had to cut yourself to bread that came ready sliced. My mother acquired a second-hand, primitive vacuum cleaner. Washing-powders appeared, and she no longer had to work on the family's laundry with unmanageable blocks of green soap. When I was little, the pieces of toilet soap that were too small to wash with were used for making soapy water for the washing-up: several of them were put into a small gauze-metal cage at the end of a handle and whisked about in hot water in the kitchen sink. The dirty crockery was then washed in this bubbly water, and rinsed under the running tap. But then in came washing-up liquids that did the job so much better. What to do with the little bits of soap then? So as not to waste them we squashed them down flat on to the surfaces of bigger bars.

There was a vague feeling around that gadgets and machines were all the time creeping into our lives from outside. Just as there were ever more cars on the roads, though still perhaps not many, so there were ever more aeroplanes in the sky, though one appeared only every now and again. In spite of the slowness of these changes I somehow acquired the idea subliminally that things in general were all the time moving forward, getting better, going somewhere. I accepted it as a continuous and welcome process, but without taking it for granted, because change was always noticeable. Among other differences, it highlighted the differences between generations. My grandfather went on using matches (Swan Vestas) after my father had started using a cigarette lighter, just as he went on using a cut-throat razor after Dad had changed to safety blades, and boots after father had changed to shoes. I was increasingly aware of the differences between the way my grandparents spoke and the way my father spoke. My grandparents pronounced Charing Cross 'Cherring Crawss', and called a car a motor, a mirror a glass, and a mantelpiece a chimney piece. There were a lot of other differences too, and years later Nancy Mitford itemised nearly all of them as U, as against non-U, but that was a misunderstanding on her part: what she was noticing was not primarily a difference between social classes, it was primarily a difference between generations – between, on the one hand, the spoken English of the Victorian and Edwardian generations and, on the other, the English of our own and more recent times.

I was aware of these differences in the world around me, not just within my family. All old people seemed to speak like my grandparents. Most of them dressed in dark clothes, the women in black, while younger adults were colourfully dressed. Most old men wore flat caps (not my grandfather, who wore a homburg) but the younger ones, including my father, wore trilbies. Up to the age of about forty most adults were thin and wiry, many of them quite scrawny, but after that they thickened out and became fat. (The very old, of whom there were not many, were skinny again.) The difference between generations was like a difference between two races: the bony, brightly dressed, noisy young and the quiet, fat, middle-aged in black. I regarded the middle-aged and old as belonging to a depressing world that had gone, though I found the old surprisingly interesting to talk to. The middle-aged were usually crotchety, but the old were friendly, and liked talking to children, perhaps because they lived alone.

Somehow, even before the war, I began to form an expectation that the future was going to mean more cheerfully coloured clothes for more people, more films, more music on records and radio, more telephones, cars and aeroplanes. There seemed to me a general direction in which the world was moving, my life along with everything else; and on the whole I welcomed it. I positively wanted things to go on opening out in this direction more and more as I got older – it came to seem the natural and proper order of things. I had always assumed that the process of growing up would carry me out into a big wide world beyond Hoxton, and I saw this as part of the process. My father's powerful stories based on news photographs filled me with a lively sense of a world full of drama that was going on around us and changing every day. The radio, to which I listened increasingly, was about worlds elsewhere, as were the newspapers. Our Sunday motoring trips brought home to me in a physical way that there were places besides London; and our summer holidays gave me experiences of staying in different environments, whether beside the sea or a country village. I was being prepared for change without realising it.

I was surprised when my grandparents turned out to be preparing for change too. In 1938 my grandmother went down to Sussex for the day to visit an old friend who had retired there, and on her return announced that she had rented a cottage in a village, for her and my grandfather to retire to. She was much given to this sort of thing, acting on decisions that had life-changing implications for other people without consulting them. (A worse example involved my aunt Peggy as a schoolgirl: after Peggy had been a pupil at Owen's, a grammar school at the Angel, for a matter of years, my grandmother informed her one day that she had been withdrawn from the school because the family could not afford the fees, so instead of going to school that day Peggy would go out and look for a job.) In this case she had seen how her friend in retirement was living, decided that she would like to live like that herself when the time came, and found somewhere to do it. She reasoned that she and my grandfather were both now in their sixties, which was a much older age for people to be then than it is now, and they ought to be making preparation for retirement. They had both lived unusually hard lives, and were perhaps beginning to feel it. My father, in his late thirties, was chafing to run the shop. So everything fitted in. But no such retirement occurred. I find it impossible to believe that my grandfather would ever have contemplated living in a Sussex village, but in any case my grandmother's dreams were dispersed by the outbreak of war the following year, which changed everything.

She had rented the cottage for a song. We referred to it as 'the bungalow', it being one of a row of three brick bungalows put up by a speculative builder in a village called Worth. This consisted simply of one long, straggling street tucked away on a side road that was also a cul-de-sac, a couple of miles outside Crawley. But now that she had it, the question was what to do with it. I think she and my grandfather visited it occasionally on Sundays, taking the train from Victoria to Three Bridges, which is a mile from

Worth. When they were there my parents would sometimes motor down with me and Joan, and we would all have lunch and tea there together. Over the Easter of 1939, and again in the summer, I made a stay of a few days there with my grandmother – I remember how thrilled I was at being able to identify birds from a set of coloured cigarette cards I was collecting. The thing that struck me most about the bungalow was that when you opened the kitchen door you found yourself looking across a field. It was the playing field for the village children, and I played with them, mucking in immediately as I had at Loders. I was astonished to discover how much they knew about my family, including some things I did not know myself. Nothing was known at all in the village that was not known by everyone.

By that summer, in London at least, conversation among the grown-ups was entirely dominated by the prospect of war. My school told my parents that if war broke out the school would evacuate to the Midlands, though they were not sure where. It would happen in the first two days, so my parents needed to be ready to deliver me to Dalston Junction railway station at one day's notice, equipped with a suitcase containing a given list of requirements, and a label hung round my neck telling people who I was. Given that I was nine years old, my parents were none too keen on this idea. Prolonged discussion took place within the family about alternatives. Eventually it was concluded that if war came I should not accompany my school to the Midlands but would go to Worth and stay there with my grandmother, and attend a school locally. However, since none of the schools there were thought suitable for my sister, who was now nearly thirteen and at a good grammar school, it was decided that she should remain with her school if it evacuated (which it did, to Huntingdon).

The moves, when they came, were abrupt. At the end of August my aunt Peggy telephoned to tell us that war was about to begin.

A friend of hers who worked as a secretary in Whitehall had told her that Germany was about to invade Poland, and that a couple of days after that Britain would declare war on Germany. The invasion of Poland happened as predicted, and on 2 September 1939 – the day before Britain and France declared war – I was sent to Worth to stay indefinitely with my grandmother. I did not know it at the time, but in fact I was leaving Hoxton never to live there again.

POSTSCRIPT

What must always be special for me about pre-war Hoxton is that
it was my first world. For most of the period that I lived in it I
knew no other life. As I went on growing up I was to experience
several other worlds, but in each of them I had my experience of
the previous ones to draw on and compare it with. For three
months, which at the age of nine seemed almost an endless time,
I lived in Worth: it was my first experience of living away from
parents and home for more than just a holiday. And these were
the first months of the war, which made it an even more distinctive experience. Then I joined my school in Market Harborough,
where I was billeted as an evacuee with two local families for a
year and a half. While I was there my parents were bombed out
of our Hoxton home, so they moved into a flat opposite Arnos
Grove tube station, at the northern end of the Piccadilly Line.
This meant that when I visited them during the school holidays
I went not to Hoxton but to a suburb in which I had never lived,
and where I did not know anyone.

At the age of eleven I became a pupil at a unique school,
Christ's Hospital, an all-boarding school that for hundreds of years
had been in the City of London, but by this time had moved to
Sussex. Since its foundation in 1552 it had specialised in giving
a first-class education to children who could benefit from a
boarding school but not pay for one, and was now taking them
two or three years younger than other public schools and teaching

339

them for that much longer. The range of opportunities it offered was astonishing – in my last year it sent me as an exchange boarder for a term to one of the best *lycées* in France, the Lycée Hôche in Versailles. Having taken me in as a Cockney kid at the age of eleven, it turned me out just short of my eighteenth birthday with an unusually good education and a scholarship to Oxford. Before going on to university I had, like all boys of my generation, to put in military service, so I spent a year in counter-intelligence work in Austria.

When I went up to Oxford in October 1949 I was nineteen. This means that before I was even out of my teens I had experienced life in a Sussex village, a Leicestershire market town, a London suburb, an English public school, a French *lycée*, a small Iron Curtain frontier-town between Austria and Yugoslavia, then Graz, and now Oxford University. It was a many-sided preparation for life, for which I have been abidingly grateful. But before any of those things, there were nine and a half years in Hoxton, during most of which I had not the remotest conception of those other worlds, or of any other life. Because of the uniquely non-comparative nature of that experience there are some respects in which I think of pre-war Hoxton as my Garden of Eden – a whole and enclosed, exclusive and unprecedented world out of which I was expelled into the rest of my life. I was not invariably happy in it, and I did not think of it as a paradise; but I was happy for most of the time, and I had the kind of innocence that comes from not knowing of anything else. I took everything for granted as being life itself, the world, the way things are. I have carried this world around inside me ever since, invisible but always there. I believe that somewhere there is a small part of me that has never left it, and that lives in it still.

But of course Hoxton itself has changed out of all recognition. I have already mentioned how most of it was destroyed and swept away, first in the blitz, then in the post-war slum-clearance programmes. The rubbishy buildings that went up then are now up to half a century old and are themselves run-down, though completely different from pre-war Hoxton. Even the people look different now, because a large black population has moved in. Most unexpectedly, in the 1990s a part of Hoxton became a magnet for artists, and is now an artists' colony.

There were many warehouses in the Hoxton of my childhood, especially in the area nearest the City. The bomb-blasts that cleared away whole streets of slums left most of the massive, solidly built warehouses standing, and, being in use, they were ignored in slum-replacement plans. When they fell into disuse later, after the demise of the London docks, they could be rented for almost nothing. Their huge spaces and high ceilings made many of them ideal for conversion into artists' studios. Painters and sculptors were able to find space for their special needs more cheaply here than anywhere else in the middle of London. As I write, that part of old Shoreditch that includes the southern half of Hoxton is the most fashionable artists' colony anywhere in Britain. Artists have moved in in such numbers that bohemian cafés and clubs, ethnic restaurants, even an art cinema, have come into existence to serve them; the pubs have made themselves over to cater for them, and the whole district has been transformed. This is the area of which Hoxton Square is the centre. Nor is it only visual artists who have come to work here. The building in Pitfield Street which for me was a swimming bath and public library is now in daily use for rehearsals by English National Opera. The Royal Shakespeare Company advertises its courses for drama students as taking place 'in fashionable Hoxton'. And, talking as we are of students, Hoxton Market is now home to one of the campuses of a new university. The area has returned, you could say, to something nearer what it was in the late sixteenth and early seventeenth centuries. But these changes together make up an environment that people in the Hoxton I knew would have found impossible to conceive.

So there is a double sense in which this book is about a vanished world: it is about the vanished world of my childhood, but it is also about the vanished world of pre-war Hoxton, and all the things it represented, if sometimes at their most extreme, in a vanished England.

AFTERWORD

I am aware that in portraying people as they appeared to me as
a child I have probably done injustice to one or two individuals.
I am thinking particularly of Roy Taylor and Mr Lowe, who I
expect were not at all as absurd as they appeared to my infant
self, but were more ordinarily human. There must, in any case,
have been more to them than I perceived. If they or their loved
ones read this book I hope they will forgive me and remember
that I was, after all, only a child.

AFTERWORD

I am aware that in portraying people as they appeared to me as a child I have probably done injustice to one or two individuals. I am thinking particularly of Roy Taylor and Mr Lowe, who I expect were not at all as absurd as they appeared to my infant self, but were more ordinarily human. There must, in any case, have been more to them than I perceived. If they, or their loved ones, read this book I hope they will forgive me and remember that I was, after all, only a child.